At Home in the Whedonverse

At Home in the Whedonverse

Essays on Domestic Place, Space and Life

Edited by JULIETTE C. KITCHENS

McFarland & Company, Inc., Publishers
Jefferson, North Carolina

LIBRARY OF CONGRESS CATALOGUING-IN-PUBLICATION DATA

Names: Kitchens, Juliette C., 1976– editor.
Title: At home in the Whedonverse : essays on domestic place, space and life / edited by Juliette C. Kitchens.
Description: Jefferson, North Carolina : McFarland & Company, Inc., Publishers, 2017. | Includes bibliographical references and index.
Identifiers: LCCN 2017020237 | ISBN 9781476667027 (softcover : acid free paper) ∞
Subjects: LCSH: Whedon, Joss, 1964—-Criticism and interpretation. | Home on television. | Home in motion pictures.
Classification: LCC PN1992.4.W49 A83 2017 | DDC 791.4302/33092—dc23
LC record available at https://lccn.loc.gov/2017020237

BRITISH LIBRARY CATALOGUING DATA ARE AVAILABLE

ISBN (print) 978-1-4766-6702-7
ISBN (ebook) 978-1-4766-2982-7

© 2017 Juliette C. Kitchens. All rights reserved

No part of this book may be reproduced or transmitted in any form or by any means, electronic or mechanical, including photocopying or recording, or by any information storage and retrieval system, without permission in writing from the publisher.

Cover image © Stock Finland

Printed in the United States of America

McFarland & Company, Inc., Publishers
  Box 611, Jefferson, North Carolina 28640
  www.mcfarlandpub.com

Table of Contents

Acknowledgments — vii

Introduction. Locating Home: Unraveling the Domestic Entanglements in the Whedonverse — 1
JULIETTE C. KITCHENS

Genius, Billionaire, Playboy, Prometheus: Transhumanism and Proxemics in the Works of Joss Whedon — 11
DUSTIN DUNAWAY

It's Joss Whedon's World and We're All Just Livin' in It: The "Closed Frame" of the Whedonverse — 27
KIRK HENDERSHOTT-KRAETZER

Broken but Home: Institutions, Control and the Non-Place in *Dollhouse* — 48
CATHERINE PUGH

Seeking Safe Haven: Shelter and Self-Protection from *Afterlife* to *Avengers: Age of Ultron* — 68
VALERIE ESTELLE FRANKEL

Domestic Space and Identity: Joss Whedon's Futuristic Frontier in *Firefly* — 87
MELANIE A. MAROTTA

Scythe Matters: Performing Object Oriented Ontology on Domestic Space in *Buffy the Vampire Slayer* — 104
JULIE L. HAWK

Deliver Us from Evil: Demons, Feminism and Rhetorical Spaces in *Buffy the Vampire Slayer* — 122
VICTORIA WILLIS

vi   Table of Contents

Militarization of the Domestic Space: Positioning Buffy as a   142
    Post-Feminist Heroine through the Lens of Choice Feminism
        KAREN WALSH

Classrooms, Classrooms Everywhere, but Not to Slay   165
    or Think: The Domestic Learning Environments
    of *Buffy the Vampire Slayer*
        MELANIE A. JENSEN *and* KYLE WILLIAM BISHOP

A Home at the End of the World: The Future of Domesticity   182
    in the Whedonverse
        LISA K. PERDIGAO

About the Contributors   199

Index   201

Acknowledgments

This collection has been a deeply personal journey for me, both as a scholar and as a fan. In part, the subject matter has created as many complications as it has rewards. After all, how does one write about home and not become entangled in her own understanding of it—material or otherwise? Add to that the focus on the Whedonverse home—of which there are many, seemingly endless representations—and the task becomes delightfully overwhelming. For this reason, this project needed to be a collection; it needed to represent the various contexts and constructs home creates and exists within. This purpose is brilliantly fulfilled by the scholars whose work is collected here. I extend my deepest gratitude to the contributors who made this project possible. The smart, thoughtful treatment of the Whedon homes we know and love—and some that we are only now discovering—have brought an idea into reality. I am grateful for their care and compassion in handling this subject and remain in awe of the many perspectives exposed within these essays.

This collection came together in part because of the organizations that supported the idea and, for some, offered a venue for our work-in-progress. My gratitude to members and officers of the Whedon Studies Association, International Association for the Fantastic in the Arts, and the Popular Culture Association for believing in this project and for spreading the word. Through these organizations, I connected with several of the collection's contributors and have made lasting friendships.

I am also grateful to my colleagues who supported me throughout this project. My deepest appreciation to Julie Hawk for her ongoing feedback, compassion, and levity. For the summer morning cafe work sessions and the hallway Q&A, I am grateful to Star Vanguri, Kelly Concannon, and Molly Scanlon. Your generosity in sharing your experiences as editors and writers encourages me and keeps me grounded.

Finally, I would like to express my appreciation to my family. My gratitude to Derek for the re-watches of the 'verse(s) and the conversations about the many homes within them, and for his support and patience throughout this project. Creating a home with you is an amazing journey. And finally, I would like to thank Mom, Brian, and Kim for teaching me that home requires compassion and understanding.

Introduction
Locating Home: Unraveling the Domestic Entanglements in the Whedonverse

JULIETTE C. KITCHENS

> Well, this is nice. It's a little bare, but a dash of paint, a few throw pillows—call it home.—Buffy Summers, "Welcome to the Hellmouth"

In the Whedonverse(s), home is never simple. As in the real world, home is where our beloved characters grow up, find their voices (and sometimes lose them), suffer incredible loss, celebrate victory, live truths (and lies), discover family, and fight like hell to survive. In the 'verse, home often offers a stable setting for the greatest changes, yet home is an unfixed location. It isn't simply the suburban home, the underground zen den, the ship in space. It can move beyond a structure, embodied in relationships with people, with places, with things. Home reaches into the past, fiddles around with the present, and speculates on the future. Joss Whedon's *Much Ado About Nothing* (2013) adapts Shakespeare into a modern setting while maintaining original dialog. *Firefly* (2002–2003) and *Serenity* (2005) suggest that when Earth is used up, descendants several generations removed will mirror the cultural, political, and economic strife witnessed by contemporary audiences. *Angel* (1999–2004) adeptly traverses narrative ground spanning the lifetime of a 200-plus-year-old vampire, illustrating that while fashion and architecture changes, humanity kind of doesn't. *Fray* (2001–2003), an eight-issue comic book series that expands the Slayer narrative beyond *Buffy the Vampire Slayer*, reaches far into the future to represent the notion that some ideals never die and the girl still doesn't need saving. And *Dollhouse* (2009–2010) offers one of the most complex representations of time, space, and home in Whedon's works. The imprints allow Dolls and identity constructs to traverse time and space with minimal awareness.¹ Compounding the spatiotemporal complexity of the series, the multiple representations of home embedded in the narrative are as intricate and as intimate as the neurological architecture that maintains a Doll's imprint. Each of these Whedon productions tinkers with time and fixates on notions of home—what it was, what it is, what it could be.

To say that various domestic representations feature prominently throughout the Whedonverse is somewhat underselling the role of home within it. Home, in all its embodiments, frequently complicates the narratological and rhetorical structures of the 'verse as well as audiences' contemporary ideological and sociopolitical assumptions. It is a space (or a thing, person, feeling, or time) that often blurs private and public purposes and unites domestic and commercial goals. In both *Buffy the Vampire Slayer* (1997–2003; hereafter *BtVS*) and *Angel* the distinctions between public and private domains diminishes as characters create home-spaces from public, often commercial, locations. The Magic Box, a retail shop, becomes home base for the Scoobies, ultimately housing a training facility for Buffy and the gang's library of magic. Yet, within the same series, domestic space is transformed to serve a more publicly-oriented purpose. In season seven of *BtVS*, Buffy converts the Summers house into a Potentials dormitory that houses dozens of would-be (soon-to-be) Slayers. Buffy's home space mirrors her increasingly complicated roles as Slayer, sister, friend, and leader. Similarly, Angel's private and public purposes are inextricably woven together throughout the *BtVS* spin-off series *Angel*. Initially he lives in the basement of Angel Investigations. In season two, Angel moves into the Hyperion, an abandoned hotel that becomes both the base of operations for Team Angel and a domicile for several of its members. The televised series concludes with Angel living in a penthouse in the Los Angeles branch of the evil law firm Wolfram & Hart. Angel, a character deeply bound to humanity through his soul and yet always apart from it (because he is a vampire), repeatedly attempts to create private, familiar, intimate connections with public, often commercial, spaces. It is not until the comic book series *Angel and Faith* (2011–) that we find Angel attempting to create a home in a traditional dwelling (in a contemporary timeline).

In *Firefly* and in *Dollhouse*, representations of home play significant roles narratively and rhetorically, creating visual and textual conflict between what can be considered private and public. Proclaiming that *Serenity*, as the "tenth crew member," is the only non-expendable character on the show (Pascale 210), Whedon solidifies the complex shape of home in his work. Because the Firefly-class ship is home to the crew—carrying all of the sentimentalities and pragmatics associated with traditional domestic spaces—and yet also transportation to travelers and a functional work space for all on board, *Serenity* contests dichotomized readings of domestic locations as either public or private. Beyond the black, the Central and Outer planets offer complicated representations of home that are socio-politically charged, whether it is through the overtly patriarchal representations of privilege in "Trash" or "Shindig" or the subversively feminist brothel in "Heart of Gold" (Amy-Chin). Similarly, *Dollhouse* invites viewers into a space that is neither fully domestic nor commercial, but rather a simulacrum of both (Nadkarni; Scott). Inside the Los Angeles Dollhouse, the Dolls' "home" remains as illusory as the service they provide, positioning audiences to move beyond the environmental location in order to consider the biological and metaphysical manifestations that we might also consider "home."

In challenging rote notions of domestic locations, the Whedonverse also reminds us that we fight to protect home. *The Avengers* (2012), *Avengers: Age of Ultron* (2015), and *Agents of S.H.I.E.L.D.* (2013–), or the MCU Whedonverse, prominently feature a narrative of struggle and sacrifice in order to save the world—our home. Although these stories expand our domestic space intergalactically, we are faced with the destruction and salvation of domesticity on macro- and micro-levels. While characters fight for and save the planet, cities, and families throughout the MCU Whedonverse, audiences are also confronted with potential domestic conflicts and complications that arise from environmental and biological entanglements. Both *Avengers* films present mass urban destruction (New York City and Sokovia, respectively) that is addressed, albeit somewhat superficially, in *Age of Ultron* and in *Agents of S.H.I.E.L.D.* Further, a primary plot point throughout *Agents of S.H.I.E.L.D.* has been the creation, protection, and regulation of the Inhumans. As with *Dollhouse*, Whedon watchers are positioned to question the ways in which "home" is embodied and also the external influences that shape our biological spaces. As the franchise unfolds, *Agents of S.H.I.E.L.D.* also provides central ideas of traditional and nontraditional homes and families with Hawkeye's farmhouse playing a vital role for the Avengers and Coulson's team of agents finding their home in the bunker or on the "Bus." While these spaces often echo those seen throughout his productions,[2] within the MCU Whedonverse, these homes help connect audiences to the characters inhabiting them.

Home also offers a space in which Whedon *others* audiences, creating subversive commentary on the nature of the audience while nodding to our cultural fascination with the intimacy of home.[3] Films such as *The Cabin in the Woods* (2012) and *Much Ado* offer complimentary expressions of audience voyeurism through domestic locations. In *The Cabin in the Woods*, the producers "watch" the students in the house of horror as they struggle to survive. Yet the voyeurism is not merely embedded in the actions of the observers who watch the students while placing bets on their sins and survival; more importantly, it also exists in the metacommentary of the audience watching the observers watch the students (Canavan). As viewers, we access the cabin through observing the facility that houses the producers (i.e., the observers within the narrative). The cabin itself becomes the subject space of a horrific reality TV experience; filtered through a series of lenses, this horror/reality show suggests that someone is always watching the watcher. Shifting the voyeuristic perspective, in *Much Ado*, Whedon invites the audience into his own home, but through a lens that is under his control. Here, the audience surveys the intimate spaces of Whedon's life, but they are masked by script and production. We connect with the modernity of the space while we are simultaneously distanced by the expression of the text and the screen that ensures we remain on the outside of the home. Solidifying the familial nature of domestic space in Whedon's labor of love, he brought together a kindred crew to imbue the set (his home) with familiarity (Lanier).[4]

There are myriad examples of home throughout the Whedonverse(s), each adding to and complicating their narrative. As this collection demonstrates, there is no single definitive representation of "home" in the 'verse; home can be structure, body, space, object, idea, or illusion. This complexity, then, affords us opportunity to explore the many ways home is produced, challenged, and embodied.

Domestic Entanglements

> Love keeps her in the air when she ought to fall down. Tells you she's hurting before she keens. Makes her a home.—
> Malcolm Reynolds, *Serenity*

This collection uses the representations, locations, purposes, and elements of home and domesticity throughout the Whedonverse to explore, specifically, the various entanglements embedded and enacted in these spaces. Using spatial, narrative, rhetorical, social, and speculative theories, the essays that follow collectively demonstrate the materialism of home through its enmeshed subjectivity—regardless of how "home" is defined or framed. Bruno Latour suggests that entanglements offer outcomes that impact more than the actants involved for an extended duration of time. Entanglements may involve agents that span a variety of realms, including but not limited to the biological, technological, social, cultural, fictional, and/or political. When individual actants inter-relate and create—whether the creation is physical or conceptual—the resulting object, environment, or idea reaches beyond the moment of engagement and the locus of exigency. The entanglement takes on its own agency and *becomes*.

One of the more important interpretations of "entanglement," at least for the sake of this text, follows object-oriented and new materialist frameworks. Home, more often than not, is considered a non-spatiotemporal phenomenon attached to a specific location. That is, a dwelling can be a home to anyone at any time, but not all dwellings are homes, and a single dwelling can be a home during one time and not during another. Moreover, a person may make one dwelling a home, move, and make another dwelling an extension of the previous as it becomes home.[5] Therefore, while there is no binding singular spatial or temporal location for a home, the concept takes on a material object state when embodied or enacted. Because of this object-material nature, it can be useful to view this collection through new materialist and object-oriented lenses. Within these bodies of theories, notable philosophers such as Graham Harman, Ian Bogost, Levi R. Bryant, Karan Barad, and Jane Bennett grapple with the meaning and results of entanglements. Bryant, aligning with Barad, suggests associating the term with "diffraction patterns" in which no single object is a single actant, but rather objects with individual agency.[6] Bennett pushes this concept further with her notion of "vital materiality," which complicates "the capacity of things ... not only to impede or block the will and designs of humans but also to act as quasi agents or forces with trajectories, propensities, or tendencies of their own" (viii).

While not every essay in this book explicitly aligns with object-oriented philosophy or new materialism, they collectively create a sense of the vast entanglements embedded in domestic spaces. Together they demonstrate that the Whedonverse consistently displays domiciliary signs of entanglement through the subjectivity of objects, contestation of public and private spheres, and hybridity generated within complex relationships. That is, the Whedonverse illustrates the diffraction patterns of home. The intended purpose of this collection exposes the agency in and the dynamism of our environments. As we become an increasingly biotechnologically diverse culture, understanding and revising our conceptualization of home often means repurposing how we frame the biological, environmental, social, cultural, and technological agents that function in a continuum of entanglements.

Coming Home

> Why do you have to go back in the wedge? Why don't you come home?—Echo, "Omega"

This collection initially situates domestic environments broadly, positing that these spaces reflect psychological, ideological, physical, and cultural constraints. Each of the first three essays frame home locations as spaces of conflict, exploring sites throughout the Whedonverse in relation to agency. In "Genius, Billionaire, Playboy, Prometheus: Transhumanism and Proxemics in the Works of Joss Whedon," Dustin Dunaway centers representations of personal space, technology, and relationships in order to explore the ways in which Whedon interrogates the foundations of humanity. Acknowledging Whedon's feminist frame but focusing on his use of humanism, Dunaway's essay reminds us that home is a locus of humanity and serves as a key spatial marker of the impact technological entanglements carry. Using the scope of Whedon's televisual and filmic productions, Dunaway ultimately argues that the physical space represents the power currency of the occupants, which he concludes is central to the chaotic struggle of human agency and transhuman control.

In "It's Joss Whedon's World and We're All Just Livin' in It: The 'Closed Frame' of the Whedonverse," Kirk Hendershott-Kraetzer explores production design as a reflection of characters' lack of agency in Whedon's films *Much Ado, Serenity, The Avengers,* and *Age of Ultron*. He posits that while Whedon masks the "closed frame" within these productions with characters functioning as if they have agency, the restricted environments in each production indicate a variety of confinements for both the characters and the creator(s). Extending his spatial study to Buffy, Angel, and the Dolls, Hendershott-Kraetzer develops a persuasive portrait of the restlessness of the domestic Whedonverse.

"Broken but Home: Institutions, Control and the Non-Place in *Dollhouse*" explores the multiplicity created through the aesthetics of purposed space in the show's two-season run. Catherine Pugh suggests that the show situates the Los Angeles Dollhouse as a total institution, illustrating that it is presented aesthetically as serene and vulnerable while the filmic transitions suggest that control, trauma, and fragmentation are inherent to the Dolls' domicile. The paradoxical images of the Dollhouse's schizophrenic space suggest surreptitious boundaries and echo real-world post-traumatic, dissociative states. Using Echo's final reintegration into the 'House as evidence, Pugh argues that the disconnection among imprint, original personality, and Doll-state consciousness is somewhat reconciled once the narrative uncovers the Dollhouse as a non-place.

The next essay turns our attention to the potential refuge of various domestic representations in the Whedonverse. "Seeking Safe Haven: Shelter and Self-Protection from *Afterlife* to *Avengers: Age of Ultron*" demonstrates that homes often are spaces of feminist empowerment and that characters throughout the 'verse often must fight to recover these spaces as their own. Valerie Estelle Frankel argues that while the physical home is often rejected for the fray, despite the many heroes throughout the 'verse who seek the safety and peace that it offers, they often create sanctuary through their relationships with others.

The following three essays offer varied perspectives on identity and alternatively purposed domestic locations. "Domestic Space and Identity: Joss Whedon's Futuristic Frontier in *Firefly*" applies Homi Bhabha's concept of the unhomely to explore the crew's continuously blurred gender constructs as reflected in the domestic surroundings they inhabit on the *Serenity*, which straddles the ideological (and actual) space between the central planets occupied by the patriarchal Alliance and the lesser-controlled outer worlds. Melanie A. Marotta argues that because the crew exists in liminal space—that which is both public and private, ever moving and changing—they create similarly liminal gender identities that allow them to form a functional community. Marotta's analysis of the multi-purpose domestic and commercial space of *Serenity* and the transference of blurred purposes on the planets the crew encounters builds on our understanding of Whedon's feminism and encourages further consideration of alternative locations for domestic spaces throughout the 'verse.

In "Scythe Matters: Performing Object Oriented Ontology on Domestic Space in *Buffy the Vampire Slayer*," Julie L. Hawk uses vital materialism (Bennett) to consider the Slayer's scythe as an object in its own right, providing agency and autonomy from the anthropocentrically-driven constructs that privilege the subject's perspective. Hawk argues that the scythe, a critical character within the *BtVS* narrative world, and its power reach beyond its connection to the Slayer as a tool of destruction or protection; it is a home space for the Slayer power and for magic. Directly considering the significance of domestic entanglements, Hawk reminds us that home is not merely a passive location in which events happen to or within; in fact, domiciliary agency is an active empowerment with equal ability to act upon and in collaboration with its inhabitants and environment.

"Deliver Us from Evil: Demons, Feminism and Rhetorical Spaces in *Buffy the Vampire Slayer*" argues that Buffy's feminist agency emerges not in traditional public locations, but in domestic spaces. Victoria Willis posits that Buffy's rhetorical power is located in the parlor rhetoric she engages in the Summers home. Willis demonstrates how Whedon provides examples of heternormative, traditional rhetoric and its oppressive constructs while simultaneously pushing at the privileges inherent to the patriarchy in order to highlight a feminist rhetoric capable of inhabiting traditional spaces in nontraditional ways. Juxtaposing speeches delivered by male antagonists, the Mayor, the Master, and Jonathan Levinson, Willis illustrates the lenses through which the audience receives Buffy's speeches and the impact on feminist agency within the Buffyverse provided by the domestic location of her delivery.

The following two essays repurpose domestic locations in order to explore the ways in which Whedon multitasks through home spaces. In "Militarization of the Domestic Space: Positioning Buffy as a Post-Feminist

Heroine through the Lens of Choice Feminism," Karen Walsh continues the collection's discussion of Whedon's feminist agenda by tracing how Buffy's domestic locations mirror her evolution as a post-feminist representation in her struggle to find work-life balance and "have it all." Focusing on the season nine and ten comics, Walsh suggests that enhanced militarization of Buffy's home signals an increasing acceptance of her roles as both a leader and a nurturer. Further, as the Slayer encounters socionormative shifts, the purpose her domestic location serves is merged intentionally with increasingly social and economic goals. The result is a mutable public image of home, often mobilized and weapons-ready, that resists a narrative of chaos in order to embrace one of choice.

The relationship between home locations and learning spaces is considered in "Classrooms, Classrooms Everywhere, but Not to Slay or Think: The Domestic Learning Environments of *Buffy the Vampire Slayer*." Focusing on the television run of *BtVS*, Melanie A. Jensen and Kyle William Bishop argue that while slaying is the primary objective in the Slayer's narrative, teaching and learning provide the backdrop against which Buffy's journey is set. Jensen and Bishop address the multitude of learning spaces throughout the show's seven seasons, focusing on how each offers Buffy and the Scoobies hybrid locations that equally prioritize the ideals of the home and of the educational institution. Because of this, *BtVS* models hybrid institutional-domestic learning spaces that can inform real world teaching practices. They demonstrate that Sunnydale High's library is the initial domestic learning environment and suggest it serves as the most traditional representation of education. However, as the series progresses, the Slayer and crew struggle to find an ideal learning space until the final season, when the Summers house becomes both a domestic space and a training environment for the Potential Slayers. Ultimately, Jensen and Bishop conclude that *BtVS* is a study in pedagogical approaches through its use of different domestic spaces.

In the final essay in this collection, Lisa K. Perdigao suggests that the MCU Whedonverse repositions home as we have come to know or recognize it in Whedon's works. Using the work of Kristin J. Jacobson, Perdigao deftly identifies the elements of neodomestic fiction operating within specific home spaces in order to locate character realities and conflicts that destabilized notions of domesticity. In "A Home at the End of the World: The Future of Domesticity in the Whedonverse," Perdigao argues that the impossibility of establishing stable traditional domestic environments for the MCU characters ultimately positions them to move beyond nostalgic conceptualizations of home in order to reclaim progressive notions that offer possibility and purpose.

This collection is not intended to be an exhaustive study of domestic space or place, nor does it tap into all of the ways in which the agency of home (or that which is informed by home) impact narrative and rhetorical structure, character development, and world creation. However, at the heart of this collection is the desire to encourage deeper critical consideration of the home spaces existing in the Whedonverse as well as those which we embody and those with which we are entangled.

NOTES

1. The original identities of the volunteers are placed on a wedge and stored throughout the duration of their contract with the Dollhouse so that their bodies may be used for imprints. When they are re-imprinted into their bodies, they are relatively unaware that any time has passed. Bodies functioning in a Doll-state seem similarly unaware or perhaps merely unconcerned with where they are or with time as it passes.

2. Consider the parallels between the farmhouse and Summers' home circa season six and seven of *BtVS*—both are constantly under construction and serve as respites for the team. Another parallel is seen between the S.H.I.E.L.D. Airborne Mobile Command Station (more commonly known as the "Bus") and the Firefly-class ship *Serenity*, both of which provide protection and defense from outsiders while serving as both home and work space.

3. See Martin Heidegger, "Building, Dwelling, Thinking," Mary Douglas, "The Idea of a Home: A Kind of Space," and Juhani Pallasmaa, "Identity, Intimacy, and Domicile," for a more thorough discussion of the intimacy of the home.

4. Whedon regulars such as Amy Acker (*Angel* and *Dollhouse*), Alexis Denisof (*BtVS Angel* and *Dollhouse*), Nathan Fillion (*BtVS*, *Firefly*, and *Dr. Horrible's Sing-Along Blog*), Clark Gregg (*The Avengers* and *Agents of S.H.I.E.L.D.*), and Fran Kranz (*Dollhouse* and *The Cabin in the Woods*) appear alongside a host of notable Whedon-production players to form a [fan] family within the home that exists outside of the story. Playing on Matt Hill's term "hyperdiegesis," Alyson Buckman referred to this as "hyperdiegetic casting" in her presentation "'We Are Not What We Are': Hyperdiegesis in the Whedonverse" at the 6th Biennial *Slayage* Conference on the Whedonverses (Hautsch, McGee, and Nadkarni).

5. For more on the spatiotemporal nature of home, see Gaston Bachelard, *The Poetics of Space*, Olivier Marc, *Psychology of the House*, Irene Cieraad, "Anthropology at Home," and Tim Ingold, "Building Dwelling, Living: How Animals and People Make Themselves at Home in the World."

6. See Bryant's "Entanglements & Diffraction Patterns" for an extensive philosophical account of "entanglements."

WORKS CITED

Amy-Chinn, Dee. "'Tis Pity She's a Whore: Postfeminist Prostitution in Joss Whedon's *Firefly*?" *Feminist Media Studies* 6.2 (2006): 175–189. Web. 5 Jan. 2016.
Bachelard, Gaston. *The Poetics of Space*. Trans. Maria Jolas. Boston: Beacon Press, 1994. Print.
Bennett, Jane. *Vibrant Matter: A Political Ecology of Things*. Durham: Duke University Press, 2010. Print.
Bryant, Levi R. "Entanglements & Diffraction Patterns." *Larval Subjects*. 2 May 2010. Web. 19 March 2016.
Canavan, Gerry. "'Something Nightmares Are From': Metacommentary in Joss Whedon's *Cabin in the Woods*." "*We Are Not Who We Are*": *Critical Reflections on* The Cabin in the Woods. Ed. Kristopher Karl Woofter and Jasie Stokes. Spec. Issue of *Slayage: The Journal of Whedon Studies* 10.2–11.1 (2012). Web. 28 Dec. 2015.
Cieraad, Irene. "Anthropology at Home." Introduction. *At Home: An Anthropology of Domestic Space*. Ed. Irene Cieraad. Syracuse: Syracuse University Press, 1999. Print.
Douglas, Mary. "The Idea of a Home: A Kind of Space." *Social Research* 58.1 (1991): 287–307. Web. 10 Sept. 2016.
Hautsch, Jessica, Masani McGee, and Samira Nadkarni, eds. "Much Ado About Whedon: Report on the 6th Biennial *Slayage* Conference." Sacramento, The Whedon Studies

Association: June 2014. *Slayage: The Journal of Whedon Studies* 12.2–13.1 (2014). Web. 5 Jan. 2016.
Heidegger, Martin. "Building, Dwelling, Thinking." *Poetry, Language, Thought.* Trans. Albert Hofstadter. New York: Harper & Row, 1971. Print.
Ingold, Tim. "Building Dwelling, Living: How Animals and People Make Themselves at Home in the World." *Shifting Contexts: Transformations in Anthropological Knowledge.* Ed. Marilyn Strathern. New York: Routledge, 1995. Web. 20 May 2016.
Lanier, Douglas M. "'Good Lord, for Alliance': Joss Whedon's *Much Ado About Nothing*." *Représentations: La revue électronique du CEMRA* (2014): 117–142. Web. 28 Dec. 2015.
Marc, Olivier. *Psychology of the House.* Trans. Jessie Wood. London: Thames & Hudson, 1977. Web. 20 May 2016.
Pallasmaa, Juhani. "Identity, Intimacy and Domicile: Notes on the Phenomenology of Home." The Concept of Home: An Interdisciplinary View, a symposium. University of Trondheim, Norway. 21–23 Aug. 1992. Web. 10 Sept. 2016.
Pascale, Amy. *Joss Whedon: The Biography.* Chicago: Chicago Review Press, 2014. Print.
Nadkarni, Samira. "'In My House and Therefore in My Care': Transgressive Mothering, Abuse, and Embodiment." *Joss Whedon's* Dollhouse: *Confounding Purpose, Confusing Identity.* Ed. Sherry Ginn, Alyson R. Buckman, and Heather M. Porter. Lanham, MD: Rowman & Littlefield, 2014. 81–97. e-text.
Rogers, Scott. "Joss Whedon's *Dollhouse* and Joss Whedon's *Dollhouse.*" *Journal of the Fantastic in the Arts* 22.2 (2011). Web. 5 Jan. 2016.

Genius, Billionaire, Playboy, Prometheus
Transhumanism and Proxemics in the Works of Joss Whedon

DUSTIN DUNAWAY

The rapid expansion of technology over the last half century has left the humanist areas of study—particularly philosophy, religious studies, political science, and social psychology—struggling to keep up, so it should come as no surprise that a humanist writer and scholar like Joss Whedon would be so interested in what exactly makes humans *human*. Literary antecedents since Prometheus have sought to answer the question of what happens when humans take on the properties of gods. If intimacy requires weakness and vulnerability, do we lose intimacy if we become stronger? If we lose this intimacy, what happens when we try to forge the interpersonal relationships that are the core of domestic life? These questions are central to the ethos that runs throughout Whedon's work (Whitten). For his part, Joss Whedon answers the question in exploring humanity through a group of characters who are struggling with transhumanity: a chosen Vampire Slayer, a tortured vampire with a soul, a human blank slate, and a genius playboy billionaire philanthropist with a suit of armor powerful enough to bring peace to the Middle East.

In a culture that increasingly ties our identity to online avatars, PIN and bank account numbers, credit report scores, and standardized test results, our various identities become simulacra to our physical bodies. A life that is primarily lived through interactions on Facebook, Instagram, Snapchat, and text is one that will live on long after the physical body is dead. For some, this transcendence to something "more than human" is an ideal humanity should strive for (Winner 386). In examining domestic entanglements then, it becomes important to acknowledge that, as our identities continue to uncouple from our corporeal bodies, our assorted "homes" become central to what remains of our physical humanity. As a result, transhumanism connects to our environment and proxemics as we attempt to express our humanity through what is left of the physical space we embody. As a writer and director, Whedon explores the implications of humanism and transhumanism using physical space both as an overt narrative device and as part of his *mise en scène*. One key theme throughout Whedon's work is that humanity is best represented in the ways we treat the people around us. Our interpersonal relationships, the ones that leave a lasting impact on those we meet are what allow us to retain the best part of our human identity. In a body of work that almost exclusively focuses on transhumans, Whedon spotlights the importance of interpersonal communication and the creation of intimate connection with others as defining factors in humanity. This essay will investigate Whedon's exploration of humanity (and its conflict with transhumanity) through his use of domestic space and environment as symbols for characters' interpersonal relationships. It contains three main sections: the science of proxemics and environment as forms of nonverbal code, proxemics' relation to the Western cultural phenomenon of domesticity, and an examination of symbolic proxemics in Whedon's work. The section on Whedon's work is divided into subsections on *Alien: Resurrection, Buffy the Vampire Slayer, Angel, Dollhouse,* and the two *Avengers* films.

Proxemics and Environment

Joss Whedon rarely hides his themes for long. The metaphors in *Buffy the Vampire Slayer* (1997–2003) and *Angel* (1999–2004) quickly became apparent as they challenged the gender roles of traditional horror fare. Whedon's primary theme, though, is not merely feminism. It is the value of human dignity, regardless of gender, race, or orientation. Part of this theme comes with narrative inquiry into how we dehumanize other humans by violating their basic human rights. One such violation is through proxemic violations, or the violation of space.

Anthropologist Edward T. Hall, who is widely credited for inventing the term, defines proxemics as "the interrelated observations and theories of man's use of space as a specialized elaboration of culture" (*The Hidden Dimension* 2). Hall suggests that the study of proxemics communication is important because behavior is largely reflected and regulated in the layout of personal and public space ("Proxemic Behavior" 1003–1004). Hall distinguishes between two categories of proxemics: the area immediately around a person (personal space), and territory, that to which a person can lay claim (Moore 130). Hall further divided personal space into four proxemics zones or "reaction bubbles": intimate distance, personal distance, social distance, and public distance (Moore 130). The science of proxemics has been applied to everything from street harassment of women in major cities to "buffer zones" at abortion clinics (Hern 3–5). Proxemics relates heavily to humanity in that the relational dialectic between closeness and autonomy is regulated by the distance we keep between others and ourselves. Hall notes that humans tend to feel anger, anxiety, or discomfort when ownership over their space is challenged (*The Hidden Dimension* 96–97). One way in which humans deal with these feelings of angst is to dehumanize the person who is challenging their space (Sommer 101). Robert Sommer imagines a subway car in which everyone's personal space is being invaded. The only way to survive psychologically is to pretend that the other person is an inanimate object, thus dehumanizing them (Sommer 101). In an era of the internet, the entirety of the online experience becomes a contested space. Internet users feel an ownership over their personal information, data, and ability to traverse the World Wide Web in peace. However, users also find that navigation impeded by spammers, phishers, and trolls. This, coupled with the asynchronous and anonymous nature of the internet, has led to a dehumanizing effect (Konrath 188). It is at this nexus of empathy, dehumanization, technology, and contested space (virtual or otherwise) that we find Joss Whedon operating.

Proxemics Role in Domesticity

While Whedon's themes generally are feminist and progressive, his main subjects are generally the fundamental interpersonal relationships between characters. What may separate Whedon from his contemporaries is his willingness to give equal weight to various forms of relationships. Many writers focus solely on romantic relationships (following the old adage "sex sells"). Whedon certainly presents romantic relationships (Buffy, Willow, and Xander each explore multiple relationships in *BtVS* alone), but he also explores the complexities of sibling or para-sibling relationships (Buffy/Dawn, Buffy/Willow, Buffy/Faith, Angel/Spike) as well as generational relationships (Buffy/Giles, Buffy/Joyce, Ripley/Call). The complexity of these relationships often owes itself to both the emotional and physical closeness the characters enjoy. When Whedon rings truest to the audience, he is at his most valuable. It is at this point when we recognize the truisms of human nature.

Most human cultures, indeed most mammalian cultures, rely on the idea of a family unit that lives together as the building block of society. Unlike our reptilian and insect cousins, most mammal species thrive in altruistic environments. This means we, as a species, value physical closeness. Of course, this comes at a cost. As we allow others into our physical space, we also make ourselves vulnerable to attack. Therefore, we tend to limit our space to those with whom we share a close bond or with whom we make some form of social exchange (Homans). Those we perceive as offering benefits are allowed into our space. This means that those we perceive as not offering benefits, or worse, offering harm in some way, are categorized as outgroupers and excluded from our space. Whedon recognizes these violations can be played for laughs, horror, or the agony of dehumanization.

Proxemics as Symbols of Domestic Identity

Alien: Resurrection

Although the collaborative nature of the film likely makes this the least "Whedonesque" of the works studied here, *Alien: Resurrection* (1997), the fourth film in the horror/sci-fi franchise, nevertheless bares many of the markings of a Whedon project. It contains self-referential humor, strong female leads, and a philosophical narrative on what constitutes humanity. Like the previous films in the series, *Alien: Resurrection* benefits from a claustrophobic, enclosed space and a group of characters forced to interact with one another, despite differences in class, race, gender, and worldview. It is here where we see Whedon's use of physical space and proxemics as a narrative device first manifest. The plot centers on protagonist Ellen Ripley's clone teaming with a group of mercenaries to prevent the xenomorph aliens from reaching Earth.

In the opening lines, Whedon establishes the ships as displaced symbols for the respective crews. The USS *Auriga* is vast and "majestic," a powerhouse of military might. The rogue ship *Betty* is described as "a small vessel, it is every bit dirty and jerry-rigged as the *Auriga* is pristine" (*Alien: Resurrection* "Early Draft" 14). Whedon's fetishization of environment and its representation of the identity of his characters become apparent in the first act of the film. The films do not just symbolize the crew, they are extensions of the crew's identity and psychological state, a trick Whedon would later repeat in his space western *Firefly* ("Out of Gas"). The *Auriga* serves as the vessel carrying Dr. Wren and his associates who are responsible for cloning Ripley and her alien spawn. As such, it is sleek and sterile. Its form follows function. Its only personality is the absence of personality, the perfect representation of a group of military scientists who have no purpose outside of their mission. Because it is a military vessel, though, it serves as a domestic environment for those aboard, pushing them into various roles—masculine, feminine, paternal, maternal, leader, and follower. Conversely, the *Betty* represents the ragtag group of mercenaries in the same way that *Serenity* would half a decade later. It is the embodiment of the underdog. As *Betty* docks with the *Auriga*, Whedon describes the differences:

> One by one the crew files out. Seeing them en masse, we get a clearer view of what separates them from this Environment. They're not wearing uniforms. They're an eclectic, fiercely indivualist [sic] group, their look varied—spots of bright color showing through militarian space gear [*Alien: Resurrection* "Early Draft" 21].

It is this set of characteristics that differentiates, through representation in their environment, the values and philosophies of the two crews.

When Ripley's clone is first introduced, she is encompassed in a dark chamber. As a clone she is a newborn, complete with Ripley's personality and memories, yet still disoriented from being brought back into the world. It is 200 years after the events of *Alien³* (1992). As the audience enters the story, Ripley has essentially achieved the transhuman state. Although she perished at the end of *Alien³*, intentionally throwing herself into a smelting furnace to prevent the birth of a new xenomorph, she is reborn here over 300 years after her natural birth. Whedon portrays this immortality as a curse rather than a blessing. Ripley is not human and not just transhuman. She is an alien-human hybrid. As with Lovecraft's "fish-men," Ripley has achieved a sort of deathlessness by becoming something hideous. Witness Ripley's exchange with Annalee Call:

> CALL: I've read Morse—I've read all the banned histories. She gave her life to protect us from the beast. You're not her.
> RIPLEY: If I'm not her. What am I?
> CALL: You're a thing. A construct. They grew you in a fucking lab.
> RIPLEY: But only God can make a tree.
> CALL: And now they've brought the beast out of you.
> RIPLEY: (smiling) Not all the way out [*Alien: Resurrection* "Early Draft" 28].

Call disputes whether the person she is talking to can even be considered Ellen Ripley. Of course, in the narrative, Ripley does not choose immortality, nor is she given a choice in her resurrection. Ripley is not treated as human so much as property of the military who uses her as an involuntary brood mare and organ donor. Although not explicitly stated, Whedon's implication is that immortality has the unintended consequence of diminishing the value of life. Certainly, the military does not value the failed clones that preceded Ripley's successful resurrection: "Numbers one through seven. The first failed efforts to clone Ripley. They are lined up like museum exhibits—or side show freaks.... Each one more horrifying than the last, and the last the worst of all" (*Alien: Resurrection* "Early Draft" 79). In the same way that Victor Frankenstein did not anticipate the consequences of his creation because he does not view it as human, Dr. Wren fails to value "Ripleys 1–7" as humans, leaving them to suffer. Number Seven actually begs Ripley to destroy them all, like Frankenstein's creation, deciding that death is preferable to an existence of suffering. As Scheper-Hughes notes, in a transhuman era, the ethics of phenomena like global organ trade become blurred (145). Whedon, whose body of work was still practically in its naissance, shows an immediate distrust for bureaucracy (corporate or military) when it comes to its ability to value human dignity. This becomes a running theme in Whedon's humanism—a system, whether governmental, mystical, or environmental cannot truly be, nor understand, human nature. The result is friction between those who adhere to a systemic view and those who value individual humanity above all else.

Buffy the Vampire Slayer

Easily the most studied of Whedon's work, and certainly his most durable television endeavor, is *Buffy the Vampire Slayer* (hereafter *BtVS*). Equal parts horror, soap opera, and teen-angst drama upon its debut, *BtVS* occupies a fortified locus in popular culture thanks to intense interdisciplinary academic scrutiny and the increase in streaming outlets for which *BtVS* seemed to be created (Arpe & Stafford). While *BtVS*' brand of third-wave feminism and the characters' tendency toward post-structuralist language (sometimes referred to as "Buffyspeak") have been the most salient fodder for analysis, it is Whedon's penchant for representing what it means to be a human being that makes *BtVS* timeless. The character of Buffy Summers is Whedon's stand-in for the concept of retaining humanity in the face of enormous power, responsibility, and temptation. Whedon often positions Buffy as the human center in opposition to her transhuman foes and, on occasion, her transhuman allies. In the fourth season, Adam's puzzlement over the human condition drives him to attempt to create a simulacrum of a human family, bringing Buffy's patchwork family back together. Faith Lehane's insecure nihilism accentuates Buffy's humanist moral center in season three. Willow Rosenberg's anguished anxiety and suffering leads to a rage-filled revenge path and causes her rift with Buffy's compassionate restraint in season six. Because of their enormous power, these antagonists represent a transhuman counterpoint to Buffy's ethical core, and in each case, the antagonist argues that they have transcended the morality of mortal humans due to this power. As Bill McKibben postulates, transcending humanity into transhumanity—whether technological in the case of Daryl ("Some Assembly Required") and season four's Adam, or mystical in most other cases—jeopardizes the social order by making the human experience less meaningful (72).

This is not to say that Whedon's humanism is always positive; in fact, it is quite the opposite (Hinze; Loftis). According to Whedon, "Ultimately, stories come from violence, they come from sex. They come from death. They come from the dark places that everybody has to go" (Longworth 213). "Place," as used here, clearly means a metaphorical space, but it also refers to the physical space around the characters. Often, the violence, sex, and death come from the very environment that Whedon, himself, creates. Moreover, that struggle between protagonist and violence, sex, and death are *represented* in the environment, both physically and spatially. The danger from the environment often is represented by the most benign of signifiers—a middle-class home, well-to-do high school and a teen-centric nightclub. Hitchcock recognized the horror that is best represented in the banal, and Whedon uses this to maximal effect.

Perhaps not surprisingly, while Buffy's home is a central focus of the show, much of its use is in character building rather than staging for mystical conflict. When we first meet Buffy Summers in "Welcome to the Hellmouth," she awakens from a prescient nightmare in her new home in Sunnydale, California. As Whedon describes the room: "it's only half decorated: there are still boxes as yet unpacked in the corner" ("Welcome to the Hellmouth"). Indeed, the audience finds that we have joined the story on Buffy's first day at a new school after flaming out (figuratively and literally) at her previous school in Los Angeles. "You burned down the gym," Principal Flutie puzzles upon meeting her ("Welcome to the Hellmouth"). Although Flutie promises her a fresh start, his treatment of her school records from Himbry High indicates that she is already on thin ice from day one. Further compounding the first-day-of-school-as-nightmare scenario, Buffy runs afoul of Cordelia Chase, Sunnydale's Queen Bee, by talking with Willow Rosenberg and Xander Harris. To make matters worse, the "curse" of being a Slayer, which she so desperately wanted to leave behind in Los Angeles, has followed her to Sunnydale. "*Buffy* is about growing up," Whedon explains (Robinson). If we accept BtVS as a metaphor for the transition from adolescence to adulthood, then Buffy's first day is the nightmare scenario every teen dreads on their first day of school—in trouble with the principal, social pariah, and inescapable responsibility. All of this, however, is symbolized in the first scene when Buffy awakens in the unpacked bedroom. Whedon, who often uses the symbolism in Buffy's dreams to fuel the narrative, positions the unpacked boxes as a symbolic cue to the audience of life transition. Buffy, like her bedroom, exists in a limbo not fully immersed in the Los Angeles of her youth, nor the Sunnydale of her womanhood. Not only does this give the audience an idea of who Buffy is, but it portends the show to follow. Buffy is presented to us as a human being in flux and someone who simply is not ready for the challenges of life. This lack of conscientiousness and preparedness is something Buffy is routinely chided for by Rupert Giles in the first half of season one. Compare this, then, with later episodes in season one and into season two. As Buffy matures, both as a Slayer and as a woman, Whedon allows her room to fill in with pictures, clothing, her slaying equipment, and brighter lighting. As the shades of her character fill in, so too does her living space.

The most salient metaphor in the pre-collegiate seasons is the use of Buffy's home as a stand-in for her body. Proxemically, Buffy's home is safe in the first three seasons. Despite the fact that she is the scourge of the demon underworld, demon attacks on her home are uncommon. On the rare occasions when the forces of evil violate Buffy's domestic space, it is because someone within the house has dabbled with demonic forces (see "Dead Man's Party"). We see in various instances that Buffy is highly protective of her space. Although she expects her mother to have access to her room, she hides the artifacts that symbolize her Slayer-self in a trunk during the first two seasons. At this point, this part of herself is secret from her mother. When she finds Joyce's boyfriend snooping through her Slayer kit, Buffy's reaction denotes less worry that he knows her secret identity and more outrage over the violation of her personal space ("Ted"). Much of this attitude can be attributed to the stereotypical teenager's desire for privacy during a period of identity formation, but it is important to recognize that Buffy Summers identity formation travels along two parallel tracks: teenage girl and transhuman superhero. In many instances, these two tracks must progress independently of one another and, in a recurring theme for the first two seasons, they often interfere with one another. Whedon symbolizes this by having Buffy literally compartmentalize her Slayer world within her domestic world.

This becomes an important point when viewing Buffy's relationship with her vampire boyfriend Angel. Buffy first invites Angel into her home in the first season. Not only does she invite Angel into her home, she invites him into her bedroom—a place he spends most of his visits. If Buffy's room represents her identity in this first season, then allowing Angel in symbolically represents her desire for intimacy with someone who can understand the dichotomy of being a transhuman superhero and a tortured teen. Not only does she keep her trunk full of weapons as part of her duties as Slayer, she keeps all the trappings of a normal teenage girl. Although we see many people interact in Buffy's room, including her mother, the Scoobies, and even counterfeit foreign exchange student "Ampata" ("Inca Mummy Girl"), only Angel needs specific verbal permission to enter her domestic space. That his entry requires explicit rather than implied permission creates a situation in which Buffy must verbally and overtly make her domestic space vulnerable to him. It is perhaps not surprising in Whedon's work that Angel is the most dangerous person in her circle, and not just from a physical violence perspective. Angel is the character with whom Buffy becomes most intimate. In the episode titled "Angel," Buffy mistakenly thinks Angel has violated her privacy by reading her diary. She chastises him for it before he corrects her, but we see the dialectic between Buffy's desire for intimacy and her reluctance to share her true feelings. This dialectic shifts from subtext to text when Buffy and Angel sleep together for the first time, causing the curse that restored his soul to be broken. Angel's evil counterpart Angelus is happy to exploit both the intimacy of Buffy's emotional connection to Angel and the intimacy of her domestic space. In fact, Angelus is most "at home" when he uses violations of domestic space to disturb and torture psychologically. Willow, who had spoken with Angel in her room near her fish tank, later finds her fish killed and left as a message. When Angelus kills Jenny Calendar, he specifically leaves her body in the bed at Rupert Giles' home to taunt him. Later, Angelus approaches Joyce outside of Buffy's home and reveals that he and Buffy slept together, intentionally violating Buffy's privacy. Once Angel's soul is restored, we see a gradual return to intimacy between Buffy and Angel, and he is again allowed into her home when their relationship resumes. Again, though, we see that the tense dialectic between Buffy's desire for an intimate relationship with Angel in season three, and her fear that she will once again be hurt. Tellingly, most scenes in which Angel and Buffy share intimate conversations in season three take place not in Buffy's home, but in Angel's crypt.

The push-pull pattern repeats with Spike in seasons five and six. Spike, although he is missing his soul, earns Buffy's trust by being significantly less dangerous at first. The Initiative-installed chip in his brain renders him both helpless and (theoretically) harmless. His willingness to aid the Scoobies and protect Dawn makes Spike seemingly safe. However, once Spike develops feelings for Buffy and is able to harm her, she removes his ability to enter the home. The scene's emotional impact comes from Spike's feel of shock, betrayal, and, most importantly given Spike's history, rejection. Buffy's and Spike's relationship comes at a different point in Buffy's development. As a result, the symbolic meaning behind Buffy's home is different, but its importance to her psyche and relationships is no less impactful. When Buffy engages in a yearlong relationship with Riley Finn, she does not have to offer affirmative consent, and that, in many ways, diminishes the weight of their relationship. Even Buffy notes that Riley is less dangerous and that makes him less attractive to her on an emotional level ("Something Blue"). The danger, while necessary, is secondary to Buffy's need and willingness to engage in a relationship fully and intimately. However, without the danger of being hurt, Buffy's consent is meaningless. The nexus of emotional consent and proxemic consent becomes apparent in "Seeing Red," an episode that features Spike attempting to rape Buffy. She fights him off and kicks him out of the house, ending their romantic relationship. Again, like Angel, Spike does not return until he regains his soul. During the rape attempt, Spike saw Buffy as dehumanized, an object to be possessed—something that would make his psyche whole.

Situated on a "hellmouth" (a portal that bridges the human world and mystical hell world beneath), Sunnydale High serves as the battleground for most of Buffy's early fights against evil. The school itself is fairly typical. Whedon's script direction even notes that the school and its students "could be from anywhere in America" ("Welcome to the Hellmouth"). Given its status as "Anywhere, U.S.A.," Sunnydale High's inherently rigid social structure makes a perfect environment for the criticisms of becoming "more than human." After all, companies that sell cosmetics, acne treatments, hair products, and weight gain/loss programs have made billions targeting the high school demographic with impossible (often-inhuman) beauty standards and then offering consumers the promise of achieving these standards. On some scale, these products exist to mitigate the "imperfections" of humanity. One key tenet of transhumanism is the attainment of physical perfection (Murphy). Of course, ultimately, the drive to attain physical perfection is to improve our social value. One vital part of relationship formation is the concept of matching (Hatfield et al.). As our social value increases, our perceived ability to engage in social relationships increases (Dion, Berscheid & Walster). This allows those of high value to find domestic partners of high value (Walster et al.). In fact, when one examines many of the motives of Sunnydale students, one sees that an almost-obsessive need to maintain domestic relationships is at the core of their actions. When Xander dabbles in witchcraft in "Bewitched, Bothered, and Bewildered," it is because he wants to maintain his relationship with Cordelia. Chris, of "Some Assembly Required," wants to maintain his relationship with his brother. Pete drinks a Mr. Hyde–potion to become hypermasculine and maintain his relationship with Debbie ("Beauty and the Beasts"). The drive to form and retain romantic relationships is central to forming social identity in teens. At Sunnydale High, the same drives exist, but the solutions are turned up to eleven.

In Whedon's domestic relationships, as in real life, neither force nor social value alone can maintain a relationship. Successful relationships depend primarily on how well-adjusted the individuals involved in the relationship are. At Sunnydale High, where most of the people Whedon introduces to are transhuman in some form or another, this "normalcy" becomes a dialectic between the power they have as transhumans and the powerful hegemonic forces of traditional high school life. In the third episode of the first season entitled "Witch," Buffy and friends contend with a witch bent on reclaiming her former high school glory by switching bodies with her teenage daughter and sabotaging the cheerleading team. It is here where Sunnydale High opens up and begins to resemble the typical high school, and it coincides with the first instance of Buffy attempting to engage in acts that allow her to retain her humanity. Buffy, seeking an identity outside of "The Slayer," tries out for the Sunnydale High cheerleading squad. It is here where we see the dialectic between Buffy's humanity (social and self-actualizing needs) and

Buffy's status as a transhuman. "You have been chosen to destroy Vampires, not wave pom-poms at people," Giles scolds, clearly expecting to embrace her. "I'll still have time to fight the forces of evil, okay? But I want to have a life. I want to do something normal," she tells Giles ("Witch").

The library at Sunnydale High operates on its own level, apart from the school proper, and, as such, warrants its own analysis. In many ways, it seems like its own private world for the "Scooby Gang." Sunnydale students rarely come seeking books, and when they do, it is used as comic cannon fodder. "Does this look like a Barnes & Noble?" Xander Harris asks two students who wander in timidly ("Passion"). The library, therefore, becomes the perfect base of operations for the Scoobies. It encompasses antiquity and modernity with both ancient books and computers. When technopagan Jenny Calendar arrives on campus in "I, Robot.... You, Jane," it is no wonder she acts as a bridge between Rupert Giles (antiquity) and Willow Rosenberg (modernity). More than merely a base of operations, the library becomes a central home to many of the characters. With very few exceptions ("Passions" being most notable), the library acts as a home for the character of Rupert Giles. Even Whedon himself noted that when Giles talked to Buffy in the hall or at the Bronze, it gave off an "icky" vibe ("Welcome to the Hellmouth" DVD Commentary). It is in the library where Giles forms a fatherly relationship with Buffy, Xander, and Willow. The library also offers Giles' primary venue for his flirtation with Jenny Calendar in the first two seasons. Similarly, the audience rarely sees Xander Harris' room prior to the fourth season, and we never meet his family outside of disembodied voices. In many ways, the library serves as Xander's home and the Scoobies his family. Even Willow develops her first real relationship with the demon Moloch on the library's computer. Indeed, invasions into the library, as with the Master's army in the first season or Mayor Wilkins in the third, are nearly incursions on the level of invasions of Buffy's home.

Angel

Angel, a spinoff to *BtVS* featuring the titular character, sees this same proxemics-as-humanity motif, although on a far more overt level. Angel, who is relegated to the sewers of Los Angeles during the day and a basement apartment at night, finds himself struggling to atone for the sins he committed as a full transhuman. When precognitive demon Doyle (Glenn Quinn) and Sunnydale's Cordelia join him in his mission, Angel finds a road to humanity through his interactions with them. Early in the series, everyone lives in separate apartments. Cordelia and Doyle each inhabit small "hole-in-the-wall" apartments, and Angel lives by himself in an apartment that connects to the office. His apartment is intentionally Spartan. Few things symbolize a "home," save for some items of Asian décor. It is an emptiness that is symbolic of Angel's internal self at the beginning of the series. He has just left Buffy behind in Sunnydale and is starting over as an "avenger of the night." Like Angel, Cordelia originally lives in a smaller apartment that symbolizes her losses in Sunnydale. In season three of *BtVS*, Cordelia's father lost everything due to tax evasion. Also like Angel, Cordelia struggles to move on by moving into a new, larger apartment (which, of course, is haunted). Unlike Angel, who sought solitude, Cordelia seeks to recapture her Queen Bee status, this time in Hollywood. As the season progresses, however, Cordelia comes to appreciate her newfound friendships more than her status. The "Phantom Dennis," who also occupies Cordelia's apartment, becomes a much-needed friend and roommate for Cordelia.

The second season sees Angel and company move into the abandoned Hyperion Hotel. Again, the hotel is haunted in early episodes, but the important shift comes in the dynamics. All of the characters in Angel's life now have a shared home. The group starts functioning as a unit. The emotional bonds become tighter, and the intimacy among characters begins to grow. This continues, despite difficulties, through the end of season four with many additions moving into the hotel. The Hyperion Hotel itself is filled with history and acts both as metaphor and as sounding board to externalize the internal struggles of its characters. In many ways, it serves the same purpose as the hellmouth under Sunnydale High. Whatever psychological or emotional issue the characters are undergoing manifests through the history of the hotel. Unlike Sunnydale's library or Buffy's home, however, the hotel never becomes sanctuary. This demonstrates that many of the characters in *Angel* are more damaged and vulnerable than the characters in *BtVS*. Angel regrets the many malevolent things he did as a vampire. Like Xander Harris, former Watcher Wesley Wyndham-Price is insecure about his masculinity in a world of superpowered transhumans ("Billy"). Charles Gunn feels the pull of his roots as well as the responsibility for his younger sister's death ("War Zone"). Fred Burkel deals with the isolation her intelligence has created as well as the real, lived isolation of being stuck in Pylea ("Heartthrob"). Connor, who was raised by a vampire hunter in a hell dimension, constantly demonstrates that he distrusts his father to a pathological degree ("Home").

In *Angel*'s final televised season, Angel Investigations takes over the malignant law firm of *Wolfram & Hart*. It is a dramatic shift in tone for the series and in its *raison d'être*. Narratively, the change offers its characters challenges to their values. These value questions are also challenges to the relationships the characters engage in. Characters begin to question each other's motives. Contrary to the ending of *BtVS*, the group in *Angel* finds themselves fractured and facing a hopeless battle against the end of the world. It is a markedly different result than *BtVS*' empowering final episode.

Dollhouse

Whedon's fourth major foray into an ongoing television series, *Dollhouse* (2009–2010), is the most significant in terms of transhumanist philosophy and space. The series follows Echo and a cohort of "Dolls" who serve as programmable fantasy-fulfillment for the rich and powerful on behalf of the Rossum Corporation. When the dolls are not active, they are housed in the "Dollhouse," a series of sleeping chambers and Japanese design. Production Designer Stuart Blatt explains the set as "these people are being pampered like world-class athletes, kept ready for whatever the next assignment is" (Fernandez). The comfort of the dollhouse reinforces Whedon's thesis for the show: "The idea of the show is what I consider any good fantasy to be—your worst nightmare and your greatest dream. And the nightmare is: I don't know who I am. I'm exploited. I'm trapped. I'm helpless. And the dream is: I have no burdens, and I spend all of my time eating really good food and getting massages in the nicest place in the world" (Fernandez). We see the disharmony of power and diminished human value—the dolls (or "actives") can be programmed to be geniuses, black-belt martial artists, sexual dynamos, or any combination of desirable traits, but they have value only in as much as they serve the already-powerful. If Whedon's early work questioned how one forms a domestic relationship with someone when one's agency is unparalleled, then *Dollhouse* ponders the question "How can a relationship form when one partner views the other as disposable?" *Dollhouse*'s first season—inadvertently or not—becomes a critique of the burgeoning trend of hookups and internet pornography. If one can use another person to gratify their every wish, why risk emotional attachment? Rossum programs the dolls to fulfill fantasies, so there is no chance of rejection for those who fear taking a risk. In essence, Rossum has created a series of "Buffybots" in the same way Warren Mears created girlfriends in the *BtVS* episodes "I Was Made to Love You" and "Intervention." The series narrative takes a shift toward grander conspiracies late in the first season, but the early episodes question the how intimacy can truly exist when one side (generally, the woman) has no agency.

Avengers and Avengers: Age of Ultron

Easily Joss Whedon's most commercially successful works are the couplet of Disney/Marvel films *Avengers* (2012) and *Avengers: Age of Ultron* (2015). The first film features the titular supergroup forming to combat an incursion from the Norse trickster god Loki who has amassed an alien army. Although the cast is ensemble, Tony Stark (the progenitor of the Marvel Cinematic Universe) takes center stage throughout. Interestingly, Stark's only true superpower is that he is inhumanly wealthy, something into which he was born.

It is unsurprising, then, that he deals with power better than his peers do. When we first meet him in *The Avengers*, he is putting the finishing touches on a Trump-style tower with his name on it. Stark is not someone who shies away from the spotlight. It is in this first Stark scene where Whedon shines as a scribe of banter. Although Pepper Potts is a "love interest" role, Whedon presents her as an equal in terms of her wit. This relationship grounds Tony's humanity, and it is the first thing later writers jettison in making him more of a threat to the world.

Stark's character arc continues in *Age of Ultron* and the non–Whedon work *Iron Man 3*. After the events at the Battle of New York in *Avengers*, Tony faces panic attacks and an overwhelming sense of helplessness. His brush with death at the end of the first film has paralyzed him emotionally. Tellingly, Pepper Potts only makes a cameo during a conversation on "Who has the best girlfriend?" Instead, the focus of *Age of Ultron* becomes the dysfunctional family that is the Avengers. Brother figures Tony Stark and Steve Rogers have intense philosophical differences that are not reconciled by the end of the film. Bruce Banner sees himself as the dangerous "black sheep" of the family, and banishes himself despite overtures from Natasha Romanoff. Clint Barton gives precedence to his own, real-life family. It then falls to para-siblings Ultron and Vision to give the film its most Whedonesque touches. Whedon explores the idea of sibling relationships through both transhuman beings, both created inadvertently by Tony Stark. In many ways, their relationship resembles the dichotomy between Angel and Spike. They have comparable abilities, but only Vision has a soul. Ultron and Vision meet for a dialogue near the denouement. Their conversation reveals the brotherly relationship they feel. "Stark wanted a savior and settled for a slave," Ultron grouses. "I suppose we're both disappointments," Vision tells Ultron. "Humans are odd. They think order and chaos are somehow opposites and try to control what won't be," he continues (*Age of Ultron*). As with many Whedon characters—including Anya Jenkins (*BtVS*) and River Tam (*Firefly*)—the transhumans are able to summarize the virtue of the human spirit due to their outsider status.

Whedon offers few direct answers on domestic entanglements. After all, Whedon's work is notorious for never giving couples a happy ending. While his work does deal primarily with "more than human" characters, the consistent thread is the struggle to maintain intimate relationships under circumstances that work against them and the value those relationships have to the people who engage in them. Whedon's work says relationships are dangerous. Whedon's work says intimacy and vulnerability are dangerous. Whedon's work also says, ultimately, that those relationships are worth the danger.

Works Cited

Alien³. Dir. David Fincher. Twentieth Century Fox, 2002. Film.
"Angel." *Buffy the Vampire Slayer: The Complete First Season*. Episode 7. Writ. Joss Whedon. Dir. Joss Whedon. The WB. 14 April 1997. Twentieth Century Fox, 2002. DVD.
Arpe, Malene, and Nikki Stafford." Why Buffy Still Slays Us." *The Toronto Star*. thestar. com. 4 March 2007. Web. 5 May 2016.
The Avengers. Writ. and Dir. Joss Whedon. Marvel Studios, 2012. DVD.
Avengers: Age of Ultron. Writ. and Dir. Joss Whedon. Marvel Studios, 2015. DVD.
"Beauty and the Beasts." *Buffy the Vampire Slayer: The Complete Third Season*. Episode 4. Writ. Marti Noxon. Dir. James Whitmore, Jr. The WB. 20 Oct. 1998. Twentieth Century Fox, 2002. DVD.
"Bewitched, Bothered, and Bewildered." *Buffy the Vampire Slayer: The Complete Second Season*. Episode 16. Writ. Marti Noxon. Dir. James A. Contner. The WB. 10 Feb. 1998. Twentieth Century Fox, 2002. DVD.
"Billy." *Angel: The Complete Third Season*. Episode 6. Writ. Tim Minear, Jeffrey Bell. Dir. David Grossman. The WB. 29 Oct. 2001. Twentieth Century Fox, 2004. DVD.
"Dead Man's Party." *Buffy the Vampire Slayer: The Complete Second Season*. Episode 2. Writ. Marti Noxon. Dir. James Whitmore, Jr. The WB. 6 Oct. 1998. Twentieth Century Fox, 2002. DVD.
Dion, Karen, Ellen Bierscheid, Ellen Walster. "What Is Beautiful Is Good." *Journal of Personality and Social Psychology* 24.3 (1972): 285–290. PDF.
Fernandez, Maria Elena. "For 'Dollhouse' on Fox, the set is one of the stars." *Los Angeles Times*. latimes. com, 1 Feb. 2009. Web. 20 April 2016.
Hall, Edward T. "A System for the Notation of Proxemic Behavior." *American Anthropologist* 65.5 (1963): 1003–1026. PDF.
_____. *The Hidden Dimension*. New York: Anchor Books, 1966. Print.
"Heartthrob." *Angel: The Complete Third Season*. Episode 1. Writ. David Greenwalt. Dir. David Greenwalt. The WB. 24 Sept. 2001. Twentieth Century Fox, 2004. DVD.
Hern, Warren M. "Proxemics: The Application of Theory to Conflict Arising from AntiAbortion Demonstrations." *Population and Environment: A Journal of Interdisciplinary Studies* 12.4 (1991): 379–378. PDF.
Hinze, Scott. "Joss Whedon—Fanboy Radio Show—Newsarama.com Recap." Whedon. info, 12 Dec. 2006. Web. 8 May 2016.
Homans, George. *Social Behavior: Its Elementary Forms*. New York. Harcourt, 1974. Print.
"Home." *Angel: The Complete Fourth Season*. Episode 22. Writ. Tim Minear. Dir. Tim Minear. The WB. 7 May 2003. Twentieth Century Fox, 2004. DVD.
"I, Robot ... You, Jane." *Buffy the Vampire Slayer: The Complete First Season*. Episode 8. Writ. Ashley Gable, Thomas A. Swyden. Dir. Stephen Posey. The WB. 28 April 1997. Twentieth Century Fox, 2002. DVD.
"I Was Made to Love You." *Buffy the Vampire Slayer: The Complete Fifth Season*. Episode 15. Writ. Jane Espenson. Dir. James A. Contner. The WB. 20 Feb. 2001. Twentieth Century Fox, 2003. DVD.
"Inca Mummy Girl." *Buffy the Vampire Slayer: The Complete Second Season*. Episode 4. Writ. Matt Kiene, Joe Reinkemeyer. Dir. Ellen. S. Pressman. The WB. 6 Oct. 1997. Twentieth Century Fox, 2002. DVD.
"Intervention." *Buffy the Vampire Slayer: The Complete Fifth Season*. Episode 18. Writ. Jane Espenson. Dir. Michael Gershman. The WB. 24 April 2001. Twentieth Century Fox, 2003. DVD.
Konrath, Sara H. "Changes in Dispositional Empathy in American College Students Over Time: A Meta-Analysis." *Personality and Social Psychology Review* 15.1 (2011): 180–198. Print.
Loftis, J. Robert. "Moral Complexity in the Buffyverse." *Slayage: The Online Journal of Whedon Studies* 7. 3 (2009): n. pag. PDF.
Longworth, James L. "Joss Whedon: Feminist." *TV Creators: Conversations with America's Top Producers of Television Drama*. Syracuse: Syracuse University Press, 2000. Print.

Moore, Nina. *Nonverbal Communication: Studies and Applications.* New York: Oxford University Press, 2010. Print.
Murphy, B. J. "How Will We Define Beauty in a Transhuman Future." *Serious Wonder: The Future Has Arrived.* Seriouswonder. com, 24 July 2014. Web. 28 April 2016.
"Out of Gas." *Firefly: The Complete Series.* Episode 8. Writ. Tim Minear. Dir. David Solomon. Fox. 25 Oct. 2002. Twentieth Century Fox Home Video, 2003. DVD.
"Passion." *Buffy the Vampire Slayer: The Complete Second Season.* Episode 17. Writ. Ty King. Dir. Michael E. Gershman. The WB. 24 Feb. 1998. Twentieth Century Fox, 2002. DVD.
Robinson, Tasha." Joss Whedon." *The Onion AV Club.* avclub. com, 8 Aug. 2007. Web. 25 April 2016.
"Seeing Red." *Buffy the Vampire Slayer: The Complete Sixth Season.* Episode 19. Writ. Steven S. DeKnight. Dir. Michael Gershman. UPN. 7 May 2002. Twentieth Century Fox, 2004. DVD.
Sheper-Hughes, Nancy. "The Last Commodity: Transhuman Ethics and the Global Traffic in 'Fresh' Organs." *Global Assemblages: Technology, Politics, and Ethics as Anthropological Problems.* Ed. Aihwa Ong and Steven J. Collier. 15 April 2008. Web. 5 May 2016.
"Some Assembly Required." *Buffy the Vampire Slayer: The Complete Second Season.* Episode 2. Writ. Ty King. Dir. Bruce Seth Green. The WB. 22 Sept. 1997. Twentieth Century Fox, 2002. DVD.
"Something Blue." *Buffy the Vampire Slayer: The Complete Fourth Season.* Episode 9. Writ. Tracy Forbes. Dir. Nick Marck. The WB. 30 Nov. 1999. Twentieth Century Fox, 2003. DVD.
Sommer, Robert. *Personal Space: The Behavioral Basis of Design.* Englewood Cliffs, NJ: Prentice Hall Trade, 1969. Print.
"Ted." *Buffy the Vampire Slayer: The Complete Second Season.* Episode 11. Writ. David Greenwalt, Joss Whedon. Dir. Bruce Seth Green. The WB. 8 Dec. 1997. Twentieth Century Fox, 2002. DVD.
Walster, Elaine, Vera Aronson, Darcy Abrahams, and Leon Rottman. "Importance of Physical Attractiveness in Dating Behavior." *Journal of Personality and Social Psychology* 4.5 (1966): 508–516.
"War Zone." *Angel: The Complete First Season.* Episode 20. Writ. Garry Campbell. Dir. David Straiton. The WB. 9 May 2000. Twentieth Century Fox, 2003. DVD.
"Welcome to the Hellmouth." *Buffy the Vampire Slayer: The Complete First Season.* Episode 1. Writ. Joss Whedon. Dir. Charles Martin Smith. The WB. 10 March 1997. Twentieth Century Fox, 2002. DVD.
"Welcome to the Hellmouth." *Buffy the Vampire Slayer: The Complete First Season.* Episode 1. Joss Whedon. DVD Commentary. Twentieth Century Fox, 2002. DVD.
Whedon, Joss. *Alien: Resurrection.* "Early Draft." Horrorlair.com, 1995. Web. 12 May 2016.
_____. "Joss Whedon: Atheist & Absurdist." 2005. YouTube. *YouTube: Broadcast Yourself.* Web. 8 May 2016.
_____. "Outstanding Lifetime Achievement Award in Cultural Humanism." Harvard Humanist Society. Harvard Memorial Church, Cambridge, MA. 10 April 2009. Acceptance Speech.
Whitten, Liam. "Humanist Hero: Joss Whedon." *Humanist Life.* humanistlife.org.uk, 25 Nov. 2014. Web. 11 May 2016.
Winner, Langdon. "Resistance Is Futile: The Posthuman Condition and its Advocates." Ed. Harold Baillie and Timothy Casey. Boston: MIT Press, 2005. 385–411. Print.
"Witch." *Buffy the Vampire Slayer: The Complete First Season.* Episode 3. Writ. Dana Reston. Dir. Stephen Cragg. The WB. 17 March 1997. Twentieth Century Fox, 2002. DVD.

It's Joss Whedon's World and We're All Just Livin' in It
The "Closed Frame" of the Whedonverse[1]

Kirk Hendershott-Kraetzer

There is a show-stopper of a shot 46 minutes into Joss Whedon's 2013 film *Much Ado About Nothing*. Beatrice, hiding in the knee-hole under the kitchen counter, listens in on a conversation between the maid Ursula and Hero, Beatrice's best friend: the two are discussing Beatrice's shortcomings, among them pride, scornfulness, being so sharp-tongued that she turns "every man the wrong side out" (3.1.68),[2] and generally being blind to Benedick, the great catch hanging right in front of her face were she wise enough to notice him.

This shot, in particular the compositional aspect of its *mise-en-scène*, is a synecdoche for *Ado*'s worldview and for the worldview of Whedon's larger body of work. With few exceptions, in the Whedonverse characters believe they act out of free will, struggle for control, believe they are in control, and appear to triumph over the forces that seek to contain or destroy them, but the way in which Whedon constructs his characters' homes and the ways in which his characters interact with their homes suggests that, in the Whedonverse, characters are endlessly stuck in worlds beyond their control.

Open and Closed Frames

In *The World in a Frame: What We See in Films*, Leo Braudy describes what he sees as the fundamental nature of how art constructs reality:

> Too often we accept a film as a window on reality without noticing that the window has been opened in a particular way ... we can't see southern France without

Cezanne's eyes or walk through parts of London without feeling the rhythms of Dickens' words.... Representational art always re-creates the world around us as a new form of visual organization [22–23].[3]

In terms of film, say, our notions of the American West have been conditioned through Westerns such as John Ford's *The Searchers* (1956): it is difficult to think of the West without reference to Ford's iconic Monument Valley landscapes, hard to think of Westerners without considering John Wayne. As Braudy puts it, films "impose structures of perception upon the audience" (46). He names these structures and "their attitudes towards all [that] they contain" the open film and the closed film. His discussion of open and closed films' features is extensive, but at heart, "the world of the [open] film is a momentary frame around an ongoing reality. The objects and characters in the film existed before the camera focused on them and they will exist after the film is over," whereas "the world of the [closed] film is the only thing that exists; everything within it has its place in the plot of the film.... Everything is totally sufficient in a closed film; everything fits in" (46–47).[4]

While provocative, "open film" and "closed film" do not adequately convey how these structures work, especially since Braudy grounds his theory in earlier examinations of how representational art shapes the way in which the audience views and understands the world. So, following Richard Barsam and Dave Monahan, I have revised open film and closed film to *open frame* and *closed frame*. In film, the frame is the border of the image, and its "first and most obvious function is to control our perception of the world by enclosing what we see within it" (199). The boundary that defines what is bordered is the crux of Barsam and Monahan's revision of Braudy: the frame is a literal structure, giving physical shape to the metaphorical "structure of perception" that conditions, or frames, our reaction to and understanding of the film and its world. For example, the director and the director of photography frame their shots, and this framing is key in crafting an open or a closed film. And the way in which the script frames the story being told through its characters, conflict and plot, in concert with the director's overall conceptual framework for the film, drives the film's design work and photography. What Braudy calls an open film is an open film *because* of its open frame; a closed film is a closed film *because* of its closed frame.[5]

Barsam and Monahan emphasize the importance of discussing frames-within-the-frame, explicit or implicit borders established within that larger visual frame, such as windows or doorways (explicit frames) or tree branches, power lines, or outstretched arms (implicit frames). The image's frame is liminal, a boundary separating the world of the film from the world of its audience and situating that filmworld in relation to the audience's lived-in world. Within a film, an internal frame might serve any variety of purposes. There is a classic example in *The Searchers*: Ethan Edwards stands in the dooryard of his family's cabin, framed by its open doorway, an explicit, sharp rectangle drawn around the character. This rectangle separates inside from outside, domestic interior from wild exterior, the civilized, peaceful people inside and the uncivilized, violent racist on the outside. The door's structure—its top and its side jambs, along with the floor—structures our perception of Ethan's personality and his relationship with his family: he is boxed in by his hatred, boxed out from those who love him.

Braudy believes that open and closed structures "reverberate on levels of meaning and subject matter that otherwise have no visual equivalent" (46). While it is true that levels of meaning and subject matter *may* have no visual equivalent, I disagree with Braudy: levels of meaning often have strong visual equivalents, as I hope I have just demonstrated, and as I aim to demonstrate further by showing how framing in the Whedonverse—the way in which it composes and frames its shots—directly relates to the closed-frame world Whedon's *Ado* characters, in fact all of his characters, inhabit.

Bard in a Box

In the Beatrice shot, the blocky, darker weight of the counter and cabinets balances the airy lightness of the dining nook, and the crouching, rumpled Beatrice balances the upright, clean lines of Hero and Ursula. This is a lovely composition for the ironic emotional dynamics of the scene. Beatrice listens to two characters discuss how her mulish pride and sharp tongue have trapped her: she will never find romantic love. Although Hero and Ursula are describing her powerlessness, Beatrice thinks she has power over them because she believes they do not know she is listening in. However, the audience knows that the conversation is a put-up job. Hero and Ursula know Beatrice is there, knows she is listening, knows she is going to be appalled by what she is hearing (3.1.1–33). Ursula and Hero, who are in control, are upright and backlit, framed by an open doorway and soft curving forms. Framed by hard angles, Beatrice hunches in shadows, not in control. The shot's architecture and the composition are strong visual equivalents for Beatrice's miserable emotional position.

The architectural elements within the frame also evoke the plot's structure. The Shakespearean playtext contains a series of cons and frames perpetrated on the characters, ideal source material for a closed-frame worldview, given that Braudy notes that closed-frame films "may involve the entrapment of an innocent bystander, the guest betrayed" (49–50). This best applies to Hero, whom Don John and his compatriots frame as a loose woman (see 2.2.11–49, 3.2.85–122 and 3.3.138–56), but also is relevant to Benedick, gulled into thinking that *his* sharp tongue and mulish pride are preventing an adoring Beatrice for proclaiming her undying love for him, to him (2.3.35–212). These put-up jobs result in further tricks and entrapments: Don John tricks Claudio, Hero's beloved, and Don Pedro, their lord, into slut-shaming Hero (4.1.10–112), which leads to Leonato, Hero's father, publically condemning her (4.1.115–54); Beatrice, enraged by Claudio's treatment of her friend, maneuvers Benedick into challenging Claudio to a duel that the younger man will almost certainly lose (4.1.255–328); a host of conspirators trick Claudio into marrying Hero, who has been playing dead and who has, by this point, been proven innocent (thereby tricking Claudio and Leonato into stewing in guilt—see 4.1.214–39, 5.1.249–82, 5.1.318, 5.3 *passim* and 5.4.1–66); and Claudio and Hero trick Benedick and Beatrice into admitting their love for each other, to each other (5.4.85–97). Characters who think they know what they are hearing and seeing are routinely cornered and caught out as a result of their assumptions.[6]

Frames and Framing in Whedon's Ado

On screen, the moment with which this essay began lasts about a second, a slender peg on which to hang one's hat. Again, this shot is a synecdoche for the whole scene and the entire film. By the time the shot appears, nearly halfway through the movie, viewers have been thoroughly indoctrinated into the nature of this particular filmworld and to the nature of the Whedonverse. Braudy notes that "often a closed film begins with a series of images that defines its nature, teaching the audience how to watch its particular world" (47). *Ado* begins with an interpolated scene set in a claustrophobic little set of rooms.[7] Whedon composes many of the shots in this scene like his film's first, juxtaposing rectilinear elements (edges of floorboards; the leg, top and sides of an out-of-focus end table in the lower right fore-ground; the straight vertical leg of a bed mid-ground left; deep back left, another straight vertical of a door frame and the hard horizontal where the floor meets the wall) with elements of rumpled casualness (cast-off pants, some women's shoes, a bra; the heavy drape of the bedspread). Empty booze bottles litter the frame's edges. This contrast of soft and curvy with hard and linear, complemented by the jetsam of a good time had by all, appears throughout the movie, and it is clear in the kitchen eavesdropping scene.

The movie's second shot continues the first's strongly geometric compositions and cements the film's frame-within-a-frame motif. The camera has pulled back and is somewhat elevated. Foreground, we see that end table again, flanked by two armchairs; both display the aftermath of a shared meal. Midground is a doorway or arch, framing the couple in the room beyond. Long draperies imply a curtained theatrical proscenium through which we watch the silent morning-after drama. Because the camera is handheld, the scene is voyeuristic. We are peeping. Braudy makes a major point of this: "Voyeurism is a characteristic visual device of the closed film" (49). And indeed, voyeurism is a through-line in Whedon's *Ado*: people peek and eavesdrop and spy, and we, the viewers, do this right along with them.[8] The composition is claustrophobic, even oppressive, establishing a visual aesthetic of people boxed in by the spaces they inhabit.

Closed films define their inner space as "geometric and architectural" (Braudy 48). That is the case in these shots, and as *Ado* progresses, we continue to see strong architectural elements framing the characters. Leonato's house has narrow hallways, and the upstairs room where Benedick is lodged is tiny, with a doorway that encloses Don Pedro and Claudio while they talk with Benedick, who lounges on a little girl's bed whose metal frame forms a sort of cage around him. This is not the only time that Benedick is boxed in. During his gulling, one shot pins Benedick within a frame three times over: he is framed by window mullions, which are framed by the legs and outstretched arms of Don Pedro and Claudio, who themselves are framed by the head, jambs, and sill of large French windows. In this scene, in which the two men frame Beatrice (describing her as loving Benedick through the report of false evidence) and trick Benedick into responding to her purported love, we see Benedick, secreted behind a shrubbery, pictured in a frame-within-a-frame-within-a-frame-within-a-frame-within-a-frame. He is not the only character trapped in a tight space. Consider Dogberry in his basement office, an already confined room with low ceilings further chopped up by cubicle partitions and too much furniture: the characters barely have room to move. This reflects Dogberry's precarious situation as a common constable charged with investigating the doings of individuals with vast resources of social and financial capital. *Ado*'s visual world mirrors the characters' predicaments; viewers not versed in Shakespearean language will see the Shakespearean entrapment theme on the screen. Even when the characters are outside, garden walls and masses of lush, impenetrable greenery enclose nearly all of the film's outdoor spaces, an "'arboreal tangle'" reflecting the "blocked male-female relationships" that populate the film (Lanier 128). As Braudy writes, the film's "style makes it difficult for the viewer ever to feel expansive and free" (49).

Trapped at Home; or, the Madwoman in the Attic and the Monster in the Basement

The closed-frame film director is "preoccupied by the limits, from without and within, that can never be escaped" (Braudy 50), and we can find examples of these limits in *Buffy the Vampire Slayer* (1997–2003), *Angel* (1999–2004), *Firefly* (2002–03), *Serenity* (2005), *Dollhouse* (2009–10), *The Avengers* (2012), and *Avengers: Age of Ultron* (2015). Throughout Whedon's corpus, external and internal forces alike bind or entrap individuals, and their entrapment is made concrete through the way in which Whedon choses to represent their homes and home lives: in a closed film, "the house ... may entrap" (Braudy 66).

In *BtVS*, *Angel*, *Dollhouse*, *Firefly/Serenity*, and the *Avengers* films, the spaces themselves are not so restrictive as they are in *Ado*. They can be tight, as with Mal's or Kaylee's quarters on the *Serenity* or Echo's sleeping pod in the Dollhouse, but they are as often expansive. Angel has an entire hotel to brood in, including a soaring lobby, a space mirrored by the central atrium in the Dollhouse and by *Serenity*'s main cargo hold.[9] However, there are less physical ways to create a sense of a compressed and claustrophobic domestic space than simply photographing small rooms on a set. Although S. Rachman and Steven Taylor note that psychologically there are only "two major elements of claustrophobia: fear of suffocating and fear of restriction" (281; see also 289), film and TV evoke these fears through a variety of means, including compacted living conditions in suburbia (Bullock 86) or the city (Mulvey n. pag.; Smith 12) or densely packed working conditions (Smith 12); dense, dark or overwhelming landscapes (Bullock 86–87; Mulvey n. pag.); being surrounded by thronging monsters (Canavan 285); a character's physical immobility or being trapped in darkness (Gentry 55 and 59); being confined with or subject to the scrutiny of family members (Oppenheimer, "Woman" 44) or neighbors (Smith 13); and any of a variety of expressionist design principles (Bullock 86–88; Orkin 56; and Titford 20, 21, and 23–24).

Compacted living conditions, along with hovering butt-insky "family" members, certainly exist in *Firefly/Serenity*, *Dollhouse*, and *Angel*, and they are increasingly the norm as *BtVS* runs towards its final season; there are more than enough thronging monsters to go around in *BtVS*, *Angel*, *Serenity*, *Avengers*, and *Age of Ultron*. But I wish to focus on the way in which Whedon situates his characters in and then photographs his spaces. Of particular interest is one of his signature shots, the "oner" or process shot, in which the camera explores a structure's space, moving from room to room and even level to level in a single, apparently unbroken run of film. Braudy describes the process shot as a key marker of the closed frame, part of the overall motif of entrapment, in this case of the viewer who "is lured into" the production's "world or just as often pulled in" through the camera's sinuous progress (49). *Angel*, *Dollhouse*, *Firefly*, *Serenity*, *Avengers* and *Age of Ultron* all feature big, showy oners (sometimes more than one, as in *Serenity* and *Age of Ultron*). Similarly, the photography in Whedon's films and TV series often plays on well-known horror film tropes, tightly framing the shots while shadowy menaces lurk in the background (or pass by in the extreme foreground), suggesting the characters' entrapment if not immanent messy deaths; another common Whedonverse visual scheme is the handheld point of view (POV) shot, where a wavery frame suggests a blood-thirsty boogem waiting to snack on the helpless shmo it is stalking. Murky shadows accentuate the ominous environs. One of these POV gems appears in *Avengers,* when the Hulk is revving up to disassemble the S.H.I.E.L.D. helicarrier: Black Widow, scared, hides amid a tangle of pipes and conduit, her head barely visible, even less so after the Hulk snarls and she hunkers down a bit more. This shot is handheld. Such stalker-vision shots notwithstanding, several of *Dollhouse*'s main motifs—hotties of both sexes parading around in their PJs, or sweaty and writhing in Topher's chair, or sweaty and writhing while being tortured, or sweaty and writhing while they're having sex with people they do not know—are voyeuristic in the extreme. The Whedonverse likes to represent its characters and position its viewers as helpless.

When they are not trapped in the frame or being ogled, Whedonverse characters are often trapped in the home. Frequently grounded, Buffy cannot seem to escape her home town, either: even death cannot keep her from being brought back. Echo always comes home to the Dollhouse, where she is a 21st century indentured servant, even to live there at the series' end, in an episode subtitled "Return." Janet K. Halfyard argues that "Echo and the other Dolls inhabit the underworld, like souls who have drunk the waters of Lethe" (51), except one does not so much inhabit the underworld as dwell there forever[10]; Martin Shuster notes that "escape from the Dollhouse itself became part of the Dollhouse experience" (236), a significant caveat being that the great escape is only ever virtual, giving the experience that special torturey tang.

Peter Tupper's discussion of the Gothic in *Dollhouse* helps us to see the Whedonverse's heavy debt to Gothic design and motifs, a major one of which is entrapment. Characters are imprisoned in attics and dungeons, both common features of Gothic architecture, ready-made metaphors for the secrets that we lock up but that seep out to haunt us.[11] The Whedonverse is peppered with such places. Driven mad by his newly returned soul, Spike sits chained and moaning in Buffy's basement early in that series' seventh season. In season four of *Angel,* Angelus sits locked in a cage in the basement of the Hyperion, dredging up all manner of icky memories for his erstwhile friends to savor. And then there is the Failsafe, created to destroy Angel and housed in the basement of Wolfram & Hart's HQ ("You're Welcome"). Ultron, in his Frankenstein's monster iteration, shambles up out of Tony Stark's basement to dribble goo and remind Tony of the perils of hubris. Over in *Firefly,* River ghosts about the ship, a lost soul trapped with the nightmare memories of her time at the Alliance "school," and she haunts Jubal Early from the "attic" of his ship in "Objects in Space." The film *Serenity* repeatedly shows her hiding and watching from above as other characters go about their lives. Then, too, there is the Dollhouse's Attic, where bad little boys and girls go to live out their nightmares repetitively until death frees them from this awful limbo ("The Attic").

Throughout, these productions stress the repression of awful memories and the desire to escape a miserable past, and this repression is given form: shackles, cages, ductwork, labs, voids, all of which exist somewhere in a home that entraps its inhabitants. In the closed frame of the Whedonverse, homes are full of monsters and no one can ever leave.

Home Is Where the Work Is

Another strong element of entrapment in the home appears when the Whedonverse collapses the home-work divide. In part this reflects a societal trend, in which "home spaces are being appropriated by work activities and objects used for work (like home PCs used for email). Mobile technologies increase the number of possible locations where work can be done" (Towers et al. 597). Beyond the home, these "work extending technologies" are "'transforming locations as diverse as public and private transport, cafés, sites of leisure, and [professional] offices'" into "'third spaces'" that are "legitimate places of work" (597). More and more, people are taking work home, working from home (telecommuting), working while waiting in doctors' offices or for other personal appointments, working on weekends, working longer.

Sometimes, Whedon offers analogous extensions of work into the home. When not getting her info face to face, Buffy's main work-extending technology is a landline: she does not own a cell—or is not shown using one—until seventh season opener, "Lessons." In fact, Buffy always brings her work home with her. Being the Slayer, she cannot leave whatever she is working on piled on her desk when she heads home for the day, but she does spend a lot of time in the series' earlier years trying to keep work out of her house (via vampire-preventing wards or by pitching the Big Bad out a window) or to get out of the house so she can do her job. However, the general direction of the series turns the Summers house into the base out of which the Scoobies operate, particularly after Joyce's death midway through season five (see, for example, "Dirty Girls").

Owing to the proximity of his residence and his office, the audience can see the difficulty Angel has separating work from home. In season one, his apartment is a short, slow elevator ride down from his work space; in season two, he moves home and office into the Hyperion, where he remains through the end of season four, at which point he moves into a luxury apartment a short elevator ride up from his work space at Wolfram & Hart. In point of fact, Angel is never really away from work, never really off duty. He may spend some of his time reading while he waits for a maiden to rescue, but for Angel, the work/home divide simply does not exist. Much the same could be said for Mal and crew in *Firefly* and *Serenity*. Mal's living space is nominally separate from his workspace, in that he has his quarters that he can retreat to ("Our Mrs. Reynolds" and "Objects in Space"), but in this he is no different from his mates. And the crew's relationship with technology is more comprehensive and mission-critical than Buffy's or Angel's: without this tech in their homes, they will die. A crucial distinction from Angel is Mal's attitude towards the lack of separation between home and work: whereas Angel's choice to live mere feet from where he works seems to derive from his driving need to combat evil and atone for the centuries of pain he wrought on others, Mal loves his work-home, and while his job is stressful, "there's no place [he'd] rather be."

Echo also works out of her home ... except her home is a glossy brothel run by the secretive multinational biotech firm to which her life and body are contractually bound. Her day job is being a Doll, but her *real* work, revealing the truth of the Dollhouse and saving all the other dolls, is secret and always under surveillance, with the constant threat of death (or worse) looming. The interior of the Dollhouse is sumptuous, the most luxurious of the Whedonverse domiciles: the place has been feng shui'd to a fare-thee-well. Even the coffin-like pods in which Echo and the rest of the dolls sleep are elegant, with polished wood, frosted-glass lids and sexy backlighting. Like Angel in his final season, Echo lives and works in hostile territory. The prime difference here is that Echo never gets down time: she is at it, day job and real work alike, 24/7, whereas the characters in *BtVS*, *Angel* and *Firefly/Serenity* get time to rest and recoup.

The blurring of the home/work divide continues in *Ado*, *Avengers*, and *Age of Ultron*. In many ways, *Ado* is an ideal source text for Whedon, a director who tends to write his own scripts, because its themes and plot allow him to keep all of the characters stuck in Leonato's house: it is about the traps of reputation and the springes of language. In *Ado*, when characters' reputations are constructed for them, that is who they are, and they have to battle to get out, give up and accept the situation, or embrace such changes as may occur as opportunities. Beatrice, Benedick, Claudio and Hero are each pinned to particular reputations early on in the action. Leonato casts Beatrice and Benedick as being involved in a "merry war" (1.1.58); separately, Benedick characterizes Beatrice as "Lady Disdain" (1.1.112) and "shrewd of tongue" (2.1.17), while Benedick is "the prince's jester, a very dull fool" (2.1.125) with a "contemptible spirit" (2.3.177). The bastard Don John is framed up as moody melancholic villain, a role he embraces (1.3.26–34). Even when others dynamite Benedick, Beatrice and Hero out of their initial public identities, they get other, newer ones through the stories that are told about them—Beatrice and Benedick as besotted lovers (2.3.91–174, and 3.1.36–37 and 77–83, respectively), Hero as trollop, a "rotten orange" who "knows the heat of a luxurious bed" (4.1.30 and 39). Like Don John, they embrace the constraints of their new roles, albeit with some initial resistance. Hero protests the identity assigned to her but does consent to be known publically as a fallen woman until she can take up *another* identity, this time as the woman wronged.[12] All of this activity makes up the characters' work in the film. Don John spreads calumnies about Hero and wrecks the lives of the happy partiers. Beatrice's and Benedick's friends trick the merry warriors "into a mountain of affection th'one with th'other" (2.1.338–39), and it is the warriors' job to fight and then to woo. Hero's job is to be publically shamed, to play dead, and then to forgive Claudio; Beatrice's job, in her role as Hero's confidante and defender, is to press Benedick to avenge Hero's slander, and it is Benedick's job to avenge that wrong. For such a festive setting, the work that goes on in and around Leonato's home is quite serious, and although no one dies, the threat of death is immanent (metaphorically for Hero, literally for Claudio).

Whedon also eliminates the distinction between home and workplace in *Avengers* and *Age of Ultron*, and, as with his other works, this does not to lead to happiness. As *Avengers* begins, Tony Stark and Pepper Potts are nearing completion of Stark Tower, their office and home. Much as with *BtVS*, *Angel*, *Dollhouse*, and *Firefly/Serenity*, home soon becomes where he does his "other" work, fighting, first Loki, then Ultron, Ultron's minions, and eventually his own team. A telling exception is made in the person of Clint Barton, Hawkeye, however. Both Avengers movies spend time investigating or at least alluding to the private lives of the various main characters, the exceptions being Nick Fury (who seems to do nothing but work) and Hawkeye, whose past work is noted but whose private life is never discussed, that is until *Age of Ultron*'s reveal that he is married, has kids, and a nice country home which he spends his down time remodeling. When the Avengers retreat there after being spanked by Ultron and Scarlet Witch, it is clear that none of his teammates, save Natasha and Fury, know about his "secret." Clint the civilian has gone to considerable lengths to keep his private life separate from the public, Hawkeye-side of his life. His home is a haven, and no one is particularly happy that the Avengers have invaded it, including those who shelter there.[13] Nor should they be happy, given the Whedonverse's track record of what happens to people who bring their work home.

Home Is Where the Hurt Is

Trauma in the home workplace is where Whedon seems to be more critically engaged in the issue of the home/work divide than simply depicting an unhappily common aspect of contemporary work: working in the home can be downright dangerous. Not only are homes where Whedon's characters work, not only are their homes where they are often trapped, but their homes/workplaces are where they are under serious threat. Heroes' homes are invaded and their denizens attacked, suggesting not only the oppressiveness of danger in the Whedonverse but in a concrete way arguing that bringing work home can be deadly.

A range of studies of the impact of work-extending technologies in the home present a grim litany of descriptors: "Home spaces are being appropriated by work activities"; "Mobile technologies" are "eroding ... work/non work boundaries"; it is an "invasion" (Towers et al. 597); blurred boundaries between the roles that an individual fills "linked with greater job-related demands and work-family conflict" (Schieman and Glavin 1344–45; see also 1353); "negative spillover ... which results in discord" (Eng et al. 105); "a potent stressor" (Schieman and Glavin 1355; see also Glavin, Schieman, and Reid 53; and Eng et al. 105–07 and 117); psychological distress and guilt (Glavin, Schieman, and Reid 51; see also Grant, Wallace, and Spurgeon 540–41). Eroded boundaries. Negative spillover. Conflict. Stressor. Guilt. Discord. Invasion. Just another day at home in the Whedonverse. The narrowing of the home/work divide that Whedon's four major television series and three major studio films seem to be following is ominous, even deadly. This effect is pronounced in Whedon's television work where, the more intertwined home and work become, the more that important characters are threatened, get injured, suffer, or die.

A rout of monsters menaces Buffy's home throughout her show's run, including Angelus ("Passion"), Joyce's reanimated corpse ("Forever"), a hoard of women driven mad by a love spell gone awry ("Bewitched, Bothered and Bewildered"), Glory ("Checkpoint"), and The First Evil ("Conversations with Dead People," among others). As the series binds home and work, characters are at greater risk. Jennie Calendar and Kendra perish early in the series ("Passion" and "Becoming, Part One," respectively), but the deaths really pile up after Buffy's mother Joyce dies ("I Was Made to Love You") and Buffy shifts her base of operations into the home: Glory brain-sucks Tara, and Warren shoots Tara later in the series ("Tough Love" and "Seeing Red," respectively), Caleb pulps Xander's eye ("Dirty Girls"), the Bringers axe Anya ("Chosen"), and First's minions kill a number of the Slayers who live with Buffy in the final season. Unlike Buffy's, Angel's home seems under constant threat. Above, I noted that Angel can seem to have a much harder time separating home from work than Buffy, but really, Angel does not want to separate the two, despite the fact that having them so connected brings him no end of grief. Demons of various stripes constantly break in, attempt to break in, infiltrate, or blow up the place ("I Will Remember You," "Dad," "The Price" and "Players," and "To Shanshu in L.A.," respectively), and this does not even begin to consider the shenanigans that plague team Angel once they take up residence at Wolfram & Hart.[14] Insofar as major characters go, the carnage is more extreme in *Angel* than in *BtVS*.

The damages are not so severe elsewhere in the Whedonverse, though like *Angel*'s various domiciles, the *Serenity* is either under threat ("War Stories" and *Serenity*), or infiltrated or invaded ("Our Mrs. Reynolds," "Objects in Space"). The ship is never blown up, though one of its engines gets ripped off, and two of the nine major characters perish in *Serenity*: Wash (impaled) and Book (gunned down). In *Dollhouse*, most of the Dolls, their handlers and other affiliated characters are physically and psychologically damaged in some way. Priya's handler serially rapes her ("Man on the Street"), Bennet Halverson loses the use of her arm in a break-in ("Getting Closer"), and Boyd, November/Mellie, Paul Ballard, and Topher die ("The Hollow Men," "Epitaph Two: Return"). A scourge of assailants infiltrate the building throughout the series' run, though "attack it from within" might better describe what happens: Alpha and Echo both wreak havoc from their positions inside the house, and in the series' final episodes we discover that Boyd has been spying on, lying to and manipulating everyone for the entire run of the series.[15] Looters ransack the Dollhouse after Rossum's scheme to provide effective immortality for those who can pony up the lucre leads to planet-wide anarchy. Comparatively, Leonato's home in *Ado* suffers only party-related damage, nothing that his household staff cannot clean up in a day or two, and it is not invaded (unless we count the horde of party-goers who descend on the place). Rather, Don Pedro invites in the snake in this garden: once there, Don John insinuates himself into the lives of those he would torment and, he hopes, destroy, repeating the Whedonesque theme of the home workplace being threatened through infiltration. No one dies in *Ado*, though there are metaphoric and literal threats, and while the playtext leaves open the possibility for considerable emotional wreckage, Whedon's film ends happily. Over and over again, though, we see Whedon questioning the collapsing of boundaries, and his inquiry is most sharp when that boundary is most narrow: when co-workers become co-habitants, when the public and private are most mixed—*Dollhouse*, *Angel* season five, *BtVS* season four's "Living Conditions" and the back half of season seven, the close quarters of the reveling weekenders in *Ado*—is when things are at their worst.[16] Clint Barton is right to want to keep these people away from his house: the victims that characterize Braudy's closed frame are thick on the ground at home in the Whedonverse.

We Are All Living in Whedon's Closed Frame

Early in *Avengers*, Captain America is getting whomped by Loki when in rockets Iron Man, complete with his own AC/DC soundtrack. Of this,

Whedon remarks, "Tony Stark. Not a man of the people. He's a man of Tony Stark. And God bless him, he's definitely a hero, definitely likes to help people, but it's his world: we're all just living in it" (Director's Commentary, *Avengers*). Through referencing Stark's irresponsibility, ego and narcissism, Whedon could be talking about the Whedonverse, in which the great dramatic irony is that most of the characters think of themselves as autonomous agents, in charge of their own fates or, at a minimum, free to resist their strictures and possibly break them, but in reality they are enmeshed in webs that they cannot break and may not even be able to see.

This is not to say Whedon is utterly committed to the closed frame. He often makes "self-conscious reference to filmmaking itself" (Braudy 47), such as the numerous gestures towards other artworks he makes in *Age of Ultron* and the reflexive attention paid to the photographer in *Ado*.[17] Both Avengers films open "outward" (Braudy 47), if "outward" means to the otherwise closed Marvel Cinematic Universe.[18] Certainly his characters do resist their various entrapments, engaging in mighty struggles for self-determination. *Dollhouse* ends "happily" in that the "lucky" Dolls "get to start over" after Topher's brain-resetting bomb bounces its signal off the atmosphere ("Epitaph Two: Return"), but those characters' autonomy comes at horrific cost. As Gerry Canavan points out, "Topher and Adelle selfishly abet the Rossum Corporation's drive for better and better technologies of control, but the rebelling Dolls' victories over Rossum ironically introduced the unstable power vacuum that made the global Dollpocalypse possible in the first place" (295–96).[19] Plus, bonus, the survivors of the de-imprinting blast still have to stay inside the wrecked Dollhouse—for a *year*—and the series' very last seconds are hardly reason for optimism: Echo, with Paul Ballard stuffed into her brain, settles into her pod for a well-earned rest. She crosses hands on her chest, and the camera slowly cranes up, revealing the familiar image of the pods arrayed like teeth on an enormous gear. Then the music playing over the final montage, Lissie's "Everywhere I Go," cuts off mid-verse, with a suspiciously long moment of silence over a black screen before the series' theme song plays over the end credits for the last time. Given Fox's overall treatment of the series, it is not unreasonable to suspect that the network lopped off the last couple of seconds if the episode were over-time. The sudden cut to black, contemporaneous with the song's abrupt end, suggests death, or maybe Echo goes to sleep. These possibilities align with various features of the closed frame: if it is Fox up to no good, this becomes an example of everything being "controlled by outside forces" (Braudy 51); if we are going to sleep or dying with Echo, then the cut to black is part of the "claustrophobic identification of our point of view with that of one character" (48); it may be an expression of "paranoia about our helplessness before events that has been the special subject of closed films since the earliest days of cinema" (54); it may be the final gesture of a television show whose style and themes make "it difficult for the viewer ever to feel expansive and free" (49). Whatever it is, the visual of Echo still in the teeth of a machine is not optimistic.

The conclusions of Whedon's other projects are also ambivalent about their characters' various homecomings. *The Avengers* ends with a member of the World Security Council telling Nick Fury, "You don't understand what you've started, letting the Avengers loose on this world," a sentiment reinforced by the mid-credit sequence featuring Thanos, happily considering his courtship of Death via challenging humans, a plot thread extended by *Age of Ultron*'s mid-credit scene, in which Thanos suits up with an Infinity Gauntlet and says, in effect, if you want something done right, you'd better do it yourself: something wicked this way comes, and Nick Fury invited it home. Whedon reinforces this bleak notion in his comments on the sound cues over Captain America's penultimate scene:

> There's a moment where I feel I got it wrong.... There's one cue that we had two versions of, and it's Cap's revelation that ... he's at home here, here in this place [the new Avengers facility]. We had a cue that expressed a kind of doubt and poignancy in that, and I suggested, "Well, what if we tried putting a version of the Captain America theme there," and everyone liked that better, and I mean *absolutely* everyone, but every time I watch it now, I go, "You know, should have had the doubt," because I don't want him saying want him to be saying, "Oh, no, it's great, I found my home," I want him to be saying, "I'm a guy who never will," and "This is not, I'm not satisfied, I'm not proud of this, that this is what I am, it's just something I've come to accept" [Director's Commentary, *Age of Ultron*].

Whedon did not want an entirely optimistic ending for his film, which he calls "a summer tent-pole movie where you actually get to say humanity is doomed." Hard to feel expansive and free about that homecoming. Over in *Angel*, our hero's defiance of the Senior Partners gets Angel's home, the entire city of Los Angeles, sucked into hell—thanks for that, hero-man—and while the series' canon extends in *Angel: After the Fall* (Lynch, Mooney and Urru), the events that end the TV run are plenty bleak, with several characters already dead, Gunn dying, and Angel wading into battle against a moil of demons. Buffy beats The First Evil and closes the Sunnydale Hellmouth, and her show ends with the promise of a little R & R and a wistful, hopeful smile from the hero, but her home got sucked into a giant crater and she is still the Slayer, back at work in *Buffy The Vampire Slayer Season Eight* where things, yup, go south in a hell of a hurry (Whedon, Jeanty, and Owens). In the first episode of *Firefly*, Mal complains that it is "getting awful crowded in my sky." That situation has not improved by the end of *Serenity*. If anything, it's gotten worse: River has found some peace; a glowing Kaylee finally gets to snog (and maybe more) with Simon; and Inara appears to have decided to return to the ship; but the widowed Zoe is in for a "bumpy" ride, and the Operative flat-out tells Mal that the Alliance's Parliament may be "weakened," "but they are not gone, and they are not forgiving." In his last close-up, Mal is shot from behind, his face turned away and most of his head in deep shadow, visuals that are tonally identical to the last shot of the ruined Operative, of whom "there is nothing left to see": Mal may be flying off to new adventures, but he is hardly whole and hale. And let us not forget that the last visual in the film is of a hunk falling off the ship, Mal's home. Things get worse in the graphic narrative continuation of the canon: the entire Alliance is actively hunting Mal and the *Serenity*, and what is left of the crew is coming apart at the seams (Whedon, Jeanty, Moon, and Story).

Among Whedon's major film and TV works, *Ado* comes closest to breaking the closed frame with its conclusion's suggestion that the world is "basically benevolent" (Braudy 66) and that "objects and characters in the film existed before the camera focused on them and they will exist after the film is over" (47). The film's wind-up includes one of Shakespeare's loveliest, most optimistic lines, "For man is a giddy thing" (5.4.106), and that charming Renaissance tradition, a dance in which everyone, from servant to Prince, gets their groove on in a happy obliteration of class difference. *Ado*'s final image, of Beatrice and Benedick kissing while the revelers dance behind them, "is not so much a capitulation to social pressure as a rapturous release from it, the creation of a social space all their own within that of the larger community" (Lanier 138). As the writer-director himself puts it, "And really the whole point of the thing is that these two have left the party, that the wild whirligig is still going around, people all around them, and they have finally learned to stop lying, stop pretending, and just admit that they are ready to need each other" (Director's Commentary, *Ado*). Yes, but. This final lightheartedness is not unmixed. A doorway frames Beatrice and Benedick, much as one did in the film's second shot: they have moved on, but they are also back where they began. Beyond that, in a variety of interviews, Whedon describes making *Ado* as a "relaxing and fulfilling ... breezy" (Orr) project after his two-year long stint on *The Avengers*, including a year away from home while filming, yet early in *Ado*'s commentary track, he describes working on the film while he was finishing work on *Avengers*: "Was this a good decision? No. Did it ruin my life? Totally." His tone is hard to read; he sounds serious, and many other remarks during the commentary reinforce the impression of the job being fun yet taxing. Whedon goes on to note that

> when I first thought of this, really thought about why would I want to make this play ... into a movie [it was] because of the darkness, because of the lying, because of the manipulation, because of the pain, the drama that Shakespeare just goes to the mattresses on, he does not hold back. When it's time for things to go wrong, they go *wrong*, it's not like cute wrong, and that sort of meanness of spirit combined with this extreme Romanticism reminded me of Billy Wilder and Preston

Sturges, particularly *The Apartment* and *Unfaithfully Yours* [Director's Commentary, *Ado*].

Whedon is clear that he was looking to "evoke a *film noir* kind of look," and he calls his movie a "*noir* comedy." Braudy positions Wilder and Sturges among his roster of closed-frame directors (52 and 63, respectively) and *noir* is a highly closed form, its themes of "paranoia and claustrophobia" (Schrader 11), its "complex," even "convoluted" temporal structures (11) and the often geometric angularity of its ever-present shadows being but a few examples. We finish the film where we began, voyeuristically peering at Beatrice and Benedick's intimate moment. They may not be stuck in a knee-hole while their friends anatomize their faults, but the open frame of the film's ending is itself framed by the closed-frame nature of its conception and its creator's fundamentally closed-frame worldview.

NOTES

1. This essay is dedicated to my wife, Lisa, who geeks out on Whedon with me.
2. All Shakespeare quotations are from the Arden Shakespeare *Much Ado About Nothing*.
3. Braudy echoes Oscar Wilde's "Life imitates art far more than Art imitates life" ("Decay" 982).
4. Open and closed do not imply value judgments but indicate "different significant points on a continuum" of representation (Braudy 46), "distinctions rather than absolute differences, a revolving door of visual meaning" (55), "part of a historical and aesthetic continuity, not antagonists but collaborators in the way they have changed our way of looking at the world" (46). These "structures of perception" are not absolute, despite Braudy's characterization of them as points, which are discrete: color and sound can open up a closed film (see 95), and thematically closed films might be shot in an open style (99).
5. For a discussion of Whedon's narrative framing, see Wilcox, "'Can I Spend the Night / Alone?'" (70–72).
6. Rhonda Wilcox examines a variety of other frames in the film. See her "Joss Whedon's Translation of Shakespeare's *Much Ado About Nothing*: Historical Double Consciousness, Reflections, and Frames," pars. 19–22 and 24–26 for a discussion of the film's use of silence and music as frames; on its uses of still photographs and picture frames to comment on "the division between ... our public faces and our private feelings," see pars. 29–30; on its use of mirrors and windows as frames, see par. 31.
7. The scene does not exist in the Shakespearean playtext but appears to build off of Beatrice's "You always end with a Jade's trick; I know you of old" (1.1.138–39) and "he lent it [his heart] me awhile, and I gave him use for it, a double heart for his single one. Marry, once he won it [my heart] of me with false dice" (2.1.255–57).
8. Whedon calls the film's photographer "creepy" in his commentary. On Jay Hunter's techniques to emphasize the voyeuristic element, see Oppenheimer, "Indie" 58. On the voyeuristic possibilities afforded by the house itself, see Lanier 133.
9. Cochran describes *Serenity*'s hold as womb-like (150), making it the creepiest womb ever: made of metal, people are constantly invading it, Mal and Co. crash the Mule into it, there's at least one gunfight in there, a herd of cows hangs out for a while, it belches fire, and its doors are strong enough to chop metal cargo containers in half.
10. Halfyard's discussion of the Eurydice myth (41) suggests that Sunnydale is a kind of underworld, a "home" that Buffy cannot leave.
11. On architecture in Gothic narratives, see Bunten *passim* and Davison *passim*. On repression in Gothic narratives, see Williams 796–97.

12. Whedon situates Hero as the woman wronged. The playtext is ambiguous: after asking to be "torture[d] … to death" if the accusations against her prove true (4.1.184), Hero remains silent for the remainder of the scene, an example of what Philip C. McGuire has termed an "open silence," a moment where a character is on stage and could speak but for whatever reason does not. Hero's silence leaves the performer and the performance considerable latitude to craft the nature of her response to the Friar's proposed scheme to rehabilitate her reputation. On Hero's silence generally, see Bate.

13. The film shows that Thor in particular feels out of place—he steps on the children's toys and wears a deeply unhappy expression while he's in the house—and he leaves to do more work almost as soon as he arrives.

14. Lorne's apartment is connected to his nightclub, Caritas. Holtz blows up both ("Lullaby"), and Gunn's former gang-mates invade Caritas' replacement and shoot it to pieces ("That Old Gang of Mine"). Doyle, Darla, Cordelia, Fred, Lindsey and Wesley all die, and Gunn is severely wounded ("Hero," "Lullaby," "You're Welcome," "A Hole in the World," and "Not Fade Away," respectively).

15. This is similar to "Inside Out's" retcon of Cordelia, revealing her to have been possessed by an evil power in "Birthday" then to have manipulated team Angel for the subsequent 27 episodes.

16. On "dirty space," the collective space where "traditional values of privacy have disappeared," see Lewis and Cho, 70 and 86–69. See Gerrits on the commingling of work and home when Buffy's first college roommate turns out to be a demon.

17. Whedon notes that *Age of Ultron* visually quotes from or is influenced by *Serenity*, *Age of Innocence*, the first-ever Frankenstein film, *The Searchers*, *Gone with the Wind*, *Hot Shots*, *The Best Years of Our Lives*, *Rio Bravo*, *Zulu*, *Dawn of the Dead*, *The Ultimates*, and *Miller's Crossing* (Director's Commentary, *Age of Ultron*).

18. Whedon's unhappiness makes it seem as if he were trapped in this particular "house." On the stresses of the production, see Ritman; on Whedon's conflicts with Marvel, see Robinson; on his feelings about the final cut of the film, see Whedon, Director's Commentary, *Age of Ultron*. Regarding Whedon being trapped elsewhere in the studio system, particularly with respect to FOX, see Rogers 159 and Havrileski n. pag.

19. In contrast to Canavan, see Vinci 244–45 and Moylan 83.

Works Cited

"The Attic." *Dollhouse: Season 2*. Episode 10. Writ Maurissa Tancharoen and Jed Whedon. Dir. Marita Grabiak. Creat. Joss Whedon. Fox. 18 Dec. 2009. Twentieth Century Fox, 2010. DVD.
The Avengers. Writ. and Dir. Joss Whedon. Marvel Studios, 2012. Blu-ray.
Avengers: Age of Ultron. Writ. and Dir. Joss Whedon. Marvel Studios, 2015. Blu-ray.
Barsam, Richard, and Dave Monahan. *Looking at Movies: An Introduction to Film*. 5th ed. New York: W.W. Norton, 2016. Print.
Bate, Jonathan. "Dying to Live in *Much Ado About Nothing*." *Surprised by Scenes: Essays in Honor of Professor Yasunari Takahashi*. Ed. Yasunari Takada. Tokyo: Kenkyusha, 1994. 69–85. Print.
"Becoming, Part One." *Buffy the Vampire Slayer: Season 2*. Episode 21. Writ. Joss Whedon. Dir. Joss Whedon. Creat. Joss Whedon. The WB. 12 May 1998. Twentieth Century Fox, 2009. DVD.
"Bewitched, Bothered and Bewildered." *Buffy the Vampire Slayer: Season 2*. Episode 16. Writ. Marti Noxon. Dir. James A. Contner. Creat. Joss Whedon. The WB. 12 Feb. 1998. Twentieth Century Fox, 2009. DVD.
"Birthday." *Angel: Season 3*. Episode 11. Writ. Mere Smith. Dir. Michael Grossman. Creat. Joss Whedon and David Greenwalt. The WB. 14 Jan. 2002. Twentieth Century Fox, 2009. DVD.
Braudy, Leo. *The World in a Frame: What We See in Films*. 1976. Chicago: University of Chicago Press, 2002. Print.
Bullock, Emily. "Something in the Dark: The Tale of Ruby Rose and the Tasmanian Gothic." *Metro Magazine* (Spring 2014): 84–91. Web. 1 Jan. 2016. PDF.

Bunten, Pete. "Capturing the Castle." *The English Review* 20.3 (2010): 2–5. Web. 9 Feb. 2012. PDF.
Canavan, Gerry. "Zombies, Reavers, Butchers, and Actuals in Joss Whedon's Work." *Joss Whedon: The Complete Companion: The TV Series, the Movies, the Comic Books and More*. Ed. Mary Alice Money. London: Titan Books, 2012. 285–97. Web. 1 June 2016. PDF.
"Checkpoint." *Buffy the Vampire Slayer: Season 5*. Episode 12. Writ. Douglas Petrie and Jane Espenson. Dir. Nick Marck. Creat. Joss Whedon. The WB. 23 Jan. 2001. Twentieth Century Fox, 2009. DVD.
"Chosen." *Buffy the Vampire Slayer: Season 7*. Episode 22. Writ. Joss Whedon. Dir. Joss Whedon. Creat. Joss Whedon. UPN. 20 May 2003. Twentieth Century Fox, 2009. DVD.
Cochran, Tanya R. "*Firefly* and *Serenity*: An Introduction." *Reading Joss Whedon*. Ed. Rhonda V. Wilcox, Tanya R. Cochran, Cynthea Masson, and David Lavery. Syracuse: Syracuse University Press, 2015. 149–52. Print.
"Conversations with Dead People." *Buffy the Vampire Slayer: Season 7*. Episode 7. Writ. Jane Espenson and Drew Goddard. Dir. Nick Marck. Creat. Joss Whedon. UPN. 12 Nov. 2002. Twentieth Century Fox, 2009. DVD.
"Dad." *Angel: Season 3*. Episode 10. Writ. David H. Goodman. Dir. Fred Keller. Creat. Joss Whedon and David Greenwalt. The WB. 10 Dec. 2001. Twentieth Century Fox, 2009. DVD.
Davison, Carol Margaret. "Gothic Architectonics: The Poetics and Politics and Gothic Space." *Papers on Language and Literature* 46.2 (2010): 136–52. General OneFile. Web. 17 Feb. 2012. PDF.
"Dirty Girls." *Buffy the Vampire Slayer: Season 7*. Episode 18. Writ. Drew Goddard. Dir. Michael Gershmann. Creat. Joss Whedon. UPN. 15 April 2003. Twentieth Century Fox, 2009. DVD.
Eng, Wylie, Sarah Moore, Leon Grunberg, Edward Greenberg, and Pat Sikora. "What Influences Work-Family Conflict? The Function of Work Support and Working from Home." *Current Psychology* 29.2 (2010): 104–20. Web. 18 May 2016.
"Epitaph Two: Return." *Dollhouse: Season 2*. Episode 13. Writ. Maurissa Tancharoen, Jed Whedon and Andrew Chambliss. Dir. David Solomon. Creat. Joss Whedon. Fox. 29 Jan. 2010. Twentieth Century Fox, 2010. DVD.
"Forever." *Buffy the Vampire Slayer: Season 5*. Writ. Marti Noxon. Dir. Marti Noxon. Creat. Joss Whedon. The WB. 17 April 2001. Twentieth Century Fox, 2009. DVD.
Gentry, Ric. "Another Meditation on Death: An Interview with Oliver Stone." *Film Quarterly* 60.4 (2007): 54–60. Web. 27 Oct. 2015. PDF.
Gerrits, Jeroen. "When Horror Becomes Human: Living Conditions in *Buffy the Vampire Slayer*." *MLN* 127. 5 (2012): 1059–70. Web. 6 March 2016. PDF.
"Getting Closer." *Dollhouse: Season 2*. Episode 11. Writ. Tim Minear. Dir. Tim Minear. Creat. Joss Whedon. Fox. 8 Jan. 2010. Twentieth Century Fox, 2010. DVD.
Glavin, Paul, Scott Schieman, and Sarah Reid. "Boundary-Spanning Work Demands and Their Consequences for Guilt and Psychological Distress." *Journal of Health and Social Behavior* 52.1 (2011): 43–57. Web. 18 May 2016.
Grant, Christine A., Louise M. Wallace, and Peter C. Spurgeon. "An Exploration of the Psychological Factors Affecting Remote E-workers' Job Effectiveness, Well-Being and Work-Life Balance." *Employee Relations* 35.5 (2013): 527–46. Web. 18 May 2016.
Halfyard, Janet K. "Hero's Journey, Heroine's Return? Buffy, Eurydice, and the Orpheus Myth." *Reading Joss Whedon*. Ed. Rhonda V. Wilcox, Tanya R. Cochran, Cynthea Masson, and David Lavery. Syracuse: Syracuse University Press, 2015. 40–52. Print.
Havrileski, Heather. "Trapped in the Dollhouse." Rev. of *Dollhouse*. *Salon*. Salon Media Group, Inc., 12 Feb. 2009. Web. 19 May 2016.
"Hero." *Angel: Season 1*. Episode 9. Writ. Howard Gordon and Tim Minear. Dir. Tucker Gates. Creat. Joss Whedon and David Greenwalt. UPN. 30 Nov. 2009. Twentieth Century Fox, 2003. DVD.
"A Hole in the World." *Angel: Season 5*. Episode 15. Writ. Joss Whedon. Dir. Joss Whedon. Creat. Joss Whedon and David Greenwalt. UPN. 24 Feb. 2004. Twentieth Century Fox, 2009. DVD.

"The Hollow Men." *Dollhouse: Season 2.* Episode 12. Writ. Michele Fazekas, Tara Butters and Tracy Bellomo. Dir. Terrence O'Hara. Creat. Joss Whedon. Fox. 15 Jan. 2010. Twentieth Century Fox, 2010. DVD.
"I Was Made to Love You." *Buffy the Vampire Slayer: Season 5.* Writ. Jane Espenson. Dir. James A. Contner. Creat. Joss Whedon. 20 Feb. 2001. Twentieth Century Fox, 2009. DVD.
"I Will Remember You." *Angel: Season 1.* Episode 8. Writ. David Greenwalt and Jeannine Renshaw. Dir. David Grossman. Creat. Joss Whedon and David Greenwalt. The WB. 14 Dec. 1999. Twentieth Century Fox, 2003. DVD.
"Inside Out." *Angel: Season 4.* Episode 17. Writ Steven S. DeKnight. Dir Stephen S. DeKnight. Creat. Joss Whedon and David Greenwalt. UPN. 2 April 2003. Twentieth Century Fox, 2009. DVD.
Lanier, Douglas M. "'Good lord, for alliance': Joss Whedon's *Much Ado About Nothing*." *Représentations: La revue électronique du CEMRA*, Dec. 2014. Universite Stendhal. 117–42. Web. PDF.
"Lessons." *Buffy the Vampire Slayer: Season 7.* Writ. Joss Whedon. Dir. David Solomon. Creat. Joss Whedon. UPN. 24 Sept. 2002. Twentieth Century Fox, 2009. DVD.
Lewis, Tyson, and Daniel Cho. "Home Is Where the Neurosis Is: A Topography of the Spatial Unconscious." *Cultural Critique* 64 (2006): 69–91. Web. 1 Jan. 2016. PDF.
"Lullaby." *Angel: Season 3.* Episode 9. Writ. Tim Minear. Dir. Tim Minear. Creat. Joss Whedon and David Greenwalt. The WB. 14 Nov. 2000. Twentieth Century Fox, 2009. DVD.
Lynch, Brian (w), Stephen Mooney (p, i), and Franco Urru (p, i). *Angel: After the Fall.* Vol. 4 of 4. San Diego: IDW, 2011. Kindle edition.
"Man on the Street." *Dollhouse: Season 1.* Episode 6. Writ. Joss Whedon. Dir. Andrew Straiton. Creat. Joss Whedon. Fox. 20 March 2009. Twentieth Century Fox, 2009. DVD.
McGuire, Philip C. *Speechless Dialect: Shakespeare's Open Silences.* Berkeley: University of California Press, 1985. Print.
Moylan, Katie. "'Nothing is what it appears to be': Event Fidelity and Critique in *Battlestar Galactica* and *Dollhouse*." *Science Fiction Film and Television* 5.1 (2012): 67–84. Web. 6 March 2016. PDF.
Much Ado About Nothing. Writ. Joss Whedon. Dir. Joss Whedon. Lionsgate, 2013. Blu-ray.
Mulvey, Laura. "Gimme Shelter." Rev. of *Blackboards. Sight & Sound* 11.1 (2001): 26–28. Web. 27 Oct. 2015.
"Not Fade Away." *Angel: Season 5.* Episode 22. Writ. Jeffrey Bell and Joss Whedon. Dir. Jeffrey Bell. Creat. Joss Whedon and David Greenwalt. The WB. 19 May 2004. Twentieth Century Fox, 2009. DVD.
"Objects in Space." *Firefly: The Complete Series.* Episode 14. Writ. Joss Whedon. Dir. Joss Whedon. Creat. Joss Whedon. Fox. 13 Dec. 2002. Twentieth Century Fox, 2014. DVD.
Oppenheimer, Jean. "An Indie Twist on Shakespeare: Jay Hunter Takes a Bare-Bones Approach to Joss Whedon's *Much Ado About Nothing*." *American Cinematographer* (July 2013): 56–63. Web. PDF.
_____. "A Woman on the Verge: Ed Lachman, ASC Reteams with Director Todd Haynes on the HBO Miniseries Mildred Pierce." *American Cinematographer* (April 2011): 42–51. Web. 27 Oct. 2015. PDF.
Orkin, Martin. "Film and the Uncanny, Shakespeare Making Possible Things Not So Held, Communicating with Dreams." *Sederi* 21 (2011): 49–70. *SEDERI: Spanish and Portuguese Society for English Renaissance Studies.* The Spanish and Portuguese Society for Renaissance Studies, 3 March 2016. Web. 6 March 2016. PDF.
Orr, Christopher. "Joss Whedon on the 'No Brainer' of Modernizing *Much Ado About Nothing*." *The Atlantic.* The Atlantic Monthly Group, 7 June 2013. Web. 3 June 2016.
"Our Mrs. Reynolds." *Firefly: The Complete Series.* Episode 6. Writ. Joss Whedon. Dir. Vondie Curtis Hall. Creat. Joss Whedon. Fox. 4 Oct. 2002. Twentieth Century Fox, 2014. DVD.
"Passion." *Buffy the Vampire Slayer: Season 2.* Writ. Ty King. Dir. Michael Gershman. Creat. Joss Whedon. The WB. 24 Feb. 1998. Twentieth Century Fox, 2009. DVD.
"Players." *Angel: Season 4.* Episode 16. Writ. Jeffrey Bell, Elizabeth Craft and Sarah Fain. Dir. Michael Grossman. Creat. Joss Whedon and David Greenwalt. The WB. 26 March 2003. Twentieth Century Fox, 2004. DVD.

"The Price." *Angel: Season 3*. Episode 19. Writ. David Fury. Dir. Marita Grabiak. Creat. Joss Whedon and David Greenwalt. The WB. 29 April 2002. Twentieth Century Fox, 2004. DVD.
Rachman, S., and Steven Taylor. "Analyses of Claustrophobia." *Journal of Anxiety Disorders* 7 (1993): 281–91. Web. 9 March 2016. PDF.
Ritman, Alex. "Joss Whedon: 'Avengers' Sequel Was a 'Nightmare' Due to Expanded Superhero Cast." *The Hollywood Reporter*. The Hollywood Reporter, 3 April 2015. Web. 4 June 2016.
Robinson, Joanna. "Joss Whedon Says His Battle with Marvel Got 'Really Unpleasant.'" *Vanity Fair*. Condé Nast, 5 May 2015. Web. 4 June 2016.
Rogers, Scott." Joss Whedon's *Dollhouse* and Joss Whedon's Dollhouse." *Journal of the Fantastic in the Arts* 22.2 (2011): 153–70. Web. 6 March 2016. PDF.
Schieman, Scott, and Paul Glavin. "Education and Work-Family Conflict: Explanations, Contingencies, and Mental Health Consequences." *Social Forces* 89.4 (2011): 1341–62. Web. 18 May 2016. PDF.
Schrader, Paul. "Notes on Film Noir." *Film Comment* 8.1 (1972): 8–13. *HarvardKey*. Harvard University, 2016. 3 June 2016. PDF.
The Searchers. Dir. John Ford. Warner Bros., 1956. Film.
"Seeing Red." *Buffy the Vampire Slayer: Season 6*. Writ. Stephen S. DeKnight. Dir. Michael Gershman. Creat. Joss Whedon. UPN. 7 May 2002. Twentieth Century Fox, 2009. DVD.
"Serenity." *Firefly: The Complete Series*. Episode 1. Writ. Joss Whedon. Dir. Joss Whedon. Creat. Joss Whedon. Fox. 20 Dec. 2002. Twentieth Century Fox, 2014. DVD.
Serenity. Writ. Joss Whedon. Dir. Joss Whedon. Universal, 2005. DVD.
Shakespeare, William. *Much Ado About Nothing*. Rev. ed. Ed. Claire McEachern. London: Bloomsbury Arden Shakespeare-Bloomsbury, 2016. Print.
Shuster, Martin. "What It Means to Mourn: *Dollhouse* and Aporia." *Inside Joss' Dollhouse: From Alpha to Rossum*. Ed. Jane Espenson. Dallas: Smart Pop, 2010. 233–45. Print.
Smith, Paul Julian. "Men in Trouble." Rev. of *Lebanon* and *Eyes Wide Open*. *Film Quarterly* 64.1 (2010): 12–13. Web. 1 Jan. 2016. PDF.
"That Old Gang of Mine." *Angel: Season 3*. Episode 3. Writ Tim Minear. Dir. Fred Keller. Creat. Joss Whedon and David Greenwalt. The WB. 8 Oct. 2001. Twentieth Century Fox, 2004. DVD.
Titford, John S. "Object-Subject Relationships in German Expressionist Cinema." *Cinema Journal* 13.1 (1973): 17–24. Web. 27 Oct. 2015. PDF.
"To Shanshu in L. A." *Angel: Season 1*. Episode 22. Writ. David Greenwalt. Dir. David Greenwalt. Creat. Joss Whedon and David Greenwalt. The WB. 23 May 2000. Twentieth Century Fox, 2003. DVD.
"Tough Love." *Buffy the Vampire Slayer: Season 5*. Episode 19. Writ. Rebecca Rand Kishner. Dir. David Grossman. Creat. Joss Whedon. The WB. 1 May 2001. Twentieth Century Fox, 2009. DVD.
Towers, Ian, Linda Duxbury, Christopher Higgins, and John Thomas. "Time Thieves and Space Invaders: Technology, Work, and the Organization." *Journal of Organizational Change* 19.5 (2006): 593–618. Web. 18 May 2016.
Tupper, Peter. "Joss Whedon's *Dollhouse*: 21st Century Neo-Gothic." *Inside Joss' Dollhouse: From Alpha to Rossum*. Ed. Jane Espenson. Dallas: Smart Pop, 2010. 47–60. Print.
Vinci, Tony M. "'Not an apocalypse, the apocalypse': Existential Proletarianism and the Possibility of the Soul in Joss Whedon's *Dollhouse*." *Science Fiction Film and Television* 4.2 (2011): 225–248. Web. 6 March 2016. PDF.
"War Stories." *Firefly: The Complete Series*. Episode 10. Writ. Cheryl Cain. Dir. James Contner. Creat. Joss Whedon. Fox. 6 Dec. 2002. Twentieth Century Fox, 2014. DVD.
Whedon, Joss. Director's Commentary. *The Avengers*. Marvel Studios, 2012. Blu-ray.
_____. Director's Commentary. *Avengers: Age of Ultron*. Marvel Studios, 2015. Blu-ray.
_____. Director's Commentary. *Much Ado About Nothing*. Lionsgate, 2013. Blu-ray.
_____. Director's Commentary. *Serenity*. Universal, 2005. DVD.
Whedon, Joss (w), Georges Jeanty (p), and Andy Owens (i). *Buffy the Vampire Slayer Season Eight*. Vol. 1 of 8. Milwaukie, OR: Dark Horse Books, 2007. Kindle edition.

Whedon, Zack (w), Georges Jeanty (p), Fábio Moon (p), and Karl Story (i). *Serenity: Firefly Class 03-K64: Leaves on the Wind.* Milwaukie, OR: Dark Horse Books, 2014. Kindle edition.
Wilcox, Rhonda V. "'Can I Spend the Night / Alone?' Segments and Connections in 'Conversations with Dead People.'" *Reading Joss Whedon.* Ed. Rhonda V. Wilcox, Tanya R. Cochran, Cynthea Masson, and David Lavery. Syracuse: Syracuse University Press, 2015. 70–83. Print.
_____. "Joss Whedon's Translation of Shakespeare's *Much Ado About Nothing*: Historical Double Consciousness, Reflections, and Frames." *Slayage: The Online Journal of Whedon Studies* 11.2/12.1 (2014): n. pag. Web. 21 Dec. 2016. PDF.
Wilde, Oscar. "The Decay of Lying: An Observation." *The Complete Works of Oscar Wilde.* Ed. J. B. Foreman. New York: Perennial Library-Harper & Row, 1966. 970–92. Print.
Williams, Anne. "The Horror, The Horror: Recent Studies in Gothic Fiction." *Modern Fiction Studies* 46.3 (2000): 789–99. Web. 9 Feb. 2012. PDF.
"You're Welcome." *Angel: Season 5.* Episode 12. Writ. David Fury. Dir. David Fury. Creat. Joss Whedon and David Greenwalt. The WB. 4 Feb. 2004. 2004. Twentieth Century Fox, 2005. DVD.

Broken but Home
Institutions, Control and the Non-Place in Dollhouse

Catherine Pugh

Writing on the opening title sequences of *Dollhouse* (2009–2010), David Kociemba notes that from the outset, "Whedon emphasizes place rather than character, genre or world," evidenced by Whedon's name appearing in an overhead shot of the Dolls' sleeping pods. In a show where identity and autonomy are unstable and unpredictable, Kociemba argues that "physical space grounds the series" (180).

Whedon's other primary series all feature a home as one of the central locations: the Summers' house in *Buffy the Vampire Slayer* (1997–2003),[1] the Hyperion hotel in *Angel* (1999–2004), and *Serenity* in *Firefly/Serenity* (2002–2003; 2005). The Dollhouse is an institution, yet, like *BtVS*, *Angel* and *Firefly*, the characters within form a family. Renee St. Louis and Miriam Riggs note that candidates for becoming Dolls rarely have enough community ties to warrant being missed; often they are drawn from outsiders or those already embedded in institutions (prisoners, the mentally ill, soldiers) (10). Additionally, most, if not all, of the staff have their own quarters in the Dollhouse. St. Louis and Riggs write, "The Dollhouse is thus *home*, making the people in its walls family, and situating Adelle DeWitt as the female figure of power in the family element of the tale, likening her to a mother" (11). Echo, Priya and Anthony spend much of the series attempting to leave the Dollhouse in one way or another, but by the final episode, they are forced to reunite and return. Once inside the Dollhouse walls, trapped for a year, they must adapt to their new family dynamics (Anthony and his estranged family; Echo and Ballard).

The Dollhouse itself is spa-like, designed to stimulate an atmosphere of peace and tranquility. Its open-plan design allows the camera smooth and flowing pans across the space, with every feature or area organically leading to another. The Dolls glide through the 'House, and the spectator glides with them, unhurried, untroubled. The use of wood, muted color palette and soft recess lighting suggest comfort, luxury and natural beauty. A strong sensation of Zen is implied; the Dolls practice yoga by a small pool, eat nutritious, healthy food, exercise, get massages, paint, and cultivate bonsai trees. However, as Adelle DeWitt points out in the first episode, nothing in the world of *Dollhouse* is what it appears to be. Just as Caroline's "clean slate" always leaves the mark of what was on it before, the sinister roots of the Dollhouse can be found within the space itself. The 'House may appear tranquil at first glance, but the uncanny and often disturbing aspects of Dollhouse technology quickly begin to seep through.

The Dollhouse is what Erving Goffman would view as a "total institution": a "place of residence and work where a large number of like-situated individuals, cut off from the wider society for an appreciable period of time, together lead an enclosed, formally administered round of life" (Goffman xxi). The central features of total institutions determine,

> [first,] all aspects of life are conducted in the same place and under the same single authority. Second, each phase of the member's daily activity is carried on in the immediate company of a large batch of others, all of whom are treated alike and required to do the same things together. Third, all phases of the day's activities are tightly scheduled, with one activity leading at a prearranged time into the next, the whole sequence of activities being imposed from above by a system of explicit formal rulings and a body of officials. Finally, the various enforced activities are brought together into a single rational plan purportedly designed to fulfil the official aims of the institution [Goffman 6].

Additionally, Goffman sets out five characteristics of a total institution, all of which can be used to refer to the Dollhouse. In the first, inmates can be viewed as incapable and harmless, such as those in care homes and orphanages, just as the Dolls are described as vulnerable and child-like. Alternatively, inmates can be viewed as incapable, yet presenting an (often unintended) threat to the community, such as in sanitaria and mental hospitals. There are several instances in *Dollhouse* where Dolls and Actives become unintentionally dangerous. For example, Alpha sets off a pulse which temporarily turns all Dolls violent and in "Echoes" a toxin alters the Actives' consciousness. Furthermore, Anthony and (supposedly) Priya are admitted to the Dollhouse in part to treat mental illness. In other total institutions, the inmates are seen as intentionally dangerous, such as prisons, prisoner of war and concentration camps. Similarly, when the Dollhouse was first established, it used prisoners as Actives and Caroline volunteers in order to avoid terrorism charges.

Total institutions can also be thought of as beneficial for work-like tasks, including military barracks and boarding schools. In the case of the Dollhouse, Actives are "trained" or "upgraded"; given beneficial skills that can, in several cases, be used outside the parameters of the imprint, such as with Echo, Victor and the Tech-heads. Finally, a total institution can be seen as beneficial in terms of a retreat, although it can also function to train and indoctrinate, particularly in a religious context (abbeys, monasteries and convents). The Dollhouse is endorsed by Rossum (and Adelle in particular) as a retreat, yet includes high levels of indoctrination—not only through the imprinting process, but also in the call-and-response script.

The Dollhouse functions as a total institution, providing care and protection while simultaneously indoctrinating and controlling its inmates. On the surface an image of luxury and serenity is offered, however, the design of the 'House suggests boundaries, control and an expectation of obedience. Furthermore, the Dollhouse uses imagery associated with real-life institutions, such as asylums, and horror iconography in order to foster an uneasy atmosphere of surveillance and voyeurism. By utilising institutional and horror discourse, alongside the dream-like quality of the 'House, *Dollhouse* "gives you a sense of tranquillity, but also a sense that there is something in it that you can't quite see" (Whedon, "Designing the Perfect Dollhouse").

Horror Spaces and Haunted Houses

The design aspects of the 'House particularly reinforce Goffman's ideas on the institution as supposedly beneficial while promoting indoctrination, to the point where an outwardly therapeutic space morphs into a horror landscape. While the central hub presents a spa-like ideal of harmony, openness and free-flow, there are visual clues suggesting strict boundaries (that are ultimately destabilised and transgressed), discord and secret spaces, more akin to the horror genre than science fiction or fantasy. This is supported by the text itself; Bronwen Calvert notes that "aspects of horror intrude into the narrative—even in scenes or storylines that play as strongly comic or pleasurable" particularly in the "destabilization of identity ... [where] viewers are invited to find pleasure in viewing a monstrous body that transgresses boundaries" ("Viewing Pleasure and Horror" 115).[2] Applying Barry Curtis' theories on dark places establishes the Dollhouse as a haunted house (underlined by numerous references in the dialogue and episode titles).[3] Curtis proposes that a "haunted house" can be "the lingering presence of some repressed social group, or a demonically malevolent individual, possessed by a force that is antagonistic to the protagonist's present life" (10). These "dark places" are "powerful metaphors for persistent themes of loss, memory, retribution and confrontation with unacknowledged and unresolved histories" (10) rife with anxiety about becoming possessed and losing autonomy (4). The Dollhouse itself features multiple references to traditional horror spaces; castles, laboratories, asylums, basements and dreamscapes.

Topher's workspace both supports and subverts the stereotype of the mad scientist's laboratory.[4] Blue flashes of light occur during treatments reminiscent of lightening from numerous *Frankenstein* films, while Topher's toys and games cause the Actuals in "Epitaph One" to mistake the workspace of a genius for a child's playroom.[5] Yet as both Erickson and Nylin suggest, it is Alpha's makeshift "Chair" in the warehouse that is presented as a more iconic mad scientist's laboratory. The dirty and chaotic equipment is made out of whatever Alpha could find and held together by duct tape in direct contrast to the professional, well-maintained and clean Dollhouse treatment room. The pristine Dollhouse allows "those in control of this technology [to] laud its advancement and benefits because its 'clean' appearance allows them to view it and its uses as altruistic 'helping' and 'doing good'" (Calvert, "Mind, Body, Imprint" 7). Erickson and Nylin draw comparisons between Alpha's Chair and *Frankenstein* primarily due to the "lightening," climatic music, and Alpha's theatrical performance. Yet these features also appear in Chair sequences within the Dollhouse, although in a less gothic manner. Additionally, as Calvert argues, the Dollhouse Chair sequences are not without horror:

> [Sierra] is linked to the chair with a web of wires that have been inserted not only into her head but also over her entire body. The room is in low light, while noise and flashes of light punctuate Sierra's gasps and cries of pain as her original personality is "wiped" to allow her to work as a doll.... The chair and the imprint room are similarly shot in an episode in which former security head Dominic has his personality "wiped" before being taken to "the Attic," ... the scene is also shot with a hand-held camera, making it indistinct, off-balance, and difficult for the viewer to interpret. That this is a fearsome fate is underlined by Dominic's suicide attempt in the chair, as well as his muffled screams and the frozen expressions of the other characters present [Calvert, "Mind, Body, Imprint" 8].

Notably, Topher rejects his workspace after guilt drives him insane. In "Epitaph Two," Adelle notes that he does not go into the treatment room any more. Instead, "he has created a living space in one of the old sleep pods; books and artifacts surround his nest in what seems to be an effort to bring himself some comfort.... As he jumps into his old bed (with childlike zest), he wraps himself in an old blankie" (St. Louis and Riggs). By banishing the horror space and creating a domestic space, with the comforts of childhood and family, Topher is able to find some peace.

Transparency and Open Spaces

Architects from the 1920s argued that phobias such as agoraphobia and claustrophobia were caused by urban environments. Therefore, as Anthony Vidler writes, "reviving the late eighteenth-century myth of 'transparency,' both social and spatial, modernists evoked the picture of a glass city, its buildings invisible and society open. The resulting 'space' would be open, infinitely extended, and thereby cleansed of all mental disturbance: the site of healthy and presumably aerobically perfect bodies" (51). Initially, this theory appears to extend to the Dollhouse. It is filled with healthy, beautiful young people, free from anxiety, content to wander through their comfortable surroundings. The free-flowing and borderless 'House invites transparency and infinite possibilities. There are parallels between the structure of the Dollhouse itself and the minds of the Dolls who live within it. Not only are the Dolls "transparent"—examined and created through brain-scans, GPS and live bio-readouts—but there is no limit to who they can become. Furthermore, several characters throughout the series refer to "Dollhouse architecture"—the subject's neural implants that allow personality imprints. Installing Dollhouse architecture into a person permanently transforms them into a Doll, just as it appears that almost anyone who spends time in the 'House is either revealed to be a Doll (Whiskey, Alpha, November, Victor) or ultimately becomes one (Ballard, Boyd, Dominic, Topher, Terry).[6] As Calvert notes, "the consequences of embodied enhancements cannot be erased or forgotten" a sentiment put far more bluntly by Ballard: "once a Doll, always a Doll" (Calvert, "Mind, Body, Imprint" 9; "The Public Eye").

The open-plan and spacious design of the 'House suggests that it is accessible and forthcoming, yet it is a place full of secrets and concealment, reflecting the people who live and work within it. The offices of Claire Saunders and Topher Brink, although ostensibly part of the open-plan design, are obscured. Frosted glass, panelling and low light allow the offices to look transparent, yet it is much easier for the occupant to see out than for anyone else to see in. Furthermore, Topher's office is on the upper floor, allowing him to gaze over his creations while remaining detached. While he can see everything beneath him, those on the lower floor (where the Dolls live) have a restricted view of his workspace.

Conversely, there are spaces within the 'House which should offer a level of privacy but in fact only present an illusion of it. The showers, for example, are gender-neutral, open and set into a circle. In several scenes, semi-nude Actives are seen having massages, with only a translucent series of banners (if anything) separating them from the main floor. Close-circuit television cameras (CCTV) survey every inch of the central hub. Not only is everything recorded, but it is kept and can be brought forth for analysis at any time (such as Victor's "man-reactions" in "True Believer"). The dangers of hidden space in a supposedly open house reach a crux in the episode "Man on the Street." The Dollhouse staff encounter difficulties identifying Sierra's rapist as despite the presence of cameras, the assaults have not been caught on tape. It is eventually revealed that there is a blind spot in the surveillance and that one of the frosted glass panels in the 'House can slide back, hiding the people behind it even when it is closed.

Therefore, there is an air of voyeurism that hovers over the Dollhouse from the outset. As a total institution, the Dollhouse is rife with surveillance and a subtle sense of unease even underneath the luxury. Imagery of Eden is called upon, arguing that the Dollhouse is not just a safe place, but a haven, a suggestion that is always quickly shut down, such as in this exchange from "Briar Rose":

> ALPHA/KEPPLER: They told me this was going to be the new Eden.
> BALLARD: Eden wasn't a prison.
> ALPHA/KEPPLER: What, are you kidding? The apples were monitored.

Even the peaceful atmosphere fostered in the 'House is undermined by an eerie disquiet. Various characters pick up on this, quickly contextualizing tranquility into horror. Caroline wonders, "When does the hankering for tasty brains kick in?" ("Omega") while a self-aware Victor, after encountering a "normal" Doll for the first time, immediately announces, "We're all gonna die" ("Needs").

Surveillance is reinforced in the opening titles, which assimilate close-circuit television cameras zooming in for close-ups of Echo. Kociemba notes, "[Echo] is heavily objectified in both seasons' sequences.... The camera of the opening title sequence is strongly reminiscent of the controlling male gaze" (187). Similarly, Joel Hawkes writes, "cameras and screens fill *Dollhouse*; the practices of watching, viewing, and seeing are integral to the show, mimicking the destructive and constructive male gaze, the similar gaze of the television viewer, the security of the Dollhouse and that of our own CCTV society, and our reliance on electronic screens. In these we watch ourselves" (156).

However, there is not only a male gaze at work in the Dollhouse, but an institutional one that also seeks to objectify. Aspects of the Dollhouse are reminiscent of the Panopticon design by Jeremy Bentham in the 18th century. Bentham proposed the Panopticon as a structure for institutions. It included a circular design with a so-called "inspection house" at its center and cells/rooms around the perimeter. The staff in the inspection house would be able to see all areas of the institution. The inmates, on the other hand, would not be able to tell whether or not they were being watched at any given moment. Bentham's theory suggested that, as the inmates would never know when they were being observed, they would be forced to act as though they were always being observed, allowing the institution to employ only a single watchman.

Echoes of the Panopticon also appear in the curved shape of the 'House. The main living areas are circular, so that the Dollhouse itself forms into a series of circles (or possibly even spirals). Yet these pleasantly rounded spaces are juxtaposed with squares, straight lines and angles, such as the pool in the center of the Dollhouse floor, lighting fixtures, panelling, plants and swathes of fabric. These lines appear sharp against the softness of the 'House, dividing space and drawing boundaries in a place that supposedly has neither. They suggest linearity and modernity, but also offer undercurrents of conformity, puppetry and machinery. There is a distinct irony in this environment; a space that tries so hard to be comforting and act as a safe home yet contains features suggestive of an institution or factory. The Dolls are ostensibly treated as human (albeit infantilized), but the space they live in marks them as non-human or cyborg.

Boundaries

The blurring, transgression and redrawing of boundaries is a recurring theme in *Dollhouse*. The 'House is a space that suggests no boundaries, yet is constrained by them. There is a significant change in the lighting design between seasons one and two of the show. During season one, the lighting is much brighter and more revealing, almost like an airport waiting room (as Whedon notes on the commentary for "Vows"). By season two, however, many of the lights in the main 'House have been removed. As well as reflecting the darker tone of the second season, this also creates shadowy crevasses for characters to retreat into. Echo is able to have dangerous but covert conversations with handlers Ballard and Boyd, such as her exchange with Ballard at the end of "Vows." Under the darkness of the stairs, they discuss Echo's ability to remember her former imprints, a conversation that could be destructive for both of them if overheard. At one point during this sequence, the camera is placed low behind Echo and Ballard, where the wall should be. The two characters are situated in the shadowy foreground, framed by the staircase, while in the background the activities of the brightly lit 'House continue. This technique creates a paradoxical sensation of both collusion and voyeurism; the spectator is a hidden witness to this clandestine conversation, yet watches not only Echo and Ballard, but also the 'House itself, from an upward angle in the same way that the Actives look up at Topher's laboratory. The 'House—like Echo—is being (re)constructed from a different angle; it is becoming the object of the gaze rather than the subject.[7]

There are many shots in season one that place the spectator on the higher floors or in Topher's laboratory, looking down. Indeed, this is how the floor of the 'House is first introduced in the series: with a sweeping establishing shot gazing down from Topher's office before moving onto the floor itself. There are comparatively few shots from the Dolls' point of view, looking up at Topher's laboratory or the upper floor, and even those are somewhat vague. For example, in "A Spy in the House of Love," Echo and Sierra stare up at the hidden events occurring in the laboratory as Laurence is prepared for the Attic. However, they are given no information, nor do they seek it.

Generally speaking, characters positioned on the upper floor are in power as they are privy to information or surveillance and are therefore able to easily objectify those on the lower floor (usually Dolls). This is in keeping with structures such as the Panopticon and Goffman's total institutions, where there are high levels of surveillance and "a basic split between a large managed group, conveniently called inmates, and a small supervisory staff" (7). Although the majority of the Dolls appear oblivious (or at least unconcerned) to this arrangement and the attitude of the staff, the "aware" Dolls note the difference. This can cause the Dolls to feel unease, while some of the staff (Laurence Dominic in particular) are equally threatened by the mask-like effect of the Doll state. Goffman continues, "Each grouping tends to conceive of the other in terms of narrow hostile stereotypes, staff often seeing inmates as bitter, secretive, and untrustworthy, while inmates often see staff as condescending, highhanded and mean. Staff tends to feel superior and righteous; inmates tend, in some ways at least, to feel inferior, weak, blameworthy, and guilty" (7). Underlining this sentiment, a somewhat self-aware Echo confronts Topher in "Needs": while Topher insists that he is "just the science guy," Echo points out that he is "up here. Looking down on everyone. Playing God."

Incidentally, Echo climbs the stairs when curiosity gets the better of her ("Ghost") or when she offers help ("A Spy in the House of Love"). As she does so, the camera is placed at a high angle suggestive of Hitchcock texts such as *Psycho*.[8] Curtis proposes, "The staircase, the metaphoric vehicle of ascent and descent ... mediates the distribution of space, connecting public to private, evident to secret" (60). In the 'House, stairs act as a portal and a way of sectioning off the "staff"/public space from "Doll"/private space. In an ordinary household, the stairs tend to lead to the bedroom, the space of privacy, infinite dreaming and safety. However, in the Dollhouse, this is reversed as the sleeping pods are downstairs. Echo's expeditions up the stairs are also reminiscent of the hero's journey as written about by Joseph Campbell. For example, Echo has to return to her Doll state, sleeping in a coffin-like pod before ascending the stairs in order to find identity and become "real." Navigating the Attic can be viewed an inversion of the hero's journey, similar to *Dollhouse*'s treatment of fairy tales. Additionally, stairs have a particular resonance in horror spaces, acting as warnings (going up or down into the unknown, the strange or the psyche). Unlike normal domestic spaces, Echo does not traverse the stairs in order to sleep, dream or explore the unconscious; she travels upstairs in order to wake up.

The 'House contains many cameras but very few mirrors, with usually reflective surfaces such as glass being frosted or distorted in some way. These become obstacles to stabilizing the Dolls' identity. Curtis writes, "There are many barriers to establishing what is real—mirrors, glass, veils, the effects of light that dematerialize and animate objects" (60). Furthermore, the lack of reflection invokes Jacque Lacan's work on the mirror stage, a fundamental landmark of development in the infant where the ego is formed through a process of objectification. The child recognizes themselves in the mirror, but only as a fragmented body; in order to see itself as whole, the child learns to identify with the image. The distorted reflections in the Dollhouse therefore echoes the emptiness of the Dolls; the only way that they can achieve identity is by acting as mirrors themselves, reflecting back their clients' desires.

As relationship dynamics change within the 'House, boundary systems evolve alongside them. In his book *Class, Codes and Control*, Basil Bernstein discusses boundary maintaining procedures through the symbolic ordering of domestic space, specifically in terms of what he called *positional* and *person-centered/person-orientated* families. He argues that positional families have formal physical and social boundaries, where the identity of its members is drawn from the individual's age, sex, and status within that unit (father, mother, child, and so on). Person-centered families, on the other hand, have weak or flexible boundaries. Therefore, relationships between members are based on evolving differences and qualities rather than status or function.

At the beginning of *Dollhouse*, the 'House has a positional structure. Actives are clearly Actives, with set parameters for behavior that are never exceeded, whether in Doll state or once imprinted. The spectator, and the Dolls themselves, may not know which characters are Dolls, but those in power have absolute knowledge and control. Similarly, every member of staff is acutely aware of his or her role and place in the hierarchy and perform accordingly. Even Claire Saunders/Whiskey, who is both a Doll and a staff member, behaves according to social expectations. In Doll form she is a perfect blank slate, the most requested Active in the 'House. As Claire she is the model of a compassionate physician. However, "Omega" and "Vows" demonstrate the breakdown of Claire, as well as her more unpleasant side, such as shouting at Victor that he is "ugly" and "disgusting" and later seemingly offering Echo a lollipop before eating it herself. As the original Dr. Saunders was the one to offer lollipops to his patients, this moment closes the space between personalities. It asks whether the boundaries between personalities are beginning to blur along with Claire's mental health; whether it is another indication of Doll-state anxiety along with the ominous black stains in Sierra's paintings.

A primary characteristic of total institutions is the movement of people in organized groups, reinforcing the depersonalization of inmates. Furthermore, as Goffman writes, "when persons are moved in blocks, they can be supervised by personnel whose chief activity is not guidance or periodic inspection ... but rather surveillance—a seeing to it that everyone does what he has been clearly told is required of him, under conditions where one person's infraction is likely to stand out" (6–7). Therefore, space and boundaries become particularly important, determining not only the structure of the institution (both sociologically and architecturally) but also reinforcing the us-and-them mentality that is so potent between "inferior" inmates and "superior" staff in a parallel of the positional domestic formation. Goffman notes that total institutions are in fact "two different social and cultural worlds ... jogging alongside each other with points of official contract by little mutual penetration" (9), demonstrated in *Dollhouse* by the closed-off spaces of Topher and Saunders' offices from the central hub. These are places where Dolls are not meant to wander and Topher and Saunders rarely leave. Characters rarely stray outside of their designated physical spaces. Bennett Halverson is even surprised that the L.A. Dollhouse allows the Actives as much freedom as they do, noting that in the Washington Dollhouse "we keep ours more like veal" ("Getting Closer").

However, the boundary structure of the Dollhouse gradually becomes more person-centered, reflecting Echo's development into an individual rather than a Doll. Bernstein writes that in person-centered families, "the members would be making their roles rather than stepping into them" (185) which is exactly what Echo achieves, creating her own personality from scratch. Although she can "step into" other imprinted personalities, she insists that, "You're always talking to Echo" ("Stop-Loss"). In season one, imprints are strictly monitored and, with the exception of Echo, do not bleed into the Doll state. Actives do not deviate from their assigned parameters, either physically or emotionally, and for the most part, staff stay within their own spaces. In season two, however, not only can Echo freely move between imprints, she has developed her own, dominant personality, separate from imprints or Caroline, based on her own experiences. Other Dolls, such as Victor and Sierra, develop personalities separate from but connected to their originals. Others still, like Anthony and the Tech-heads, pick and choose from the upgrades available to them. With this freedom of individuality comes a freedom of space: Actives begin to wander off or leave their assignments and even Topher and Saunders leave the Dollhouse, returning with drastically altered personalities.[9]

In terms of communication, Bernstein suggests that positional families focus on the general attributes of a person, and therefore "[speech] symbolizes the boundaries given by the formal structure of the relationships" (185). This is demonstrated clearly in the formal call and response exchange hardwired into the Actives, particularly after returning to the Doll state ("Did I fall asleep?") and the one phrase guaranteed to stop whatever they are doing ("Would you like a treatment?"). Furthermore, Goffman notes that in total institutions, dialogue between staff and inmates is formal and repetitive, often "conducted in a special tone of voice" (8) just as the Dollhouse staff use a softer tone when talking directly to the Dolls. Specifically, Topher scolds Ivy on her cold delivery of the post-imprint script in "A Spy in the House of Love," telling her that it "may seem inconsequential, but it's the first thing an Active hears after a memory wipe. It's got to be pleasant."

In the Dollhouse, words have weight. Words reinforce boundaries, control behavior and can even unlock hidden powers. For example, in the episode "Man on the Street" Adelle unlocks Mellie's sleeper program with the phrase "There are three flowers in a vase." As the show continues, and the 'House becomes more person-centered, the strict, confining boundaries of words begins to lessen, and with it, their authority. Trigger phrases become subverted or ignored, such as Echo asserting "I don't want to fall asleep, even for a little while" ("The Left Hand"). Hawkes notes that although the word "best" becomes a trap, its potency is lost when its meaning is questioned in "Briar Rose" and ultimately it is decreed that, "no one is their best in here" ("Vows").

Dreaming Space

The Dollhouse is not only a functional space, it is also a dreaming space, a place where both dreams and nightmares are realized. Gaston Bachelard envisions the house as a vertical image created through the polarity of the attic and the basement/cellar. For Bachelard, the attic represents shelter, clarity and rationality, whereas he proclaims the basement the "*dark entity* of the house": subterranean, irrational, a place that evokes "buried madness, walled-in tragedy" and casts shadows even under the brightest lights (18, 20). Readers of horror immediately recognize the basement as a place of terror: from the work of Poe and Lovecraft to contemporary film (including Whedon's *The Cabin in the Woods*), the basement remains an iconic horror space.

Yet, in *Dollhouse*, it is the Attic that represents the more overt threat. While the Dollhouse itself exists in the basement several storeys underground, broken dolls, rogue agents and other people who need to be quietly boxed away are sent to the Attic. This is a "mental suck," resulting in "whatever hell you imagine" ("A Spy in the House of Love"; "Stop-Loss"). Bachelard identifies both the attic and the basement as dreaming spaces, where construction can take place. He notes that "the dreamer constructs and reconstructs the upper stories and the attic until they are well constructed ... when we dream of the heights we are in the rational zone of intellectualized projects" (18).

Dollhouse reverses Bachelard's image of the attic as a place of rationalization and the basement one of terror. The Dollhouse Attic is an irrational space. When the audience is finally allowed to see inside ("The Attic") it is an uncanny maze of overlapping nightmares; the traumatized remnants of the sleepers that create it. The dreamers construct their own nightmares in an attempt to intellectualize their deepest fears as that is all they have left. But in doing so, they rationalize nightmares into reality. Calvert writes that inside the Attic,

> there is confusion about what is real and what is nightmare. The various nightmare experiences are grounded in embodiment with extremes of heat and cold (in Tony's and Echo's nightmares) and images of the body including feeding and dismemberment (in Echo's and the Japanese man's nightmares), corpses (in Priya's nightmare), and attacks with knives and guns throughout [Calvert, "Cyberpunk Echoes" 21].

The Attic is a mirror image of the Dollhouse; whereas the Dollhouse projects the client's greatest desires onto an object, the Attic projects the subject's greatest fears onto a space. It is this place that Echo (and others) must navigate, not only to unravel the mystery of the Dollhouse, but to ready herself for the final showdown with the Rossum Corporation. As in other texts that take place inside the mind, such as *The Cell* (2000), *Identity* (2004), *Inception* (2010) and *Dreamscape* (1984) as well as several sequences in *Buffy the Vampire Slayer* and *Serenity*, a traumatic journey through a disturbing mental landscape leads to enlightenment. The Attic brings with it knowledge and clarity that cannot be gained in the real/physical world.

Despite being in the "basement," it is the Dollhouse itself that appears rational, structured as it is around technology, rules and hierarchy. It does not take long for this space to be revealed as nightmarish in its own way, however. Here, dreaming takes on several different meanings. There are the dreams of the clients and the Actives, as well as the strange, unreal quality of the central hub. Bachelard writes that, "for the cellar, the impassioned inhabitant digs and re-digs, making its very depth active. The fact is not enough, the dream is at work. When it comes to excavated ground, dreams have no limit" (18). Echo, as the impassioned inhabitant, consistently digs not only through the memories she retains (as well as the memories of the imprints), but through Rossum, investigating the corporation. However, it is not just Echo and the other Actives that are affected by this dreaming space. The Dollhouse contains Topher's "playroom" where his creative imagination can run free (with ultimately disastrous results) and, upon seeing the Actives in their doll state for the first time, Ballard proclaims, "My whole life isn't real" ("Briar Rose").

However, the Attic of the Dollhouse is not physically the attic of the building. Logic suggests that the Attic exists somewhere between the 'House floor and the offices on the upper levels in order to keep it hidden.[10] Therefore, structurally, the offices, particularly Adelle's, can be considered the true attic of the Dollhouse as they are at the highest point of the building. Reinforcing this idea, Adelle both meets with clients and plans their engagements with Actives in her office. It is a space of rationalization and cold intellect rather than the creative intelligence of Topher's laboratory, the peaceful somnambulism of the hub, or the chaotic terror of the Attic. Adelle's office is a place where a client's "heart's desire made flesh" is planned on paper, the space where fantasies and desires are first expressed, planned, realized—and paid for.

Scholars such as Valerie Estelle Frankel, Renee St. Louis and Miriam Riggs, Ian G. Klein and K. Dale Koontz have written about *Dollhouse* in relation to mythology or fairy tale. There is an overreaching mystical iconography at work in the Dollhouse, particularly in expressions of slaying monsters in the basement and climbing towers towards conclusion. Indeed, Bachelard draws a parallel between the dreamer's city abode and legendary castles, "where mysterious passages that run under the enclosing walls, the ramparts and the moat put the heart of the castle into communication with the distant forest" (20). The episode "Briar Rose" makes particular use of this mythology, juxtaposing Ballard and Alpha navigating the passages and air ducts of the Dollhouse with a reading of the Prince's journey through the thorns towards Sleeping Beauty. St. Louis and Riggs note that when Ballard first comes across the exterior of the Dollhouse in this episode, "a shot fades from the corner of the building (complete with barbed wire and video camera) to the drawing of Briar Rose's castle and surrounding thorns.... Ballard thus becomes the prince, and the dolls, particularly Caroline/Echo and Madeline/Mellie/November, become the sleeping beauties to be rescued" (St. Louis and Riggs, 13).

But Echo is not the model fairy tale princess. As Frankel notes, Echo consistently rejects the various princes who try to rescue her (Ballard, Boyd, Alpha), choosing instead to save herself and those around her. As Echo builds herself, she builds a castle, becoming "a vessel ... guarding all the personalities and uniting them into a great assemblage of power" (75). The series ends with the Dollhouse and its remaining inhabitants beginning their sojourn, protected from the effects of Topher's reset pulse. The princess and her people will sleep for a year in their fortified castle before emerging into a new world. But they are not victims; this wicked spell has been chosen, not enforced. And in the final moments of the series, as Echo sleeps peacefully in her pod, she "is not a simple Doll being put away—she is the *ultimate* Doll, reintegrated with the place that is most a part of herself, the Dollhouse" (76).

Trauma, Healing Space and Asylums

Although the Dollhouse "deals in fantasy," it also a shelter. Dolls are often recruited in order to escape trauma, such as Anthony/Victor's post-traumatic stress disorder, Madeline/November's grief over her daughter's death and Priya/Sierra's supposed schizophrenia. The Dollhouse not only offers respite to broken people, but repairs their mental wounds in Topher's chair while nurturing their bodies with five-star cuisine. Therefore, the Dollhouse serves as a sanctuary; a type of retreat, haven[11]—or even asylum—for the traumatized. In "Needs," the beauty and peace of the Dollhouse prompts Madeline/November to muse, "Maybe something bad happened to use and they're helping us heal." The 'House is designed to feel safe; Topher points out that "in here, we minimize the trauma [of the mind-wipes] with throw pillows and perfectly crunchy lettuce. There's no conflict," while Adelle is adamant that "the world of our Actives must be one of constant certainty" ("Gray Hour"; "Needs").

This attitude is similar to the premise of The Retreat, a Quaker asylum built in the mid–1790s in the United Kingdom. The Retreat was known not only for its humane practices (limiting the use of restraints and emphasizing rehabilitation through kindness and domestic activities) but also for the attractiveness of its surroundings. The building and airing courts were created for beauty as it was thought to have high therapeutic value. Asylum designs moved away from prisons and workhouses, instead becoming modelled on the country house estate with its landscaped gardens. Just as the Dollhouse is steeped in luxury, asylums such as The Retreat had "living conditions [that] were more comfortable than in the average working home…. Modern facilities abounded and included water closets, running water, gas or electric light, clothes, and warm, clean, spacious and ornamented surroundings. A constant supply of wholesome and varied food was provided, with beer, cocoa and tea to drink" (Rutherford 29).

Despite the 'House being designed to protect the Dolls from trauma, it is also a traumatic space.[12] Traumatic events certainly take place there, both within the 'House itself (such as Hearn's attacks on Sierra and Alpha's attacks on everyone else) and within the imprinting process, which is "not unlike being born" ("True Believer"). Several Dolls display signs of anxiety and fear, such as Sierra's extreme reaction to Victor after Hearn's assault or Victor's collapse into Sierra's arms after a flashback to his military days ("Man on the Street"; "Belonging").

The Dolls are haunted by unresolved trauma that is so excessive it manages to bleed through the empty Doll-state, manifesting in behavior that the 'House staff find troublesome. The episode "Needs" focuses on Echo, Victor, Sierra and November as they regain their original personalities (but not memories) and escape the Dollhouse. The scenario is revealed to be part of a plan to manage the unresolved emotional needs carried by the affected Dolls, such as allowing Sierra to confront her abuser and November to grieve for her daughter. The sheer force of these powerful emotions puncture through layers of dissociation, demanding to be acknowledged. The only way to resolve them is for the Actives to leave the 'House. Once they achieve closure, their brains are programmed to release a sedative, waking up back in the house of dreams, their problems forgotten once again. The Dollhouse is a refuge from trauma, not a solution. It does not offer answers or closure, only respite through dissociation.

However, the continual recurrence of repetitive trauma inside the Dollhouse suggests that protection through dissociation is not enough. In order for recovery to take place, a site of healing must simultaneously—and paradoxically—act as a site of trauma and regression. This allows the subjects to both dissociate (and be sheltered) from trauma when needed while forcing them to confront it—or at least pieces of it, similar to the process of psychodynamic therapy that allows past trauma to be discussed in a safe space. This is particularly pertinent when considering the Attic. In order to escape from their individual nightmares, Echo, Priya and Anthony must confront and move past their fears; taking power away from the trauma also takes away the power of the Attic space. To exit the Attic itself requires accepting the ultimate fear—death. Calvert writes that "embodiment provides the way out of the Attic through (virtual) deaths that nevertheless appear and seem to feel real. Paradoxically, the deaths of the virtual bodies allow the characters to rediscover and reanimate their own bodies in the real world" (Calvert, "Mind, Body, Imprint" 21).

The Dollhouse also functions as an asylum in its institutional discourse. The level of dissociation promoted inside the 'House can lead to a sense of depersonalization similar to other medical institutions. The design and running of the Dollhouse is reminiscent of Rutherford's description of the Retreat, where despite the luxury, "privacy was minimal: eating and sleeping were communal ... there was little personal space. The day was strictly regulated by staff who were of varying competence and temperament. Patients had little to say in their activities and none in their companions" (29). Furthermore, the infamous Rosenhan experiment (Rosenhan 250–258), where several healthy people posed as schizophrenic patients in psychiatric institutions, was particularly critical of institutional depersonalization.

The atmosphere of depersonalization inside the Dollhouse becomes especially problematic as Echo develops as an individual. She begins to carve out personal space inside the 'House, such as scratching various phrases on the panel above her sleeping pod, each associated with a different imprint. This nods to tropes of horror madness, where a common feature of insanity is the desecration of space, particularly through a compulsion to write on any surface. The Dollhouse has the appearance of a therapeutic environment, yet features many of the disturbing aspects of the asylum. (Mostly) Archaic treatments of mental illness have parallels in the 'House, such as electroconvulsive therapy (the Chair), insulin injections, restraints, hydrotherapy, sensory deprivation, isolation ("A Love Supreme") and lobotomy (the Attic). The Dollhouse follows a horror discourse as well as an institutional one, aligning the 'House with the horror asylum as well as the institution itself. By including sequences that can be read as treatment for mental health that contemporary society finds disturbing, the space taps into real-life but horrific therapies and the fear of places that use them. Many fictional asylums present similar themes/problems as the Dollhouse, such as abuse, cruelty, power struggles and the search for a (sometimes constructed) identity, whether they are ostensibly "horror" spaces or not.

Non-Places

Michel Foucault discusses heterotopias: spaces where incompatible spatial and temporal sites converge. He offers the ferry as an example as it is simultaneously nowhere and somewhere, a finite space for "infinite imaginations" ("Of Other Spaces" 244). The heterotopia draws on the postmodern theory of non-space, an early account of which appears in Siegfried Kracauer's 1920 essay "The Hotel Lobby." Non-places involve people in transit, unengaged because the anonymity of the crowd disconnects their sense of self; they are spaces in-between periods of life and activity. Examples of non-places include waiting rooms, airports and shopping centers/malls; places where life—and identity—are on pause. Marc Augé argues that "a person entering the space of a non-place is relieved of his usual determinants. He becomes no more than what he does or experiences in the role of passenger, customer or driver" (Augé 83). Noting the arguable pleasure of the non-place, he states, "Subjected to a gentle form of possession, to which [the subject] surrenders himself with more or less talent or conviction, he tastes for a while—like anyone who is possessed—the passive joys of identity-loss, and the more active pleasure of role-playing" (Augé 83). This echoes not only the possible appeal of being an Active, but also the playfulness and lack of consequences that go hand in hand with the position.

However, Augé also notes the drawback of the non-place, in that it may provoke a crisis of identity. Identity in the non-place is a contract symbolized by markers such as passports, credit cards and shopping trolleys; it must be retrieved at thresholds such as check-in and counters. Once inside, the subject becomes one of a mass in an environment without temporal boundaries, "obey[ing] the same codes as others, receiv[ing] the same messages, respond-[ing] to the same entreaties" (83) in the same manner as those in the Doll-state and the depersonalized Dollhouse. If identity is somehow realized in the non-place, it is a jarring and uncanny experience, akin to waking the somnambulist out of the dream:

> What he is confronted with, finally, is an image of himself, but in truth it is a pretty strange image. The only face to be seen, the only voice to be heard, in the silent dialogue he holds with the landscape-text addressed to him along with others, are his own: the face and voice of a solitude mass made all the more baffling by the fact that it echoes millions of others.... The space of non-place creates neither singular identity nor relations; only solitude and similitude [83].

Therefore, framing the Dollhouse as a non-place can assist in reconciling imprints, the original volunteer personality and the individual in Doll-state. As the 'House becomes a waiting room for the Dolls in-between their many lives as Actives, so the Dollhouse architecture in the brain becomes a waiting room for different imprints. In Doll-state, the subject is neither truly an individual nor part of a community. Instead, they are a herd that wanders until the contract is called upon—until an identity is "checked out" in Topher's Chair.

Like the Dolls within it, the Dollhouse can become many things. It is a deceptively simple space; designed to be beautiful, comforting and safe, yet filled with uncanny and unsettling imagery. Open, yet secretive. Natural, yet mechanical. Therapeutic, yet mad. Throughout the series, the Dollhouse becomes a reflection of Echo and vice-versa. Both become a shelter for the lost, a haven for the traumatized. They are mechanical, transgressive and mythological. Originally designed to fulfil the fantasies of others under strict surveillance, both the Dollhouse and Echo transform themselves into something more. Julie L. Hawk suggests that Echo's metamorphosis lies in her ability to fulfil her desires by relocating them: "Echo circumvented the function of desire by relocating the object thereof. She moved the object of her desire [Ballard] from outside to inside" (250). The object of the Dollhouse's affections is Echo, the object it has spent so much time gazing at, recording and examining. As Echo progresses from object to subject, she is integrated further into the 'House; her "psychic architecture" increasingly reflecting the space of the Dollhouse. The image of her fully integrated into the 'House and finally at some kind of peace is the final image of the Dollhouse: they are echoes of each other. Each switches between identities, going beyond their original parameters in order to fulfil the ultimate mandate of the Dollhouse: to be whatever is needed.

Notes

1. See Lorna Jowett, "The Summers House as Domestic Space in *Buffy the Vampire Slayer*."
2. See also Barbara Creed, *The Monstrous-Feminine*, and Donna Haraway, "A Cyborg Manifesto."
3. See "Echo," "Echoes," "Ghost," "Gray Hour," "Haunted," "Epitaph One," "Epitaph Two," and "The Hollow Men."
4. Topher refers to himself as a mad scientist in "The Hollow Men" and throughout the series, which simultaneously supports and subverts the stereotype as it is discussed in detail by Andrew Tudor in *Monsters and Mad Scientists: A Cultural History of the Horror*

Movie. The figure usually features a man more mature than Topher, both physically and mentally, and Topher does not wear the traditional uniform of a white coat (although his assistant, Ivy, does). However, Topher has a lack of empathy (at least initially), a dangerous curiosity and pathological desire for knowledge and achievement—and, of course, he does indeed go insane. See also Sören Nylin, "Mad, Bad Scientists and Cute, Curious Magicians: The Quest for Knowledge in Buffy and the Whedonverse."

    5. For a detailed analysis of the connections between *Frankenstein* and *Dollhouse*, see Devon Anderson, "Echoes of Frankenstein: Shelley's Masterpiece in Joss Whedon's *Dollhouse* and Our Relationship with Technology."

    6. "Dolls" in this context do not necessarily refer to subjects implanted with Dollhouse architecture, but rather those who have their original personality bounced around between bodies. Ballard and Boyd are physically (bodied) Dolls as Ballard is imprinted with his own (albeit edited) persona and Boyd is the Rossum co-founder imprinted into a new body. Laurence Dominic is downloaded onto a wedge before being sent to the Attic, later temporarily imprinted onto Victor in "Briar Rose." Topher's identity is imprinted onto Victor twice, allowing him to solve different problems and be in two places at once. Serial killer Terry is imprinted onto Victor and Echo after his body is in a coma. Therefore, they have experiences beyond their own bodies and emotions—experiences that they should not have. They become "Dolls" not only because they have been subjected to Dollhouse technology—invasive or not—but because their "self" is placed beyond boundaries. This puts the Dolls in the posthuman framework written about by many Whedon scholars, rather than simply referring to those with Dollhouse architecture.

    7. See work by Michael Starr, Gregory Erickson, and Sharon Sutherland and Sarah Swan for detailed analysis of Echo and the Dolls as objects.

    8. The Hitchcock "stain," as written about by Pascal Bonizter (15–31), can be found in the 'House, adding to the air of unease.

    9. However, it should be noted that whenever Topher or Saunders leave the Dollhouse hub it is because something terrible has happened or causes something equally terrible to occur. For example, Topher must leave to rescue Echo from Washington, to find information on Alpha, to be chastised and threatened by Adelle and Dominic in Adelle's office, to dismember Sierra's rapist after she kills him, to fight Rossum and as a result of kidnapping. Saunders/Whiskey is treated with more respect when she is in Adelle's office, but her supposed sanctuary at Boyd's apartment is tempered by the fact that he is manipulating her for his own ends.

    10. This is reinforced by Laurence's escape from the Attic as he is clearly seen coming down the stairs towards the Dollhouse floor.

    11. Of course, the real "Safe Haven" that appears in "Epitaph Two" is almost the complete opposite of the Dollhouse: dirty, outdoors and hard work.

    12. The Dolls are also used in order to soothe the traumatic experiences of their clients. In "Briar Rose," Echo is imprinted with a grown-up version of an abused child in order to assist in her recovery. Topher notes that "past trauma has [the girl's] emotions, reactions, intellectual development all frakked up beyond recognition. But if she gets help, really works, deals with the soup of her life, she gets to be the nice lady with the tragic past but the healthy head." In the therapeutic space of the Dollhouse, a traumatized brain can be made into a healthy one; a damaged child can be healed into the ultimate care-giver.

Works Cited

Anderson, Devon. "Echoes of Frankenstein: Shelley's Masterpiece in Joss Whedon's *Dollhouse* and Our Relationship with Technology." *Slayage: The Online Journal of Whedon Studies* 14.1 (2016): n. pag. Web. 1 Aug. 2016.

Augé, Marc. *Non-Places: An Introduction to Supermodernity*. Brooklyn: Verso, 2008. Print.

"The Attic." *Dollhouse: Season 2*. Episode 10. Writ. Maurissa Tancharoen. Dir. John Cassaday. Creat. Joss Whedon. Fox. 18 Dec. 2009. Twentieth Century Fox, 2010. DVD.

Bachelard, Gaston. *The Poetics of Space*. Trans. Maria Jolas. Boston: Beacon Press, 1994. Print.

Bentham, Jeremy. *The Panopticon Writings*. London: Verso, 1995. Print.

Bernstein, Basil. *Class, Codes and Control: Theoretical Studies Towards a Sociology of Language*. 2nd ed. Surrey: Routledge & Kegan Paul, 1974. Print.
Bonitzer, Pascal. "Hitchcockian Suspense." *Everything You Always Wanted to Know About Lacan (But Were Afraid to Ask Hitchcock)*. Ed. Slavoj Žižek. London: Verso, 1992.
"Briar Rose." *Dollhouse: Season 1*. Episode 11. Writ. Jane Espenson. Dir. Dwight Little. Creat. Joss Whedon. Fox. 28 July 2009. Twentieth Century Fox, 2009. DVD.
The Cabin in the Woods. Writ. Joss Whedon, Drew Goddard. Dir. Drew Goddard. Lionsgate, 2012. DVD.
Calvert, Bronwen. "Mind, Body, Imprint: Cyberpunk Echoes in the Dollhouse." *Fantasy Is Not Their Purpose: Joss Whedon's Dollhouse*. Ed. Cynthea Masson and Rhonda V. Wilcox. Spec. issue of *Slayage: The Online Journal of Whedon Studies* 8.2–3 (2010): n. pag. Web. 1 Aug. 2016.
_____. "'Who Did They Make Me This Time?' Viewing Pleasure and Horror." *Joss Whedon's Dollhouse: Confounding Purpose, Confusing Identity*. Ed. Sherry Ginn, Alyson R. Buckman, and Heather M. Porter. Lanham, MD: Rowan & Littlefield, 2014. 113–127. Print.
Campbell, Joseph, *The Hero with a Thousand Faces*. London: Fontana Press, 1993.
The Cell. Writ. Mark Protosevich. Dir. Tarsern Singh. New Line Cinema, 2001. DVD.
Creed, Barbara. *The Monstrous-Feminine: Film, Feminism, Psychoanlaysis*. New York: Routledge, 1993. Print. Popular Fictions Ser.
Curtis, Barry. *Dark Places: The Haunted House in Film*. London: Reaktion Books, 2008. Print.
"Designing the Perfect Dollhouse." *Dollhouse: Season 1*. Fox, 2009. Joss Whedon. DVD Feature. Twentieth Century Fox, 2009.
Dreamscape. Writ. David Loughery. Dir. Joseph Ruben. Image Entertainment, 2000. DVD.
"Echoes." *Dollhouse: Season 1*. Episode 7. Writ. Elizabeth Craft. Dir. James Contner. Creat. Joss Whedon. Fox. 30 June 2009. Twentieth Century Fox, 2009. DVD.
"Epitaph One." *Dollhouse: Season 1*. Episode 13. Writ. Maurissa Tancharoen. Dir. David Soloman. Creat. Joss Whedon. Fox. 11 Aug. 2009. Twentieth Century Fox, 2009. DVD.
"Epitaph Two: Return." *Dollhouse: Season 2*. Episode 13. Writ. Maurissa Tancharoen. Dir. David Solomon. Creat. Joss Whedon. Fox. 29 Jan. 2010. Twentieth Century Fox, 2010. DVD.
Erickson, Gregory. "From Old Heresies to Future Paradigms: Joss Whedon on Body and Soul." *Reading Joss Whedon*. Ed. Rhonda V. Wilcox, Tanya R. Cochran, Cynthia Masson and David Lavery. Syracuse: Syracuse University Press. 341–356. Print.
Foucault, Michel. *Discipline and Punish: The Birth of the Prison*. Trans. Alan Sheridan. London: Allen Lane, 1977. Print.
_____. "Of Other Spaces." *Heterotopia and the City: Public Space in a Postcivil Society*. Ed. Michiel Dehaene and Lieven De Cauter. Abingdon: Routledge, 2008. Print.
Frankel, Valerie Estelle. "All Dolled Up." *Inside Joss' Dollhouse: From Alpha to Rossum*. Ed. Jane Espenson. Dallas: Smart Pop, 2010. 63–78. Print.
"Getting Closer." *Dollhouse: Season 2*. Episode 11. Writ. Tim Minear. Dir. Tim Minear. Creat. Joss Whedon. Fox. 8 Jan. 2010. Twentieth Century Fox, 2010. DVD.
"Ghost." *Dollhouse: Season 1*. Episode 1. Writ. Joss Whedon. Dir. Joss Whedon. Creat. Joss Whedon. 19 May 2009. Twentieth Century Fox, 2009. DVD.
Goffman, Erving. *Asylums: Essays on the Social Situations of Mental Patients and Other Inmates*. 1961. New Brunswick: Transaction Publishers, 2009. Print.
Haraway, Donna J. "A Cyborg Manifesto." *Simians, Cyborgs, and Women: The Reinvention of Nature*. London: Free Association Books, 1991. 149–182.
Hawk, Julie L. "More Than the Sum of Our Imprints." *Inside Joss' Dollhouse: From Alpha to Rossum*. Ed. Jane Espenson. Dallas: Smart Pop, 2010. 247–57. Print.
Hawkes, Joel. "The Theatre of the Self: Repetitious and Reflective Practices of Person and Place." *Joss Whedon's Dollhouse: Confounding Purpose, Confusing Identity*. Ed. Sherry Ginn, Alyson R. Buckman and Heather M. Porter. Lanham, MD: Rowman & Littlefield, 2014. 141–163. Print.
Identity. Writ. Michael Cooney. Dir. James Mangold. Sony, 2004. DVD.
Inception. Writ. Christopher Nolan. Dir. Christopher Nolan. Warner Bros. 2010. DVD.
Jowett, Lorna. "The Summers House as Domestic Space in *Buffy the Vampire Slayer*." *Slayage: The Online Journal of Whedon Studies* 5.2 (2005): n. pag. Web. 1 Aug. 2016.

Klein, Ian G. "Ritual, Rebirth, and the Rising Tide: Water and the Transcendent Self." *Joss Whedon's Dollhouse: Confounding Purpose, Confusing Identity.* Ed. Sherry Ginn, Sherry, Alyson R. Buckman and Heather M. Porter. Lanham, MD: Rowman & Littlefield, 2014. 195–211. Print.
Kociemba, David. "Welcome to the *Dollhouse*: Reading Its Opening Title Sequences." *Joss Whedon's Dollhouse: Confounding Purpose, Confusing Identity.* Ed. Sherry Ginn, Alyson R. Buckman and Heather M. Porter. Lanham, MD: Rowman & Littlefield, 2014. 177–195. Print.
Koontz, K. Dale. "Reflections in the Pool: Echo, Narcissus, and the Male Gaze in *Dollhouse*." *Reading Joss Whedon.* Ed. Rhonda V. Wilcox, Tanya R. Cochran, Cynthia Masson and David Lavery. Syracuse: Syracuse University Press. 205–221. Print.
Kracauer, Siegfried. *From Caligari to Hitler: A Psychological History of the German Film.* Princeton: Princeton University Press, 1966. Print.
_____. "The Hotel Lobby." *The Mass Ornament: Weimar Essays.* Ed. and Trans. Thomas Y. Levin. Cambridge: Harvard University Press, 1995. Print.
"Man on the Street." *Dollhouse: Season 1.* Episode 6. Writ. Joss Whedon. Dir. David Straiton. Creat. Joss Whedon. Fox. 23 June 2009. Twentieth Century Fox, 2009. DVD.
"Needs." *Dollhouse: Season 1.* Episode 8. Writ. Tracey Bellomo. Dir. Félix Acalá. Creat. Joss Whedon. Fox. 7 July 2009. Twentieth Century Fox, 2009. DVD.
Nylin, Sören. "Mad, Bad Scientists and Cute, Curious Magicians: The Quest for Knowledge in Buffy and the Whedonverse." *Slayage: The Online Journal of Whedon Studies* 7.4 (2009): n. pag. Web. 1 Aug. 2016.
"Omega." *Dollhouse: Season 1.* Episode 12. Writ. Tim Minear. Dir. Tim Minear. Creat. Joss Whedon. Fox. 4 Aug. 2009. Twentieth Century Fox, 2009. DVD.
Rosenhan, David L. "On Being Sane in Insane Places." *Science* 179 (1973): 250–258. Print.
Rutherford, Sarah. *The Victorian Asylum.* Oxford: Shire Books, 2013. Print.
St. Louis, Renee, and Miriam Riggs. "'A Painful, Bleeding Sleep': Sleeping Beauty in the *Dollhouse*." *Fantasy Is Not Their Purpose: Joss Whedon's* Dollhouse. Ed. Cynthea Masson and Rhonda V. Wilcox. Spec. issue of *Slayage: The Online Journal of Whedon Studies* 8.2-3 (2010). Web. 1 Aug. 2016.
Serenity. Writ. Joss Whedon. Dir. Joss Whedon. Universal, 2005. DVD.
"A Spy in the House of Love." *Dollhouse: Season 1.* Episode 9. Writ. Andrew Chambliss. Dir. David Solomon. Creat. Joss Whedon. Fox. 14 July 2009. Twentieth Century Fox, 2009. DVD.
Starr, Michael. "'I've Watched You Build Yourself from Scratch': The Assemblage of Echo." *Joss Whedon's Dollhouse: Confounding Purpose, Confusing Identity.* Ed. Sherry Ginn, Alyson R. Buckman and Heather M. Porter. Lanham, MD: Rowman & Littlefield, 2014. 3–21. Print.
"Stop-Loss." *Dollhouse: Season 2.* Episode 9. Writ. Andrew Chambliss. Dir. Félix Alcalá. Cret. Joss Whedon. Fox. 18 Dec. 2009. Twentieth Century Fox, 2010. DVD.
Sutherland, Sharon, and Sarah Swan. "'There Is No Me; I'm Just a Container: Law and the Loss of Personhood in *Dollhouse*." *Reading Joss Whedon.* Ed. Rhonda V. Wilcox, Tanya R. Cochran, Cynthia Masson and David Lavery. Syracuse: Syracuse University. 221–237. Print.
Tudor, Andrew. *Monsters and Mad Scientists: A Cultural History of the Horror Movie.* Oxford: Basil Blackwell, 1989. Print.
Vidler, Anthony. *Warped Space: Art, Architecture, and Anxiety in Modern Culture.* Cambridge: Massachusetts Institute of Technology, 2001. Print.
"Vows." *Dollhouse: Season 2.* Episode 1. Writ. Joss Whedon. Dir. Joss Whedon. Creat. Joss Whedon. Fox. 20 Oct. 2009. Twentieth Century Fox, 2010. DVD.
"Vows." *Dollhouse: Season 2.* Episode 1. Fox. 20 Oct. 2009. Joss Whedon. DVD Commentary. Twentieth Century Fox, 2010. DVD.

Seeking Safe Haven
Shelter and Self-Protection from Afterlife to Avengers: Age of Ultron

VALERIE ESTELLE FRANKEL

The Epitaph episodes of *Dollhouse* (2009–2010) focus on the search for the mythic Safe Haven in the world of apocalypse. In fact, frequently Whedon's characters retreat to such a place, seeking shelter before returning to the fight. *Firefly* (2002–2003) especially is a story of a group of misfits fleeing civilization, finding freedom on the frontier. The heroes of *Avengers: Age of Ultron* (2015), all emotionally brutalized by Scarlet Witch, allow Hawkeye (who sees clearest) to lead them to a "safe house" that symbolizes his own practical optimism. Echoing this, the comic arc "Retreat," in *Buffy the Vampire Slayer Season Eight*, sees the team running to Tibet in search of shelter, while *Angel: After the Fall* has Spike, Lorne, and Connor creating refuges for the human survivors of L.A. Finally, the unmade film *Afterlife* sees Whedon's heroes racing into the wilderness to escape the government tracking them.

Several related tropes appear across the Whedonverse: ships mean ultimate freedom—the *Serenity*, the *Agents of S.H.I.E.L.D.* "Bus," the Runaways' *Leapfrog* from Marvel Comics. Similarly, the independent film *In Your Eyes* (2014) and television run of *Buffy the Vampire Slayer* (1997–2003; hereafter *BtVS*) both end with the heroes escaping in a bus or train, leaving their restrictive community behind and heading out into the world. In another repeat trope, the heroes find themselves attacked in the backwoods and forced to defend a single cabin as stronghold—not just in the obviously-named film *The Cabin in the Woods* (2012), but also in *Afterlife* and the television episodes "The Target" (*Dollhouse*), "Homecoming" and "Spiral" (*BtVS*), and "Heart of Gold" (*Firefly*).

Evil spaces echo through the series, from the Dollhouse to Cordelia's haunted apartment in "Rm w/a Vu" (*Angel*). The Complex in *The Cabin in the Woods*, which Joss Whedon and Drew Goddard call "the Costco of death," may be the worst (*The Official Visual Companion*). In "'It Wasn't Our World Anymore. They Made it Theirs': Reading Space and Place," Karen Sayer argues, "Just as the biological family ... is unstable and insufficient, so the biological family home is represented as a site of conflict and pain, rather than nostalgia and comfort" (111). The Scoobies begin with unhappy families who make their homes into confining spaces. Kitty Pryde/Shadowcat (*X-Men*), Simon Tam (*Firefly*), and Clint Barton/Hawkeye (*Age of Ultron*), too, chafe against their ordinary family life, and also clash with their teams. Nonetheless, the heroines (and occasionally heroes) reclaim these spaces, transforming them into bastions of safety and strength. For this is a message of all the stories, that scary places may threaten, but it is up to the heroes to take them back, and in so doing, take back the night.

The Gothic Home

Many of Whedon's heroines begin confined in domestic spaces. This entrapment within the house is a staple of the Female Gothic, with which *Dollhouse* and *BtVS* specifically have been linked.[1] The gothic genre emphasizes a dark, secret world including "what is hidden or 'shady' (forbidden relationships or actions), doubled (split personalities, secret identities, or alter-egos), or 'infected' or of doubtful purity," especially corruption of small towns and families (Mukherjea). Meanwhile, the heroine's particular struggle within the Gothic landscape represents "a coded expression of women's fears of entrapment within the domestic and within the female body" (Smith and Wallace). Locked in the home, the young woman fears she will be tied down as her mother was and forced to serve the story's powerful men.

Echoing these tropes, Peter Tupper explains that "*Dollhouse* has much in common with Gothic literature: a hostile, authoritarian society, hidden secrets, virtuous people in distress, a critique of rationalism, and an emphasis on the subjective, emotional impact of power" (51). Alpha enacts a Bride-of-Frankenstein scenario on Echo, which forces Paul to be the gallant knight mistakenly attempting her rescue. After, Echo sneaks around the Dollhouse, concealing her growing abilities. Using the hidden nooks of the place, she hides books in her sleeping pod, spies on her handlers, and protects her friends. As Tupper concludes, "Echo can be seen as a descendant of a line of Gothic heroines, women who struggled to maintain personal integrity and freedom in the face of overwhelming institutional power" (52).

The home itself is the realm of the feminine in Freudian and Jungian symbolism.[2] Joyce generally appears in the house, insisting Buffy share in the domesticity with family dinners; DeWitt is the evil queen of the Dollhouse;

and Emma Frost is the matriarch of the X-Mansion during Whedon's run. Sayer writes of the Buffyverse, "'Place' is not simply a location or a territory, but it is a phenomenon that is inseparable from the consciousness of the people who occupy it" (134). As each mother defines the domestic space, they all leave a tremendous imprint. Andrew Smith and Diana Wallace contend, "Twentieth-century Female Gothic heroines are more likely to be trapped in domestic spaces than semi-ruined castles" (5). The threat here, if not the kidnapping monster, is the home itself, representing a future as housewife.

Buffy rebels against this motherly space as she sneaks out at night to go demon-hunting—she uses the window so often that she does so as a matter of course even when Joyce is away (as shown in "What's My Line Part 1"). This reaches its peak in the season two finale, when Joyce threatens that if Buffy goes out slaying, she need not come back. Thus Buffy runs away altogether. Season four has her living in the dorms with Willow, reveling in her freedom by barely visiting home, as Faith notes acerbically while sorting Buffy's untouched mail ("This Year's Girl"). In "The Summers House as Domestic Space in *Buffy the Vampire Slayer*," Lorna Jowett observes that Buffy is rebelling against her mother's perfect homemaker life:

> Joyce is of a generation for whom (middle class) women's traditional commitment to marriage, homemaking and the family made it problematic for them to have a career outside the home. Buffy, in contrast, is of a generation for whom "equality" between women and men seems to have arrived, and (were it not for her position as the Slayer) she might expect as a matter of course to go to university or college and/or to have a career of her own, regardless of relationships, marriage, or children [par. 6].

This may be why Buffy is so desperate to leave. She is a warrior, not a homemaker, and every minute indoors with Joyce emphasizes the conventional life she longs to avoid. The dream in "Restless" shows her mother trapped in the walls of UC Sunnydale, emphasizing the constriction of her life.

While *Angel* (1999–2004) has trapped room scenarios, especially for the women in "Rm w/a Vu" and "Billy," *BtVS* shows Buffy defending herself in many more last stands, emphasizing that the home can be a hostile space for her. "Ted," in season two, has her sharing her domestic space with a Bluebeard who murdered many wives, and "Passion" sees Angelus sadistically invading her room and Willow's. Buffy and her friends are imprisoned within houses several times in episodes such as "Helpless," "Fear Itself," "Where the Wild Things Are," and "Older and Far Away." The first two of these episodes cast Buffy as uncharacteristically terrified, deprived of power and forced to save herself using subtle cleverness in a commentary on women's struggle for independence.

In season five, Buffy returns home, and the place gradually becomes the Scoobies' new base through this and the following season. Dawn is born, Willow and Tara move in, and other characters visit, like Giles, who sleeps on the whimsical sheets, or Amy, restored from her rat-self. They create a nontraditional family, another parallel with the Gothic, which often offers a subversive solution for the struggling heroine. Of course, in season six, the home is still confining. Buffy describes her life as "hard and bright and violent" ("Afterlife") while a spirit speaks to her from walls and mirrors, reminding her she should be dead. This haunting is only one of many Gothic images through the season, as all the characters lead secret lives. Buffy sneaks out at night for illicit sex with Spike, while Willow does the same to indulge her magic addiction. Neither wants to spend their nights babysitting Dawn, who is busy shoplifting to get attention. All three women feel persecuted by society's rules of jobs and proper behavior as they yearn to break free. Thus the "domestic Gothic exposes the duplicities of women's roles and the surprising paradoxes of fear and love" as the women all war with their family roles (Smith and Wallace).

Darker Gothic themes also appear. The most classic heroines battle for independence while trapped in the home—Cinderella faces off with her wicked stepmother, and the young wife of Bluebeard sneakily investigates her husband's murders. Tara parallels both as her father is shown to have raised her as a domestic drudge ("Family") and her lover, Willow, turns abusive and controlling, even to the point of wiping her memory ("All the Way"). Ananya Mukherjea explains, "The darkest moments in Tara's life occur in her closest sphere—with the family in which she grew up, with Glory's invasion of her mind, and with Willow's lies and manipulations in season 6" (par. 28). Thus episodes like "Older and Far Away" trap them all in the limiting space, emphasizing how miserable they are there. When Buffy's ex-boyfriend Riley Finn reappears and his wife Sam asks, "Got a safe house?" Buffy replies, "I have a house. I think it's safe. Sometimes you can't even leave" ("As You Were").

The Perilous Cabin

Curtis A. Weyant in "Exploring Cabins in the Whedonverse Woods" explains that there are four particular "cabin scenarios" in the Whedonverse: "The Target" (*Dollhouse*), "Homecoming" and "Spiral" (*BtVS*), and "Heart of Gold" (*Firefly*). In each, the characters flee to a cabin seeking protection. However, as they are hunted, the space provides a flimsy, illusory shelter. Weyant sees with three generic elements of the cabin scenario:

> 1) a remote location (such as a woods) that cuts off the character(s) from the rest of society; 2) a man-made construction (such as a cabin) that likewise separates the characters from the wilderness; and 3) a monstrous threat, frequently human, that lives within or originates from the wilderness. Together, these three elements provide

a focusing effect that requires the primary protagonist(s) to accept a certain wildness to survive [par. 15].

Each time, the characters discover the home offers only the illusion of safety. Still, they defend it with all the unrestrained passion of the wilderness, discovering their inner strength through the battle. Their rejection of passivity shares themes with the Female Gothic, emphasizing that they will not allow men's assault on the home to destroy them.

"Homecoming" exacerbates Buffy and Cordelia's competitiveness as they vie to be Homecoming Queen. Their rivalry turns more bloodthirsty as the vampire Mr. Trick creates Slayerfest '98, and signs up villains and monsters to hunt the two girls (incorrectly believing that Cordelia is Faith). On the run in Miller's Woods, Buffy and Cordelia take refuge in an abandoned cabin, which gives them a moment—a chance to compare anxieties about their obsession with popularity. It is their isolation that finally allows them to admit their insecurities and bond. Moments later, the monster Kulak bursts in through the window, and another villain hurls in an explosive, both destroying their sanctuary. The girls flee their temporary haven, though it gave them momentary camaraderie. Outside, they harness their savagery to fight back and defend themselves, leaving the useless house far behind.

"Spiral" sees Buffy and her friends flee Sunnydale in an RV and finally find themselves trapped in a secluded, abandoned desert gas station with the Knights of Byzantium attacking, though the Scoobies have captured their General Gregor. This is a Western-style last stand, with the knights echoing raiders on the frontier—the group of defenders is necessarily small and desperate, battling an unstoppable force. This time, too, they fail to keep their temporary home safe. Though Buffy fights with a desperation born of their distance from civilization, Dawn is stolen, emphasizing the precarious nature of sanctuary in the wilderness.

Firefly's "Heart of Gold" follows this pattern, with the team resolving to defend the besieged brothel even though (unlike in the other scenarios) the *Serenity* crew has an option of escape in their ship. Nonetheless, they nobly stay with the threatened women who refuse to leave their home. Defying the patriarchy, the brothel owner Nandi declares, "I won't let any man take what's mine," insisting that she will defend herself here at the final last stand. The prostitute Petaline, too, bravely shoots her baby's father to protect what is hers. Though Nandi dies, the heroes win their conflict against the brutality of the local men and end their rule. This shelter is the women's home and by winning, they establish it as a frontier sanctuary.

Horror often features a cabin in the woods—with good reason. The terrible place "may at first seem a safe haven, but the same walls that promise to keep the killer out quickly become, once the killer penetrates them, the walls that hold the victim in" (Clover 198). The very isolation gives the villain opportunity, even as the confines force the hero to be resourceful. Los Angeles Dollhouse client Richard Connell hires Echo to be his ultimate outdoor girlfriend in "The Target." They travel into the wilderness and enjoy white-water rafting, rock climbing, bow hunting, and sex. In their tent, after, Richard tells Echo a tale of his father's philosophy that "if you can bring down something bigger than you with just this [bow], you prove you deserve to eat it. If it gets away, it proved it deserves to live." Richard suddenly informs Echo he plans to hunt and kill her. As she flees, Echo finds a cabin, this one belonging to a dead ranger, with poisoned water left as a trap for her. As Richard reveals he is the only one in range of the radio then taunts her through it ("Prove you're not just an echo"), Echo replies, "You want proof? I'm gonna kill you! Will that prove it?" Like Nandi, she resolves to take a stand against her male oppressor. In fact, the isolation of the cabin has revealed to her that she can only survive by becoming a killer. This she does at last.

The Cabin in the Woods, the ultimate cabin scenario, stresses the group's isolation as they leave their banal college town. Jules, eager for adventure, tells Dana, "We're girls on the verge of going wild," and Marty's eager to, as he puts it, "get off the grid. No cellphone reception, no markers, no traffic cameras ... go somewhere for one goddamn weekend where they can't globally position my ass." In fact, the cabin may appear safe, but it is a warren of spy cameras atop a cellar of monstrous objects, any of which will trigger savage attacks from the forest. Its protection is, like the other shelters, an illusion: "Thus, the very existence of a remote structure is a recognition of both the deep-rooted human desire to reconnect with the idealized forests of our cultural and personal fantasies and the reality that we do not fully understand the hazards that such uncultivated places contain" (Weyant par. 13). Unlike the other stories, this cabin scenario kills off half the heroes. Only when Marty and Dana see through it, realizing the safe haven is a constructed façade over a more sinister stronghold, can they penetrate the real one beneath and end the vast evil corporation's rule.

Afterlife, Whedon's unmade nineties film, is a clear precursor to *Dollhouse*. The protagonist, Daniel Hoffstetter, dies, but his mind is imprinted on the body of a "donor" by a sinister government organization. He and fellow scientists are kept prisoner in the Tank, a secret complex below Utah, so they can continue their all-important research. After Daniel escapes, he goes on the run but discovers he has been placed in the body of notorious serial killer Jamie Snow. He reunites with his wife, Laura, and they hide in their friends' summer cabin in Connecticut. However, as with *Dollhouse*, the original body's personality is seeping through. Soon Laura finds herself trapped in the cabin with two personalities, one gentle and the other violent. Nonetheless, the story takes a surprising twist and the characters find safety in the end. In a jolting juxtaposition, this cabin offers a moment of respite as well as a concentration of the conflict within. Their escape into the wilderness makes Laura a savage, defending herself with an axe, while at the same time Daniel discovers the truth of his existence, free from civilization's lies and illusions.

In *Agents of S.H.I.E.L.D.* (2013–), Skye declares her feelings for the trained killer Ward, when the other agents leave Providence Base on a mission. When she discovers Ward is a Hydra agent and has murdered their host, Eric Koenig, she is terrified and bursts into tears that she desperately muffles. Still, she manages to conceal that she has found out and leave a warning for her friends. Allaying Ward's suspicion, she uses her fear as a defense, telling him, "You scared me. Opening up, and that kiss ... which ... was a very nice kiss, I admit.... I don't exactly over-analyze. I just act impulsively, and then I freak out after the fact" ("The Only Light in the Darkness"). She smiles, takes his hand, and appears to trust him completely. Trapped with a superior fighter, she must manipulate him to save her friends as well as herself. This she manages, even summoning the FBI while pretending to decrypt the hard drive he wants. "Hail Hydra," she smirks ("Nothing Personal").

BtVS Season Eight actually begins with a cabin standoff, as a zombie army attacks the Slayers' Scottish castle. The team, from giant Dawn to magical Willow, shows off their new powers in fighting them ("The Long Way Home"). However, this is only a taste of what's to come: their enemies grow exponentially just as their powers have, with many demon forces allying to bring them down. I have suggested elsewhere that "Buffy has been alienating herself from the girl who longed to be 'normal,' who dated and shopped at the mall. More and more, she's become leader, general, and slayer—the ultimate Shadow of her innocent teen self. She will need to realize how overwhelming her General Buffy side has become and give it up" (Frankel, *Buffy* 197). In the midst of this escalation, Buffy realizes Slayers are being targeted worldwide, with their own magic growing exponentially until they are easy to track. She decides they need to vanish, to diminish. In "Retreat" (#26–30), the Slayers all climb into a submarine, which Willow transports to a place of ultimate peace and safety—Tibet. There they find Oz, who has mastered his werewolf powers through harmony with nature. He and his family teach the Slayers to let the demonic energy pass through the self into the earth—accepting it rather than fighting. Thus in the countryside they learn the strength of peace and of war. Of course, their refuge is shattered when Twilight's forces attack and the Slayers discover that they cannot avoid the conflict. Enormous Tibetan goddesses invade the battlefield, channeling the Slayers' energy into true savagery as they attack both sides. Thus, as the wilderness magnifies their strength, the Slayers begin to realize what they have become.

From Prison to Haven

Despite all of this Gothic horror, Whedon's women fight back, reclaiming their lives and their domestic space. David Magill argues, "*Buffy the Vampire Slayer* and *Angel* rewrote Gothic fiction's centerpieces of powerfully seductive vampire males and helplessly desirous human females as a way into postfeminist debates on women's identities and social roles" (86). Buffy stomps the Fear Demon, defies Tara's "blood kin," kicks Angelus where it counts. When Ted, who's been dating Buffy's mother, tells Buffy, authoritatively, "I don't stand for that kind of malarkey in my house," she takes back her territory with the words "Teddy, this house is mine" ("Ted").

In season seven the Summers' house becomes a real safe house as Giles gathers threatened Potentials from around the world to stay with Buffy. There, they form a community, boarding up the windows and defending their territory from demons. While the heroine's entrapment in the domestic space is a metaphor for her emotional imprisonment inside herself, Whedon's heroines, or occasionally male heroes, reclaim the home, repurposing it as a place of safety and sharing it with the lost.

In designing the near-magical Dollhouse, Whedon envisioned retreats and spas that make it "all natural and wonderful and peaceful and Zen," as he explains in "Designing the Perfect Dollhouse," a season one DVD featurette. It is an institution, a place of false pleasantry, where Topher and Adelle DeWitt can silently observe every move of their subjects as they lead carefully scripted lives. Sarah Benkendorf observes in "The New Eden: Deconstructing the Los Angeles Dollhouse":

> The Dollhouse is home as much as an actual dollhouse is home. Both are places where dolls are made to act out activities typically associated with homes—eating, sleeping, showering, participating in leisure activities like arts and crafts or yoga. This creates the illusion that the dolls are actually participating in and leading normal domestic lives and that the place they are doing this in is actually home. In reality, however, the dollhouse is not home; it is simply a shell to be filled with the fantasies of the person or people pulling the strings. Rossum's fantasy is to have a house full of beautiful, empty people that can be turned into anyone at any time [par. 19].

Nonetheless, the half-aware dolls wandering its environs, vulnerable to rape ("Man on the Street"), exploitation ("Belonging"), and murder ("The Target"), offer a frightening prospect of consensual imprisonment. Further, the male overlords at the Rossum Corporation can order its matriarch Adelle to turn over its inhabitants for gruesome fates.

By the episode "Epitaph One," the status quo has reversed: The Dollhouse is a truly female space, Adelle's castle, which transforms into a place of protection as she and the former dolls meet in "circle." When it is abandoned,

Echo leaves a key to Safe Haven within—Adelle, Priya, and Priya's child have built a new Eden as a farm far from technology of any kind. In "Epitaph Two," the team returns to the Dollhouse, reestablishing it as their place of power. It looks just as it once did, with lights glowing and dolls wandering about. This time, however, Alpha has made it a place to protect the "dumbshows"— humans with their personalities wiped. According to Benkendorf, "While this Dollhouse looks like the golden age Dollhouse, it is not the same. These people are not kept there to be turned into someone else's fantasy; they are kept there for their own protection" (par. 23). Alpha has repurposed the demonic structure of the apocalypse into a tiny safe community.

When the heroes return, they all band together to stop the destruction. This time, the Dollhouse is their fortress. The male heroes (Paul, Alpha, Topher) do not rip open the Dollhouse to rescue trapped princesses as they try to do in "Briar Rose." Instead, "each prince who remains sacrifices himself to protect Echo's community" (Frankel, "All Dolled Up" 75). Paul dies defending it, Alpha leaves to ensure his old self cannot hurt anyone, and Topher detonates a bomb that will restore everyone's identities. "Reflection like an echo—put things back the way they were, minds back the way they were. I can bring back the world," Topher says, paralleling the power that made Echo into a superheroine ("Epitaph Two"). Meanwhile, as Adelle leads her people out into the world, Echo becomes the Dollhouse's new queen and protector, safeguarding those within it. In the series final scene, "she [Echo] is not a simple Doll being put away—she is the ultimate Doll, reintegrated with the place that is most a part of herself, the Dollhouse" (Frankel, "All Dolled Up" 76).

Benkendorf calls the Dollhouse "The beginning of a dramatic shift in location for Whedon's works," after the homey spaces of Buffy's house or the *Serenity*. She adds, "After the fairly dark and morally ambiguous *Dollhouse*, he moves onto even more threatening places like the hellish cabin in *The Cabin in the Woods* and the Helicarrier in *The Avengers*, waiting three years before finally (and literally) returning home in *Much Ado About Nothing*" (par. 1)

In *Cabin*, Dana and Marty find the only safe place around—the actual Complex that has been killing them all. Entering this place pushes Dana and Marty to realize the greater truth of existence—that all they have experienced has been manipulated by this corporate entity. "You shouldn't be here," the Director tells them over the intercom, but they push through nonetheless. Dana does not literally become the fortress' new ruler as Echo does, but she becomes the decider, by causing the end of the world. Thus she remakes the space from a place of scientists terrorizing teens to a place where the final girl can control all of existence.

Alien: Resurrection (1997) features the characters, including the cyborg

Call and resurrected clone of Ripley, trapped in a ship and fleeing the aliens. The ship, named the *Auriga*, references a Greek male hero and his constellation, thus casting this as a patriarchal space (Frankel, *Joss Whedon's Names* 166). The scientists on board remake Ripley and the aliens, an arrogant experiment that soon destroys them. However, the women finally claim the space for their own. With Ripley's help, Call takes over the computer and replaces it with herself, the woman judged as "less than human." When a crewmate accesses the shipboard computer, known, tellingly, as the all-powerful "Father," Call replies on the system in Father's place, retorting, "Father's dead, asshole." This is the women's space now. The last survivors, including Ripley and Call, escape on the scavenger ship *Betty*, which has "a casual, friendly name. It's a variant on the powerful Elizabeth, and also related to butt-kicking Buffy. It saves them all in the end" (Frankel, *Joss Whedon's Names* 166). Thus the heroes abandon the masculine space for the feminine one, making it their new haven.

Likewise, in *Firefly*'s "Objects in Space," *Serenity* is invaded by Jubal Early, a bounty hunter who slides through the place, locking doors and tying up crewmembers one by one. River is dealing with her own crisis as her friends turn against her and consider putting her off the ship. However, with her friends incapacitated, she takes a stand and makes the ship her own. As she proclaims over the intercom: "You're wrong about River. River's not on the ship. They didn't want her here, but she couldn't make herself leave. So she melted.... Melted away. They didn't know she could do that, but she did... . I'm not *on* the ship. I'm in the ship. I am the ship." In a similar scene in the comic book sequel *Serenity: Leaves on the Wind*, Early returns and Kaylee clobbers him with a wrench, using the ship's tools to reclaim her personal power.

In her own new apartment, Cordelia decides she does not fear Ghost-Dennis, who tries to scare her out. She proclaims, "I'm not a sniveling whiny little Cry-Buffy. I'm the nastiest girl in Sunnydale history.... The bitch is back!" ("Rm w/a Vu"). Soon enough, she and Dennis have enacted a compromise and live happily together, with Dennis turning from a monster to a friend who offers tissues and loofah scrubs.

Caritas, as well, becomes a loving haven. Its first introductions are embarrassing—the mysterious Lorne forces stoic Angel to open up and sing karaoke whenever he needs help. This is a fair analogy for counseling, but also one for returning to one's parents—there's unconditional help here, but also over-sharing and awkwardness. As is revealed later, Lorne's own dimension is a place of pain where his parents rejected him and humans are brutalized. Thus he creates the one place he can glory in his demonic face without a trench coat and hat. He is not a woman, but he is Other as a green demon from another realm, and he too recreates himself to escape the traditional gender role he was born into (in this case, entertaining rather than fighting). Moreover, like Buffy's house, Caritas protects others. When Angel and his friends aren't safe at home, they hurry there for its protective spells.

Wolfram & Hart is the enemy's evil stronghold, and as the team takes it over in season five, it corrupts them from within. The sequel comics, however, gather the scattered heroes determined to help the hopeless. In *Angel: After the Fall*, Angel lingers at a low point, with his team reduced to only Wesley the ghost. For months he has lain in the ruins of Wolfram & Hart, trapped by his injuries. The place is a prison. At the same time, his friends are constructing true havens. In particular, Lorne's region, Silver Lake, has a protection bubble and a harpy whose soothing song keeps everyone centered. It is the only place that still resembles sunlit suburbs.

The comic opens with Angel saving a looter and telling her, "Take the car and go to this address. Don't go home to take your things, don't pick up your friends. Just go" (*After the Fall* 1). Angel has sent her, as he does everyone else, to Nina, Gwen, and Connor. When she arrives, Connor tells her, "Don't be scared.... This is my family" (*After the Fall* 1). Spike too has constructed a sanctuary, though he frames himself as its demon boss complete with scantily-dressed women catering to his whims. At this time of apocalypse, Angel's friends are all forming strongholds and reaching beyond their differences to keep civilians safe.

Like Buffy, Clint Barton/Hawkeye goes out adventuring in *Avengers: Age of Ultron*, leaving his family house for the far more exciting life of a superhero. His constant remodeling at home may also emphasize his dissatisfaction with the status quo. After the Avengers are traumatized by Wanda Maximoff/Scarlet Witch, it is he, the least superpowered character, who rallies them. He directs them to "a safe house" and introduces them to his family there. This time of shelter gives the characters time to reassess—Natasha Romanov/Black Widow and Bruce Banner/Hulk consider their relationship, Tony Stark/Iron Man confronts Steve Rogers/Captain America about his visions, and finally Nick Fury confronts Stark about creating Ultron. Fury reminds them that while they are back to basics, they can still fight: "Back in the day, I had eyes everywhere, ears everywhere else. Here we all are, back on Earth, with nothing but our wit, and our will to save the world. So stand. Outwit the platinum bastard" (*Age of Ultron*). After, the team make a plan to defeat Ultron and return to combat.

Kitty Pryde/Shadowcat's home, the X-Mansion, is a bastion of nostalgia. When she returns to this place of her childhood in Whedon's *Astonishing X-Men* run, she feels a clash as the familiar halls spark memories of her teenage self arguing with teachers and growing up. In the newly rebuilt hallway, she reflects how, as she puts it, "nothing has changed." As she notes, "I'm a kid again, out of my depth—completely overwhelmed by everything here, and it isn't the Sidri, or the Sentinels, or the Brood that surround me.../It's the smaller pieces./Shards/Of me" ("Gifted"). As she tangles with the school's current matriarch, Emma Frost, she feels like a child again and worries that she cannot succeed as a teacher. Soon enough, the school is invaded and Kitty is trapped in the worst way—faced with her fears of disappearing altogether, she transforms into a ghost. Sinking through the earth into total darkness, Kitty has time to reflect. She thinks, "Being an X-Man means a lot to me ... but it doesn't always agree with me." Trudging through the water-filled caverns underground, Kitty decides, "Now it's my turn" ("Torn"). Shadows wreath her, around her arms and forehead like commando gear. Toughened, she returns to the fight, taking down the possessed Emma Frost who caused her breakdown and saving the school.

After, the X-Men travel to a terrifying alien planet called Breakworld, which has pointed a missile at Earth. As Kitty/Shadowcat and Peter Rasputin/Colossus explore, they find a momentary lull. The compassionate Aghanne offers a night's safety, a moment to hear the silence and discover a third path for themselves other than to kill or be killed. Kitty tells Peter, while seeking a night of passion, "Everything is so fragile. There's so much conflict, so much pain ... you keep waiting for the dust to settle and then you realize this is it; the dust is your life going on. If happy comes along—that weird, unbearable delight that's actual happy—I think you have to grab it while you can" ("Unstoppable"). They spend the night together, echoing the momentary peace of *BtVS*' "Touched" before Buffy's final battle.

When Kitty investigates the missile the next day, she discovers it is a tremendous bullet of alien metal that bonds with her cells. As Breakworld fires the bullet at Earth, Kitty is trapped onboard. Back on Earth, all the superheroes have been neutralized into a magical stupor. Instead of freeing herself, Kitty accepts her fate and melds deeper with the metal. Channeling her will, subtle, nonthreatening Kitty phases the entire bullet, carrying it harmlessly through the earth. Thus the smallest X-Man with the quietest power saves everyone. She ends the story still fused with the bullet as it careens into space. It has become a single cell for her, a place of such protection she cannot leave. She too has turned threats to safety, in an unexpected way.

Buffy the Vampire Slayer ends with all of Sunnydale falling away, yet the new Slayers burst out of Sunnydale after ending its threat forever. They carry their philosophy and vows of interprotection to the larger world. As the season eight comics show, most of these new Slayers, trained by Buffy, Faith, and Giles, become leaders of new Slayer strongholds across the globe. In Gothic tradition, the Slayers "defamiliarise the familiar roles and expectations of women's lives." They expose "the dangers of complacency and the losses that come with the acceptance of a limited (patriarchal) world view" to create a better world that empowers all women (Smith and Wallace). Further, driving away from the sucking pit of Sunnydale towards new horizons emphasizes their freedom of choice in a limitless world.

The Shipboard Haven

In "Out of Gas," Mal announces his plans for his new ship, saying, "Small crew, them as feel the need to be free. Take jobs as they come—and we'll never be under the heel of nobody ever again. No matter how long the arm of the Alliance might get, we'll just get ourselves a little further." As Thomas Flamson observes,

> *Firefly*, centering around the efforts of a group of distinct individuals all looking to escape the omnipresent arm of the galactic state known as the Alliance, helmed by two veterans of the losing side in the war to avoid governance by that Alliance, really could not be more about freedom if Whedon had flashed the words "Freedom is Neato!" on the screen every tenth frame [46].

It is a place of safety as crew members learn that Mal won't abandon them no matter what, and also a place of self-determination, where each crewmember can live as he or she pleases without the Alliance stopping them. This is only possible on the frontier.

Vital to *Firefly* are the communal dinners, from the one where Jayne mouths off and is ordered to leave the table to Simon's birthday celebration. Certainly similar to *BtVS* and *Angel*, this is another chosen family story, but in a single setting. Loni Peristere, a visual effects supervisor on *Firefly* and *Serenity*, describes the ship as "a place of quiet, a center where one can focus, where one might find peace or love" (120). It is haven and the open road as one.

Simon Tam, with his stiff suits and shiny shoes, never quite fits in. In "Safe," he tells Kaylee, to her disappointment, "Fun. Right, yeah. I, uh, I consider this fun. It's fun, being forced to the ass-end of the galaxy. To get to live on a piece of *luh-suh* wreck. And to eat molded protein. And to be bullied around by our *boo-tai jung tzhang duh* of a captain. It's *fun*." *Serenity* (2005) begins with Simon's decision to leave as he clashes with the family patriarch Mal. As already happened when Simon left his own parents, he is determined to protect his sister River and will sacrifice all of their family bonds to ensure this. Simon departs at Beaumonde, but River's power activates and the siblings are discovered. Mal carries River aboard and locks her up to protect her. Thus, the *Serenity*, Simon and River's home, has truly become a prison. Of course, this means confinement among the only people who love them. As the Operative seeks River, the *Serenity* is the siblings' only safety, though they are chased through the galaxy:

While providing River with an escape from the forces that try to exploit her and retool her to meet their needs, *Serenity* has also provided River with solace and kinship. Though both will never be completely fixed and will always be subjected to some level of disconnect from the rest of the crew, the crew still chooses to place their trust in both, therefore negating the need for that absolute reparation to take place. No matter how many times *Serenity* breaks down, she still remains their home [Wear par. 10].

The crew sets a course for the aptly named planet Haven. Mal explains, "We got to lay low. And I could fair use some spiritual guidance right about now." Shepherd Book welcomes them and reminds Mal about the value of faith. However, when they return, seeking a hiding place, they discover everyone's been slaughtered, the buildings burned. The Alliance and its Operative have destroyed the galaxy's last remaining haven. They are a force of ultimate evil, not only massacring innocents, but destroying all hope of safety. Mal explodes in fury, demanding they all desecrate their beautiful ship (and thus symbolically their own serenity) in order to fly into Reaver territory to dig up the Alliance's great secret. Sometimes tearing the illusion of peace apart is the only way to build a better, lasting foundation.

Meanwhile, during their final battle in the film, Simon realizes that he is always had a place of safety and comfort: "I never planned ... anything. I just wanted to keep River safe. Spent so much time on *Serenity* trying to find us a home I never realized I already had," he tells Kaylee (*Serenity*). The team win the day through their bravery, but mostly through family love. When Simon is shot, River simply utters, "You take care of me, Simon. You've always taken care of me. My turn." With that she sends in his med kit and destroys all the Reavers.

At the film's end, the team comes together and repairs their ship, cleaning, repainting, and rebeautifying. They can only continue their adventures when *Serenity* has been healed too. Zoe tells Mal, of the ship and of herself, "She's tore up plenty. But she'll fly true." Mal's final speech emphasizes the family bond that sustains their home. Mal states, "Love. You take a boat in the air you don't love, she'll shake you off just as sure as the turning of worlds. Love keeps her in the air when she oughta fall down, tells you she's hurting 'fore she keens. Makes her a home" (*Serenity*). They continue traveling as a family, one that can escape the Alliance's strictures.

Whedon offers additional stories about escaping evil domesticity to make a home onboard an ever-traveling ship. Regarding Whedon's run as a *Runaways* writer, Don Tresca says,

> At its roots, the *Runaways* storyline is a variation of the 19th-century coming-of-age texts about children or young teens who embark on a journey of self-discovery, leaving behind their family and their childhood to venture into the unknown outside world, bravely facing the adult world of responsibility. Unlike monomyth

protagonists, these child-heroes embark on a hero-journey of their own making, rather than a mythic quest that is foisted upon them [135].

Still, the first thing the young Marvel team does is build a new community that is centered around Chase's van before they graduate to the small ship his parents built, the *Leapfrog*. This ship echoes the *Serenity*'s freedom of movement, and like in *Firefly*, the team soon pick up an abused young superheroine and invite her to join them on their adventures. Whedon gives the *Leapfrog* the power to time travel back to 1907. There the team (teens Nico, Chase, Victor, Molly, Karolina and Xavin) meet Klara Prast, who is even more in need of a rescue than they once were. While she is only about twelve, she is married to an abusive man who beats her and spends her money on liquor. He has all of the power due to his adult status and physical strength (Cocca 5). Initially disgusted by Karolina and Xavin's lesbian kiss, Klara comes to realize that she can accept their way of life, so different from the religious strictures she has been taught, and leave her husband and timeline forever. Tresca notes:

> From Klara's limited perspective, the relationship between herself and her husband is a normal part of life. However, Klara's reaction to the lesbian kiss between Karolina and Xavin in which she describes the kiss as "a sin," something "disgusting" and "unnatural," while simultaneously claiming that she has been "ungrateful. I have a duty to my husband" proves that what is considered "perverted" love is very much a product of an individual's perspective, culture, and time [138].

She leaves her confining home along with her past. Aboard the *Leapfrog*, she journeys to a dazzling future and discovers trusted friends who will always protect her.

In Your Eyes offers a similar escape to Klara's, as the heroine Becky leaves her restrictive marriage and finds freedom. Thus the story emphasizes how modern relationships can be more subtly abusive. Becky says, "Philip takes care of me ... he's not being mean. He knows how funky I can get," explaining why her husband Phil has thrown out all her family photos. As she adds, "He's getting rid of the past ... chipping away at it ... all my little quirks and insecurities." He smothers her piece by piece, insisting she interest herself in domestic concerns while destroying her home around her. As he restricts her more, she transfers her affection from him to the voice she hears in her head—gentle and sensitive Dylan. Like movie-Buffy, Becky is poised on the edge of emotional growth, symbolized by her sudden new gifts, and she longs to escape her life. Elsewhere I argue,

> She has a restlessness equivalent to young River's or young Fred's—she's questing for something to complete her beyond her restrictive existence. Of course, both young women are led astray by the patriarchy as Fred's mentor strands her in Pylea or River's experiments on her. Both are rescued—by supportive Angel and gentle Simon,

who protect them in big brother fashion while encouraging them to grow in a safe chosen family of men and women. For both heroines, this is the only path from a barren reality in patriarch's world [Frankel, "The Mad Girl" 142].

As Rebecca cultivates a mental relationship with Dylan, she desperately keeps all her new independence a secret. Cautiously, she makes excuses for her distraction to Phil and to her friends, who inform on her to her husband. This becomes a Bluebeard relationship, as her husband plans a dire fate for her and she must discover how to keep herself safe. Their relationship has a power imbalance, and her struggle for freedom carries the terror and emotional pain of the Gothic genre. When Phil suspects that Rebecca is having an affair, he suddenly locks her in a mental hospital and drugs her, keeping her thoroughly under control at last. Dylan counsels her from afar on how to break out and escape. At last, she frees herself from the hospital, taking back power from her husband in a well-placed punch and ending his familial control over her forever. With Dylan, "the pair of fugitives find each other in the concealing woods, a fairytale wilderness like Buffy's desert where they can be themselves without the dictates of society. They hop a train for Canada and end their tale romantically running off together" (Frankel, "The Mad Girl" 146).

Finally, Skye in *Agents of S.H.I.E.L.D.* considers the team's plane her home, so much a safe place that she sets her locked hard drive to decrypt there in season one. On board, they all let their guard down and indulge their lighter sides—Coulson fills his office with collectables, Skye and Ward compete at Battleship, May plays practical jokes, Fitz flies his tiny robots around his bunk, and Simmons sends him off with sandwiches as the team mom. The "Bus," their plane, is an image of freedom, a safe place that can carry them throughout the world. Similar are the Helicarrier in *Avengers*, and the team's small quinjet in *Avengers: Age of Ultron* (with a "Jarvis is my Co-pilot" bumper sticker that may nod to fandom's "Wash is my Co-pilot" stickers), *Alien: Resurrection*'s Betty, Buffy's motorhome, Buffy's school bus in "Chosen," and Buffy's season eight submarine, which all carry the team to safety, protecting them along the way.

Conclusion

Certainly, Whedon has many heroes who disdain the haven to always charge into the fight. In the *Angel and Faith* comics, Faith inherits a home from Giles but quickly moves on, venturing instead into the heart of South America instead to rescue Riley. Buffy sends Dawn and Xander away, but they return for the show's final battle, as Connor does on *Angel*. The Runaways, in Whedon's collection, find their counterparts in the past, but disgustedly leave their stronghold on discovering the difficulties of history. Like many of Whedon's characters, and like *Serenity* itself, they will keep traveling, relying on the group to be their safe haven, rather than a secure base far from the world. By reclaiming and repurposing the ship or evil stronghold, they build a sanctuary, protecting themselves as well as those most vulnerable.

Notes

1. These include, among others, Michelle Callander's "Bram Stoker's Buffy: Traditional Gothic and Contemporary Culture," Anna Free's "Re-Vamping the Gothic in *Buffy the Vampire Slayer*," Leigh Harbin's "'You Know You Wanna Dance': *Buffy the Vampire Slayer* as Contemporary Gothic Heroine," Erin Hollis' "Revisiting the Gothic: *Buffy the Vampire Slayer* and *Angel* as Contemporary Gothic," and Katie Saulnier's "From Virtuous Virgins to Vampire Slayers: The Evolution of the Gothic Heroine from the Early Gothic to Modern Horror."

2. Admittedly, both theorists were quite sexist, but they were correct that this image is ingrained in thousands of years of our literature and folklore. Whedon's work often subverts this image, as this essay will explore.

Works Cited

"Afterlife." *Buffy the Vampire Slayer: The Complete Sixth Season*. Episode 3. Writ. Jane Espenson. Dir. David Solomon. UPN. 9 Oct. 2001. Twentieth Century Fox, 2004. DVD.
"Afterlife." *Write to Reel*, 15 Nov. 2013. http://writetoreel.com. Script. Web. 30 April 2016.
Alien: Resurrection. 1997. Writ. Joss Whedon. Dir. Jean-Pierre Jeunet. 20th Century Fox, 2007. DVD.
"All the Way." *Buffy the Vampire Slayer: The Complete Sixth Season*. Episode 5. Writ. Steven S. DeKnight. Dir. David Solomon. UPN. 30 Oct. 2001. Twentieth Century Fox, 2004. DVD.
"As You Were." *Buffy the Vampire Slayer: The Complete Sixth Season*. Episode 15. Writ. and Dir. Douglas Petrie. UPN. 26 Feb. 2002. Twentieth Century Fox, 2004. DVD.
The Avengers. Writ and Dir. Joss Whedon. Marvel Studios, 2012. DVD.
Avengers: Age of Ultron. Writ. and Dir. Joss Whedon. Marvel Studios, 2015. DVD.
"Belonging." *Dollhouse: Season Two*. Episode 4. Writ. Maurissa Tancharoen and Jed Whedon. Dir. Jonathan Frakes. Fox. 23 Oct. 2009. Twentieth Century Fox, 2010. DVD.
Benkendorf, Sarah. "The New Eden: Deconstructing the Los Angeles Dollhouse." *Watcher Junior* 7. 2 (Fall 2014): n. pag. Web. 30 April 2016.
"Billy." *Angel: The Complete Third Season*. Episode 6. Writ. Tim Minear and Jeffrey Bell. Dir. David Grossman. The WB. 29 Oct. 2001. Twentieth Century Fox, 2003. DVD.
The Cabin in the Woods. Writ. Joss Whedon, Drew Goddard. Dir. Drew Goddard. Lionsgate, 2012. DVD.
Callander, Michelle. "Bram Stoker's Buffy: Traditional Gothic and Contemporary Culture." *Slayage: The Online Journal of Whedon Studies* 1.3 (June 2001). Web. 30 April 2016.
Clover, Carol J. "Her Body, Himself: Gender in the Slasher Film." *Representations* 20, Special Issue (Autumn 1987): 187–228. Print.
Cocca, Carolyn. "First World 'Jail,' Second Word 'Bait': Adolescent Sexuality, Feminist Theories, and *Buffy the Vampire Slayer*." *Slayage: The Online Journal of Whedon Studies* 3.2 (Nov. 2003): n. pag. Web. 30 April 2016.
"Epitaph One." *Dollhouse: Season One*. Episode 13. Writ. Maurissa Tancharoen and Jed Whedon. Dir. David Solomon. Fox. Unaired. Twentieth Century Fox, 2009. DVD.
"Epitaph Two." *Dollhouse: Season Two*. Episode 13. Writ. Maurissa Tancharoen, Jed Whedon and Andrew Chambliss. Dir. David Solomon. Fox. 29 Jan. 2010. Twentieth Century Fox, 2010. DVD.
"Family." *Buffy the Vampire Slayer: The Complete Fifth Season*. Episode 6. Writ. and Dir. Joss Whedon. The WB. 7 Nov. 2000. Twentieth Century Fox, 2006. DVD.
Flamson, Thomas. "Free Will in a Deterministic Whedonverse." *The Psychology of Joss Whe-*

don: An Unauthorized Exploration of Buffy, Angel, and Firefly. Ed. Joy Davidson and Leah Wilson. Dallas: BenBella Books, 2007. 35–50. Print.
Frankel, Valerie Estelle. "All Dolled Up: Twisted Princes and Fairytale Heroines." *Inside Joss' Dollhouse: From Alpha to Rossum.* Ed. Jane Espenson. Dallas: BenBella Books, 2010. 63–77. Print.
_____. *Buffy and the Heroine's Journey.* Jefferson, NC: McFarland, 2012. Print.
_____. *Joss Whedon's Names.* LitCrit Press, 2014. Print.
_____. "The Mad Girl Weds the Evil Doctor: Whedonisms in *In Your Eyes.*" *After the Avengers: From Joss Whedon's Hottest, Newest Franchises to the Future of the Whedonverse.* Ed. Valerie Estelle Frankel. Chicago: PopMatters, 2015. 141–146. e-book.
Free, Anna. "Re-Vamping the Gothic in *Buffy the Vampire Slayer.*" *Screen Education* 46 (2007): 138–144. Print.
Harbin, Leigh. "'You Know You Wanna Dance': *Buffy the Vampire Slayer* as Contemporary Gothic Heroine." *Studies in the Humanities* 32.1 (June 2005): 22–37. Print.
"Heart of Gold." *Firefly: The Complete Series.* Episode 13. Writ. Brett Matthews. Dir. Thomas J. Wright. Fox. 4 Aug. 2003. Twentieth Century Fox, 2003. DVD.
Hollis, Erin. "Revisiting the Gothic: *Buffy the Vampire Slayer* and *Angel* as Contemporary Gothic." *Critical Insights: Good & Evil.* Ed. Margaret Sönser Breen. Ipswich, MA: Salem Press, 2012. 238–252. Print.
"Homecoming." *Buffy the Vampire Slayer: The Complete Third Season.* Episode 5. Writ. and Dir. David Greenwalt. The WB. 3 Nov. 1998. Twentieth Century Fox, 2006. DVD.
In Your Eyes. Dir. Brin Hill. Writ. Joss Whedon. Bellwether Pictures, 2014. Web. 30 Apr 2016. Vimeo.
Jowett, Lorna." The Summers House as Domestic Space in *Buffy the Vampire Slayer.*" *Slayage: The Online Journal of Whedon Studies* 5.2 (2005): n. pag. Web. 30 April 2016.
Magill, David. "'I Aim to Misbehave': Masculinities in the Verse." *Investigating Firefly and Serenity: Science Fiction on the Frontier.* Ed. Rhonda V. Wilcox and Tanya R. Cochran. London: I.B. Tauris, 2008. 76–88. Print.
"Man on the Street." *Dollhouse: Season One.* Episode 6. Writ. Joss Whedon. Dir. David Straiton. Fox. 20 March 2009. Twentieth Century Fox, 2009. DVD.
Mukherjea, Ananya." When You Kiss Me, I Want to Die: Gothic Relationships and Identity on *Buffy the Vampire Slayer.*" *Slayage: The Online Journal of Whedon Studies* 7.2 (Spring 2008): n. pag. 30 April 2016.
"Nothing Personal." *Agents of S.H.I.E.L.D.: Season One.* Episode 20. Writ. Paul Zbyszewski and DJ Doyle. Dir. Billy Gierhart. ABC. 29 April 2014. ABC Studios, 2014. DVD.
"Objects in Space." *Firefly: The Complete Series.* Episode 14. Writ. and Dir. Joss Whedon. Fox. 13 Dec. 2002. Twentieth Century Fox, 2003. DVD.
"Older and Far Away." *Buffy the Vampire Slayer: The Complete Sixth Season.* Episode 14. Writ. Drew Z. Greenberg. Dir. Michael Gershman. UPN. 12 Feb. 2002. Twentieth Century Fox, 2004. DVD.
"The Only Light in the Darkness." *Agents of S.H.I.E.L.D.: Season One.* Episode 19. Writ. Monica Owusu-Breen. Dir. Vincent Misiano. ABC. 22 April 2014. ABC Studios, 2014. DVD.
"Out of Gas." *Firefly: The Complete Series.* Episode 8. Writ. Tim Minear. Dir. David Solomon. Fox. 25 Oct. 2002. Twentieth Century Fox, 2003. DVD.
Owens, Andy (w), and Michelle Madsen (p). "Retreat." *Buffy the Vampire Slayer Season Eight Vol. 6.* #26–30 (July–Nov. 2009), Milwaukie, OR: Dark Horse, 2010. Print.
"Passion." *Buffy the Vampire Slayer: The Complete Second Season.* Episode 17. Writ. Ty King. Dir. Michael Gershman. The WB. 24 Feb. 1998. Twentieth Century Fox, 2002. DVD.
Peristere, Loni. "Mutant Enemy U." *Serenity Found: More Unauthorized Essays on Joss Whedon's Firefly Universe.* Ed. Jane Espenson. Dallas: BenBella, 2007. 37–48. Print.
"Restless." *Buffy the Vampire Slayer: The Complete Fourth Season.* Episode 22. Writ. and Dir. Joss Whedon. The WB. 23 May 2000. Twentieth Century Fox, 2003. DVD.
"Rm w/a Vu." *Angel: The Complete First Season.* Episode 5. Writ. Jane Espenson. Dir. Scott McGinnis. The WB. 2 Nov. 1999. Twentieth Century Fox, 2003. DVD.
"Safe." *Firefly: The Complete Series.* Episode 5. Writ. Drew Z. Greenberg. Dir. Michael Grossman. Fox. 8 Nov. 2002. Twentieth Century Fox, 2003. DVD.

Saulnier, Katie. "From Virtuous Virgins to Vampire Slayers: The Evolution of the Gothic Heroine from the Early Gothic to Modern Horror." *Watcher Junior: The Journal of Undergraduate Research in Buffy Studies* 4.1 (Nov. 2009): n. pag. Web. 30 April 2016.

Sayer, Karen. "'It Wasn't Our World Anymore. They Made it Theirs': Reading Space and Place." *Reading the Vampire Slayer*. Ed. Roz Kaveney. London: I.B. Tauris, 2001. 98–119. Print.

Serenity (Widescreen Edition). Writ. Joss Whedon. Dir. Joss Whedon. Universal, 2005. DVD.

Smith, Andrew, and Diana Wallace." The Female Gothic Then and Now." *Gothic Studies* 6.1 (2004): 1–7. Web. 30 April 2016.

"Spiral." *Buffy the Vampire Slayer: The Complete Fifth Season*. Episode 20. Writ. Steven S. DeKnight. Dir. James A. Contner. The WB. 8 May 2001. Twentieth Century Fox, 2006. DVD.

"The Target." *Dollhouse: Season One*. Episode 2. Writ. and Dir. Steven S. DeKnight. Fox. 20 Feb. 2009. Twentieth Century Fox, 2009. DVD.

"Ted." *Buffy the Vampire Slayer: The Complete Second Season*. Episode 11. Writ. David Greenwalt and Joss Whedon. Dir. Bruce Seth Green. The WB. 8 Dec. 1997. Twentieth Century Fox, 2002. DVD.

"This Year's Girl." *Buffy the Vampire Slayer: The Complete Fourth Season*. Episode 1. Writ. Douglas Petrie. Dir. Michael Gershman. The WB. 22 Feb. 2000. Twentieth Century Fox, 2003. DVD.

Tresca, Don. "Dancing in the Sky: The Value of Love in *Runaways*." *The Comics of Joss Whedon: Critical Essays*. Ed. Valerie Estelle Frankel. Jefferson, NC: McFarland, 2015. 133–145. Print.

Tupper, Peter." Joss Whedon's *Dollhouse*: 21st Century Neo-Gothic." *Inside Joss' Dollhouse: From Alpha to Rossum*. Ed. Jane Espenson. Dallas: BenBella Books, 2010. 47–60. Print.

Wear, Jordyn. "Conversation, Reflection, and Shared Alienation: Forming Relationships with the Spaceship *Serenity* in Joss Whedon's *Firefly*." *Watcher Junior* 8.1 (Spring 2015): n. pag. Web. 30 April 2016.

Weyant, Curtis A. "Exploring Cabins in the Whedonverse Woods." *Slayage: The Online Journal of Whedon Studies* 11.2 (Summer 2014): n. pag. Web. 30 April 2016.

"What's My Line, Part 1." *Buffy the Vampire Slayer: The Complete Second Season*. Episode 9. Writ. Howard Gordon and Marti Noxon. Dir. David Solomon. The WB. 17 Nov. 1997. Twentieth Century Fox, 2002. DVD.

Whedon, Joss (w) and John Cassaday (p). "Gifted." *Astonishing X-Men, Vol. 1* #1–6 (May–Nov. 2004). New York: Marvel, 2006. Print.

Whedon, Joss (w), and John Cassaday (p). "Torn." *Astonishing X-Men, Vol. 3* #13–18 (Feb-Nov. 2006). New York: Marvel, 2007. Print.

Whedon, Joss (w), and John Cassaday (p). "Unstoppable." *Astonishing X-Men, Vol. 4* #19–22 (Dec. 2006–Aug. 2007). New York: Marvel, 2008. Print.

Whedon, Joss, and Drew Goddard. *The Cabin in the Woods: The Official Visual Companion*. London: Titan Books, 2011. Print.

Whedon, Joss (w), and Georges Jeanty (p). "The Long Way Home." *Buffy the Vampire Slayer Season Eight, Vol. 1* #1–5 (Mar.–July 2007). Milwaukie, OR: Dark Horse, 2007. Print.

Whedon, Joss, Brian Lynch (w), and Franco Urru (p). *Angel: After the Fall, Vol. 1* #1–5 (Nov. 2007–Mar. 2008). Ed. Justin Eisinger. San Diego: IDW Publishing, 2008. Print.

Whedon, Joss (w), and Michael Ryan (p). *Runaways, Vol. 8: Dead End Kids* #25–28 (April–Oct. 2007). New York: Marvel Entertainment, 2009. Print.

Whedon, Zack (w), and Georges Jeanty (p). *Serenity: Leaves on the Wind* #1–6 (Jan-June 2014). Milwaukie, OR: Dark Horse Books, 2014. Print.

Domestic Space and Identity
Joss Whedon's Futuristic Frontier in Firefly

MELANIE A. MAROTTA

In *Firefly* (2002–2003), Joss Whedon's Western television series, the frontier community has been recreated in order to demonstrate that while patriarchal constructs still exist in this universe, conventional society is experiencing a metamorphosis, which is reflected by the appearance of the frontier. Emphasized in the title sequence to the series and the series itself is humanity's desertion of Earth and its colonization of a new system. Reminiscent of the European and Midwestern migration to the West is the human flight from Earth in *Firefly* towards a new utopic space. The Alliance are members of the human population who wish to remain in the traditional gendered space so they moved to the Central Planets, a space symbolic of the closed frontier. Those that choose to not conform to the Alliance's standard hierarchal design migrated to the open frontier. Some, like Captain Malcolm (Mal) Reynold's crew, elect to reside on a ship—a floating utopic space—and, when the need for goods and services dictate, briefly land on a planet. When this movement to the planets happens, the crew is often faced with adversity. They are, once again, exposed to traditional gender constructs that both demand conformity and spurn rebellious acts from the crew. Often these planetary visits conclude with a daring escape from a stereotypical Western shootout and then a communal get-together on board *Serenity*. Significantly, throughout the short-lived series, the majority of the scenes occur on the ship *Serenity*, and feature the characters in spaces traditionally thought of as public (the galley) or private (the living quarters).

Homi Bhabha's theory of "unhomely" emphasizes the relationship between liminality and space. According to Bhabha, spaces are not separate and can become both public and private, thereby blurring that which distinguishes each. For example, the *Serenity*'s living quarters are featured as private spaces reflecting the identity of the resident, but are frequently entered by other members of the crew. Bhabha observes that since spaces become liminal, there is a "redrawing [of] the domestic space" (15). As a result, if a space houses both the private and the public, thereby altering one's perception of the spaces, then gender constructs, that which is traditional, must also be blurred. Here, domestic space and a character's actions in traditionally public spaces reflect his or her liminal gender identity. Sometimes the characters are confident in their non-gendered roles, but in the case of Wash in "War Stories," the non-conformity causes confusion and even frustration for the characters because they are at a loss as to where they fit in within the confines of this new society. This essay illustrates that by Mal, Zoe, and Kaylee existing in this liminal space, they are able to rebel against conformity for their gender, thereby creating their own liminal identities and subsequently forming a functional community.

By beginning the series with the Unification War, writer and director Whedon places immediate emphasis on the role of the soldier in this new, yet familiar, frontier.[1] In a war reminiscent of the U.S. Civil War, Mal and the other soldier character, Zoe Washburn, are shown as heroic, unsuccessful underdogs, subsequently defeated by the more powerful Alliance. Whedon, in the film pre-production memo, observes that Mal "joined [the Independents] out of belief and nothing more" and that Zoe is "career army" ("Brief History"). Whereas in the Civil War the South, the Rebels, exist as the unsuccessful and underpowered side, they are also the oppressors heralding conformity to their way of life which included the enslavement of others. The North, however, the Unionists, proclaimed freedom and a unified community. Whedon is known for placing a twist on the conventional to make it modern and, in some cases, anticipate the future. In *Firefly*, those that desire a separate society, the Independents (the Browncoats), are also those that vie for a diverse and inclusive community. Whedon starts the televised series with the Unification War. By doing so, Whedon has the viewer first witness a past event rather than one from the present, thereby showing the impact of the past on current societal guidelines. The repetition of the past aids in perpetuating the American West myth and the gender constructs contained within. According to Susan Armitage, with regard to the American frontier myth specific roles for men are stressed: "mountain men, cowboys, Indians, soldiers, farmers, miners, and desperados" (9). Here, Armitage highlights the male hero, a figure that appears prominently in Whedon's series. In his series, Whedon revises what Armitage refers to as a Western "Hisland," a concept that she creates based on Charlotte Perkins Gilman's female-centric utopic story, "Herland" (9). While Whedon does offer some male-dominated television programs, often many of his series feature strong female leads. Through these characters, Whedon repeatedly presents his audience with his vision of societies that show males and females in comparable positions. Notably, when Whedon includes these non-gendered positions in dystopic spaces, this way of life is most often threatened by societal guidelines regarding traditional gender roles.

While the televised series does not begin with the depiction of the *Serenity*'s domestic space, it does start with the battle, which is symbolic as it occurs in a public yet liminal space.[2] When the opening scene of "Serenity" commences with the Browncoats being decimated in the Battle of Serenity Valley, Mal takes a leadership role, authoritatively commanding what remains of his troops to defend their posts. With reference to his own work, Joe Haldeman writes, "When *my* stories are about war, they don't celebrate it, but rather try to demonstrate its futility and insanity" (36). Whedon captures these views of war in his series as he portrays the plight of the Browncoats. Mal and Zoe's unit is slaughtered as the viewers helplessly watch, but behind the "insanity" lies the reality of the situation (Haldeman 36). In both domestic and public spaces, the safety of one's beliefs is not assured if they defer from the norm. In the film's pre-production memo, Whedon documents the reasons for the Unification War, namely assimilation and supremacy over those who refuse the Alliance's doctrine (Whedon). The war clarifies that the rebels hold non-gender specific roles in this Western-style dystopian society; these positions carry-over to the *Serenity*'s domestic space.

Clad in a dated brown trench coat and military trousers, but with a technologically-advanced laser rifle, in "Serenity" Mal attempts to inspire his regiment to defeat the Alliance, even if this means certain death. Here, the appearance of the laser weaponry intertwined with a uniform similar to that of the Civil War reminds the viewer that while this may be the future, the past is still in conflict with traditional gendered lifestyles considered to be the norm.[3] Mal truly believes that the Independents are going to send in air support, so he encourages his team to continue the battle, an act which shows Haldeman's depiction of the "futility" of battle (36). There is no safety in this space: the Alliance does not respect the Independents' choices as the *Serenity* familial community tends to do. While it is Mal's voice and the sound of explosions that the viewer primarily hears, it quickly becomes apparent that this is not a male-only battle for the rebels. As Mal relates his orders regarding strategy, it is Zoe who voices her concerns regarding his choices. Zoe also verbally pledges her allegiance to Mal and the rebellion. Whereas the Alliance soldiers are male figures that are seen only in passing, the viewer's gaze is able to rest fully on the diverse rebels' ranks. At one point as Mal leaves the foxhole to fight, Zoe calls to another soldier to assist, but he is unable as he is paralyzed with fear. This is not the first time that Mal has had to take control and save his crew: David Budgen writes that "Mal also assumes leadership after his commanding officer succumbs to nerves at the Battle of Du-Khang" (31). At Serenity Valley, Zoe picks up the rifle and fights alongside Mal, both simultaneously firing at the enemy in an effort to defend their values. Even though they are told to surrender, the viewer's gaze rests on a shocked and defiant Zoe and Mal before the camera shot cuts to the present time, which is six years after the war. By beginning with the upheaval caused by the Unification War, a case has been made in this Whedonverse for the safety offered by domestic space.

With regard to Bhabha's domestic space, on the battlefield it appears as the soldiers' foxhole; once the war concludes, it can be seen on board *Serenity*. In these domestic spaces, both Mal and Zoe rebel against traditional guidelines set forth for their gender and for their Western character types. According to both Armitage and Richard Slotkin, customarily the character of the Western soldier is featured as male. Whedon once again resists conventional Western methodology by creating two soldiers, one white male and one black female, whose character construction strays from the Western standard for that of the soldier. In the episode "Serenity," Mal runs from the foxhole to the ground-to-air missile launcher; Zoe, not Bendis, the male soldier, protects Mal from gunfire. As the airship that Mal has shot down crashes to the ground, Mal saves Zoe from certain death. Here, the viewer does not witness the male hero saving the damsel in distress, but two characters that belong to a liminal space altering stereotypical gender roles, thereby adapting to their environment. Each of Whedon's soldier characters extricates the other from danger, acts that show camaraderie rather than typical gendered behavior for figures in the American West. Whether they are fighting for the Independents or are members of the *Serenity* crew, Mal and Zoe's motivation for their actions remain entrenched in Whedon's non-gendered soldier construct. Next, in "Serenity," Mal and Zoe are featured floating in space as part of a new community of rebels.

As part of the ship's community, Mal and Zoe are not only soldiers, but also captain of the ship and second-in-command. In reference to Zoe, Whedon remarks, "She had been career army, the opposite of Mal, but she had fought under him for the last two and a half years of the war, in more than a dozen campaigns" (Whedon). Mal and Zoe's new positions on the ship are reminiscent of those during the war; however, now their lives have become more complex as they have shifted primarily to a domestic space. In his discussion of male character types appearing in nineteenth-century American frontier fiction and non-fiction, Richard Slotkin highlights the "soldier-aristocrat" as the standard soldier character, noting that he appears in both James Fenimore Cooper and Washington Irving's texts (103, 120). While both Mal and Zoe's characters contain traits of the "soldier-aristocrat" (Slotkin 103), they defer from the norm in their rebelliousness. With regard to Irving and his writings about adventurer Captain Bonneville, Slotkin observes that "Bonneville's heroism lies in his capacity to resist the spell of such wilderness, which turns lesser men into renegades" (122). In reference to Cooper's character, this male is heroic and aristocratic in his conduct—he holds "the title of officer and gentleman"—and as for his employment he holds "the traditional aristocratic professions of arms" (Slotkin 103–4). When Mal and his crew attempt to purloin Alliance goods from a defunct ship in the pilot episode, various characters refer to Mal as "captain" as he is throughout the televised series. By utilizing this method of address for Mal, the characters show that he holds a rank aboard ship and that he is respected by his shipmates just like the soldier-aristocrat (Slotkin 103–4). As Mal turns over one of the stolen meal supplements and notices that it carries the Alliance seal, he briskly returns it to the carry case. It is at this moment, when Zoe refers to Mal as "sir," that Whedon reminds the viewer that they are still, in a way, soldiers fighting for their cause. In fact, throughout the series Mal and Zoe continuously take on illegal acts together, usually accompanied by Jayne as the muscle. On board the *Serenity*, their dynamic alters to a certain degree as now their community is no longer military-based, but employment and secrecy-based. The people on the *Serenity* are there by choice and have elected to become a family in the futuristic frontier.

In the field and on *Serenity*, the soldiers appear as the rebels; however, whether military or criminal, they exist as heroes. While on the ground amidst the battle for Serenity Valley, Mal and Zoe are shown as a military company, a community rather than as individuals. The duo vies for freedom but, unfortunately, they appear much like cookie cutter soldiers. When Mal, Zoe, and Jayne return to the ship in the pilot episode and Zoe and her husband, Wash, converse, evidence is presented to the contrary. Mal and Zoe become three-dimensional character constructions, existing not just as soldier constructs. To Wash alone, Zoe expresses her distress at Mal's behavior. He responds, "Sweetie, we're crooks. If everything were right, we'd be in jail" ("Serenity"). Wash's statement reveals his surety about his position in society; the issue is that they reside in a liminal space, so there are no certainties. Zoe and Wash's physical movement away from Mal, Jane, and Kaylee is meaningful. Here, they are separating themselves from the public space, the cargo hold, and are entering a temporarily private space, a darkened hallway. This hallway leads to Wash's cockpit, the pilot's domain, and a more intimate conversation. Wash's statement to Zoe establishes his identity and shows the concrete nature of the aforementioned. He is *Serenity*'s pilot and he is Zoe's husband. Laura L. Beadling observes that "Zoe's tasks often necessitate leaving Wash on the ship, going with Mal and Jayne to face danger. In theory, this is fine with Wash, who understands his role as pilot is crucial in making their outlaw existence work: he often flies to the rescue or manages to accomplish a difficult escape" (56). Beadling captures the essence of the Wash character, revealing that Zoe's actions cause him to doubt his placement in society. While the crew is away on an adventure in "Serenity," Wash remains behind in his cockpit playing with toy dinosaurs. Beadling captures Wash saving the day (he ensures that they escape unscathed), and also his separation from the others (56). In the television series, Wash appears to enjoy his job, but in the comic "Those Left Behind" he reveals to Mal that the only reason he is the *Serenity*'s pilot is because "I got this *woman* nearby, makes me do all manner of stupid things" (Whedon, Matthews, and Conrad). Both his physical placement during the robbery and his aforementioned conversation with Mal, during which he implies that he is only on *Serenity* because Zoe is there, show that he feels he is not part of the community.

Once in space, Zoe too has difficulty reconciling her roles. As Wash suggestively tells Zoe that he would like to go away on a vacation, just the two of them, Zoe responds by noting that she will have to ask Mal for permission. To Wash, Mal is a "man," but to Zoe he is still her commanding officer ("Serenity"). As a result, Zoe's statement is logical to her, but not to her partner, who is irked by her behavior. In reference to Cooper's soldier figure, Slotkin writes, "Washington's myth involved a similar combination of aristocratic and military attributes with frontier heroism" (104). Even though Zoe's background in the television series is not clear, it is briefly documented in Whedon's pre-production memo.[4] Zoe remains true to her origins as career military (Whedon, Matthews, and Conrad); her character is dignified, assertive, and loyal. In "Safe," Zoe acts as the sharpshooter and rescues her companions from a firefight, much as she does when she is on the battlefield in the pilot episode. Zoe is certain of her choices on the field, whether it happens to be on the *Serenity*, on planet-side missions with Mal and Jayne, or in space. When she boards the ship, her certainty continues even though her circumstances alter. When Zoe and Wash speak to one another about taking a vacation, Zoe is firm in her assertion that Mal be consulted as "he's the captain" ("Serenity"). As an individual Zoe is loyal to her marriage and declares her desire to go on this trip, but as a Western soldier, Zoe honors military rank and declares her need for her commanding officer's permission before she takes leave. Zoe loves Wash and wants to be married, but Wash desires a traditional wife, behavior that Zoe attempts to replicate. Zoe is awkward when she tries to be a wife, preferring instead the freedom the gender-neutral soldier role offers her, but ultimately she feels obligated to Wash. Slotkin continues to describe Cooper's soldier as one who always "gets the girl" in the end, in particular an upper-class, well-mannered woman that he rescues from harm (103–4). Such an act emphasizes the masculine attributes of the archetype. This behavioral aspect also shows how Whedon develops the soldier character as Zoe loses her partner in the end. Regarding *Firefly*, Beadling notes, "created by Joss Whedon, an avowed feminist, the show never directly addresses feminism per se, but creates some of the most diverse, powerful, and interesting female characters on television" (55). Zoe is one of Whedon's more vibrant characters, female or male. During their discussion, when Zoe states that she must ask for leave as Mal is the captain, Wash retorts, "And I'm just the husband" ("Serenity"). Zoe attempts to stand firm in her resolve, but she waivers if only briefly. Before noting to Wash again that Mal is "the captain," she hesitates ("Serenity"). This moment in the pilot episode is the beginning to the breakdown that occurs in their relationship and develops Zoe's identity.

Nearing the close of the film, *Serenity* (2005), Wash dies after a battle with the Alliance and the Reavers, leaving Zoe behind. In multiple episodes Zoe is depicted as leaving the ship to go on adventures with Mal and Jayne while Wash remains on board to pilot the ship. Symbolically, Zoe departs the private domain that is *Serenity* to enter the public space; when she does so her identity is no longer in flux and she, once again, becomes solely the soldier. After Zoe's moment of hesitation occurs in "Serenity," friction arises in Zoe's marriage and, on occasion, she appears unsure of where she belongs in the hierarchy and of her identity. For example, in the pilot episode Mal suggests selling the stolen goods to Patience, but Zoe warns him that Patience has already shot him once and may not be willing to complete the purchase. Once Mal has been shot again, he affirms that Zoe's judgment was correct and that his confidence in Zoe as a soldier is intact. As Zoe and Wash are immersed in their discussion about their respective roles and that of Mal's, Mal enters the cockpit, asking about Inara's return. As Zoe calls Mal "sir," she gives Wash a warning glance about him making any commentary as he has, moments before, told Zoe to call Mal by this very term. By making this statement, Wash not only shows his criticism of Zoe and Mal's relationship, but also discredits the value of her military identity. In a discussion of the war veteran and the *Serenity* crew as a "surrogate family," David Budgen writes, "Mal and Zoe's bond ... is forged in combat and supersedes any of the postwar relationships" (31). When confronted with Mal and Zoe's relationship, he asserts himself in accordance with patriarchal ideals. What Wash has not realized is that the patriarchal societal construct is not utilized on *Serenity* to determine roles and his attitude towards his marriage is outdated. As Zoe silences Wash during their conversation, Wash proceeds to briefly do the same to Zoe when he makes a disparaging remark about Inara. Zoe appears very uncomfortable until she slips back into her soldier persona when responding to Mal's query.

With reference to the military aristocrat archetype, Slotkin observes that after the frontier has been closed this character will live to be the future of America, taking residence as a "squire" and having children (105). Unfortunately for Wash, he wants to have a traditional marriage in a place where such a relationship no longer exists; therefore, he must meet his demise at the close of the film. After his death, Zoe imparts on the viewer the impression that Zoe's life will be unlike that of the military aristocrat. She does, however, remain as part of the community in space. In an effort to debunk notorious typecasting with regard to the behavior of women and men on the frontier, Armitage writes that frontier women often did not see their journey to the frontier as one of excitement, rather it was monotonous and seen as a means to an end (16). She also observes that the individual is a rarity, noting the preference for the community and the family (16–17). When Kaylee questions Wash's absence at the close of the film, it is without fanfare that Zoe announces, "He ain't coming" (*Serenity*). Zoe's stoicism is matched with Kaylee's histrionics upon learning of Wash's demise. To Zoe, as with the frontier women, death is a part of life in this space and, with or without Wash, her life must continue.

Finally, in reference to historians' accounts of the frontier, Armitage writes that "women are either absent or incidental to the story" (11), a fact that Whedon drastically alters in his fictional world. Throughout the televised series, many of the characters' living quarters are featured in great detail, but Zoe and Wash's is glaringly absent of details other than a bed. The duo is shown in Wash's cockpit, his domain, and various other public spaces in the ship multiple times, but in their quarters only once. In fact, in "Those Left Behind" the other characters allude to the fact that Zoe and Wash have had sex in the cockpit, which is Wash's space and also a public space. As with their intimate conversation in "Serenity," the cockpit becomes a liminal space, one in which a romantic interlude may occur moments before they are alerted to danger. If they are not together on the ship, they are separate, existing in spaces connected to their positions in the community—Zoe as soldier and Wash as pilot. As the series progresses to its final episode, Zoe is increasingly in the field and, in "War Stories," actively attempts to keep Wash from entering her domain. While *Serenity*'s crew may be primarily made up of criminals, it is Zoe's character who always appears as heroic. Zoe skews gender constructs by rescuing Wash from being tortured by Niska. Traditionally, the soldier archetype rescues the upper-class well-mannered woman (Slotkin 103–4). Whedon places an interesting slant on the soldier character by having a female soldier rescue a representation of the patriarchy, namely Wash. In fact, once Wash dies Mal and River replace him, with River primarily flying the ship. Symbolically, with Wash's death and the implied fall of the Alliance, traditional gender roles come to an end. Zoe lives to fight another day as she is the future of the non-gendered frontier society. Like Zoe, Mal also retains his military attributes and has difficulty with the Alliance's guidelines for male and female behavior.

Mal, whether fighting for the Resistance or with the crew of *Serenity*, embodies the characteristics of the Western soldier. Like Zoe, Mal's background is largely unknown, however over the course of the series he proves himself to be a hero. In an interview for *Dreamwatch Magazine*, Nathan Fillion recounts a conversation he had with Whedon about *Firefly* and its concept. Fillion observes, "I remember asking him, 'Are we talking Cowboys in space?' and he replied, 'Well, what is a Cowboy really except someone who kinda goes out there and tries to make his way in the frontier?' The show's frontier mentality makes it a Western—the idea of setting it in a lawlessness environment where you make your own law with your gun." In the opening episode, Mal's identity is established as the rebel soldier. Mal is self-aware, but the Alliance's domination of the Independents displaces him from his societal role. As a result, Mal must adapt his persona to suit his new station in life, that of captain of a Firefly-class transport ship. Even though Mal's position has been altered, from sergeant in the military to captain of a vessel, his primary purpose remains the same. Whether enlisted soldier or recognized thief, Mal is motivated to defend his way of life and the survival of his community. The Alliance's domination of the rebels, however, alters the societal framework in place; Mal now lives in a commodity-driven social order as opposed to one dominated by personal freedoms. According to Paul Green, "Whedon admits to the influence of Han Solo from *Star Wars* as an inspiration for *Firefly* and the character 'Mal' Reynolds" (105). Both Whedon and George Lucas created characters that live as outlaws on board spaceships, only departing their vessels long enough in order to eke out the bare minimum necessary for survival. As in Lucas' empire, Whedon's Alliance have commodified the human, thereby showing the interchangeability of the Alliance member like that of the Storm Trooper. For Mal, once his side loses the war, the only option is to reside in a liminal space.

Mal's identity alters to suit the space in which he resides. We meet Mal in battle with the rebels; he is a soldier. He next appears as a member of the *Serenity* crew involved in the theft of Alliance goods; he is both a captain of a spaceship and a criminal. As Brian Stableford observes, "The hybridization of inventor fiction and westerns emphasized the importance of the myth of the frontier to American attitudes to technological development" (22). While Stableford is referencing Vernian texts here, the same could be said about Whedon's series. Whedon has split the *Firefly* universe into the futuristic, technologically-advanced Alliance, the Western frontier (the outer planets), and *Serenity*, the in between space. In "Serenity," the crew clearly establishes that Mal is the captain, both through verbal assertions and by deferring to his judgment. The issue, though, is that the ship is a liminal space, so identities are in flux. When the crew later in the episode land on Persephone, an Alliance planet, Mal's position in society is questioned. Once he speaks with Badger, the criminal who commissions the theft of the Alliance nutritional supplements, he no longer wields the same power on the ground as on board ("Serenity").

In reference to the American West, Mal's character appears reminiscent of both John Charles Frémont and Kit Carson, famed Californian explorers. First, as Slotkin discusses the Gold Rush, he observes that "it [California] became a new sort of frontier, a more advanced 'Oregon' in which the promise of untapped wealth no longer took the form of land, but was alchemically transmuted directly into the precious metal that is the basis of capital" (198). For Mal and his crew, one of the draws to the space frontier is not land, rather it is monetary gain. In fact, throughout the series many of the crew reinforce the idea that they would prefer to reside in the ship and never give any indication that planet living is desirable. After his side loses the war, Mal places himself in the role of privateer; to him, the Alliance represents an unlimited source of capital, much like California did during the Gold Rush. To many, the planets represent an off-limits site, only necessary when money is needed. Second, as previously observed, Whedon alters perceptions in place with his characters' construction. Unlike the soldier-aristocrat Frémont, who is famed for his assistance in claiming California for America during the U.S.-Mexico War, Mal was on the losing side of his war. Frémont is later court-martialed over his actions during the U.S.-Mexico War, specifically his taking on the role of governor. According to Slotkin, "His [Frémont] subsequent explorations were tainted by failure, and by the suggestion that they were undertaken not for the sake of knowledge but for publicity" (200). While Mal opens the series with a selfless act, serving in a war which could have benefitted many, he is later shown as more self-serving, driven by monetary gain. With the crew, Mal separates himself emotionally, thereby retaining a professional relationship. Mal appears as less than professional when he refers to or converses with Inara, speaks about silencing Kaylee's expressions of joy, and briefly when he discovers the Alliance seal on the food stuffs. Cracks in his cool demeanor are revealed after his interaction on Persephone's surface ("Serenity").

Once he lands on Persephone and interacts with Badger, Mal's behavior drastically changes. By exiting the liminal space, Mal no longer exists in a relatively safe and accepting environment. When Badger speaks to Mal, he disparages his role in the war, thereby he assists in altering Mal's identity. Badger refers to Mal as "sergeant," implying that even though Mal now has a ship and a new role, he is still seen as the defeated soldier ("Serenity"). When he enters an Alliance space, Mal is devalued in his current role and is subjected to Alliance bias until he departs. For example, Budgen discusses

"Bushwacked" and the mistrust that the Alliance commander has for Mal because of his position as an Independent, even going so far as to accuse Mal of Reavers' crimes (22). Throughout the series, Mal is treated poorly by many that see him as a traitor. Even though Badger degrades him, Mal retains his calm, only revealing his agitation when Jayne questions his actions. Similar to what happens to soldier-aristocrat Frémont, Mal's reputation is besmirched and he appears as a figure driven by materialistic desires. During Mal and Jayne's conversation, Mal goes as far as to not only agree with Jayne, an unwise act as Jayne is reckless, but also to decide to go to Patience to sell the goods. Zoe offers Mal names of alternative fences for their goods, but Mal refuses, noting that Patience is the best option. As they near the ship Mal tells Zoe, "Whitefall [Patience's planet] is the safest and the closest" ("Serenity"). Here, Mal begins to place the community above his own needs. Even though going to Patience means that he may die, Mal elects to go to the person that may be able to pay him enough to run the ship, therefore enabling the community to survive. After his decision is made, Mal, Zoe, and Jayne return to the ship to find the passengers boarding.

Mal's identity now alternates in this liminal space from caring captain to calculating criminal. Slotkin continues his discussion of Frémont, observing that perceptions of the man altered depending on the location (200). In the East, including Washington, D.C., he was "self-interested, vain, and moved by the same sordid concerns as everyone else in a society based upon ambition and marketplace values" (Slotkin 200). In the West, however, Frémont was "a man of heroic selflessness and pure motive" (200). As passengers board the ship, Mal and Zoe converse. Zoe, repeatedly the voice of reason, calls attention to Mal's flawed plan, that it is unwise to place passengers in the vicinity of the Alliance goods. Mal asserts to Zoe that the passengers will be unable to locate the goods and, when questioned as to why not, Mal responds, "'Cause" ("Serenity"). He even goes as far as to suggest that Zoe open fire on those passengers that appear suspicious. Mal's sardonic tone reveals that this is not a serious suggestion, but Zoe's response of disbelief at the success of his plan shows the severity of the matter. While Mal displays a certain closeness with the crew, his distrust regarding outsiders is blatantly obvious. After his interaction on the planet that subjects him to Alliance societal guidelines, Mal's behavior becomes erratic. First, Mal is shown much like the soldier-aristocrat, Frémont, is in the East: it looks like Mal's interest is only in protecting the goods, his final payment for the goods, and himself. His behavior alters once he gets a call from Wash alerting him to danger from the Alliance.

According to Slotkin, Frémont is veiled in mythos in the West, which positively aids his reputation, whereas in the East he held the same values as others and is shown as such (200). In "Serenity," when Wash alerts Mal to a problem with the Alliance, Mal is in his living quarters. In this moment, Mal appears similar to the Western incarnation of Frémont's soldier-aristocrat figure. For a moment, Mal's identity is that of the Browncoat, but in a new setting. When Wash calls Mal, he is urinating in his living quarters. The camera surveys the room as Mal exits and highlights the military décor. As the mission may be in danger, Mal swiftly completes his personal tasks and returns to his duties. As noted previously, even though the living quarters (domestic space) are traditionally considered to be private, on the *Serenity* they are liminal. At the sink, Mal splashes water on his face, an act which implies that Mal is under great pressure to perform. In reference to the mid-nineteenth century, Annette Kolodny states, "the raw frontier could still be fantasized as a realm that might nurture that quintessential American hero, the self-made man" (168). Before he separates himself from the passengers and crew, his tone as he addresses the passengers (Shepherd Book, Simon, and Dobson) alternates between professional and acerbic. He signals as to who is in charge while simultaneously threatening them with regard to the violation of his rules. When alone, his bravado slips aside and he reveals his concern. Once Wash signals that there is a problem, Mal puts aside his emotions and runs to the cockpit. As Mal is attempting to be the "self-made man" in his new frontier (168), he is also trying to be the hero he truly desires to be. Wash informs Mal that the Alliance has been secretly contacted and they are in danger as a result. His reaction to this news is significant as it is one of violence. Mal races to the cargo hold and punches Simon in the face, accusing him of being the spy. At this point, it is unclear as to whether Mal's concern is for the perceived loss of income, or because the Alliance is about to arrest the crew. Once the actual spy, Dobson, is revealed while holding Shepherd Book at gunpoint, Mal is visibly relieved that Dobson is not there for the *Serenity* crew, or the goods; instead, he wants Simon as he is a fugitive. Mal eagerly offers him Simon, but is dismayed to find that this act of diversion is not successful. In the melee that follows, Kaylee is shot; here, Mal's compassion towards Kaylee earns him the admiration of his community. While Mal, throughout the televised series, is never able to secure his fortune, he does grow as a character. In "Serenity," Mal refuses to leave Kaylee's side after she has been injured; he continuously speaks to her, thereby ensuring that she remain conscious. Several episodes later, in "Out of Gas," as Mal attempts to save the ship from being destroyed he remembers how the crew came together and transformed from individuals to being a family. Finally, Mal and River conclude the film flying into the proverbial sunset with River primarily taking control of the ship. While the Alliance societal construct may impact Mal's identity by driving Mal to behave irrationally, the influence of the domestic space permits Mal to become more accepting, trusting, and family-oriented. Whereas Mal is portrayed as the protector figure on the ship, Kaylee is the center of the domestic sphere.

While the focal point of the series tends to be on Mal's character, it becomes clear that Kaylee is just as critical to *Firefly*'s communal structure. In "Out of Gas," as Mal is suffocating to death on the ship he reminisces about meeting the other crew members. Symbolically, when he remembers meeting Kaylee for the first time it is her voice that is primarily witnessed. While there is great emphasis placed on Kaylee as the engineer in the opening episode, the viewers learn in this episode that she is not Mal's original engineer. Because there is a mechanical issue with the ship, Mal seeks Bester, the engineer, only to discover that he is not alone. Mal yells for Bester only to find Bester and Kaylee having sex; here, only Kaylee's back is seen by the viewer. While Bester converses with Mal he is shirtless; Kaylee gets fully dressed and then verbally addresses the issue with the ship. Consistent with the construction of the soldier characters, Whedon also updates the character of the pioneer woman. In her discussion of frontier women, Kolodny examines sentimental fiction and domestic texts from the mid–1850s, noting the women's traits portrayed within. In reference to the letters of Sarah Everett, who migrated to Kansas during the 1850s, Kolodny states, "Sarah Everett's fear of growing old before her time, of losing the capacity for feminine coquetry, was a fear that most women (and men) associated with westward emigration" (174). As Kaylee turns towards the men, offering her technical knowledge about repairing the ship, the viewer observes the back of her lace bra and her flowered dress. Because *Serenity* is a liminal space, Kaylee is permitted to take on a traditionally male position in this new American West and make it non-gendered. For the Kaylee character, Whedon takes Western notions about women as reflected in Kolodny and alters them.

When Kaylee is first shown in this episode, she is open about her sexuality while also appearing modest and feminine. Kolodny documents Everett's worry that the environment is causing her to age, and also that feminine clothing is inappropriate for her setting (174). Here, Everett's statement shows her as unsure with regard to social conventions in her new setting and her discontent with the West (Kolodny 174). It is telling that Kaylee's character only wears dresses while on the planet or, in this episode, before she becomes part of the crew. Once she becomes part of *Serenity*'s community and lives on board the ship, she tends to be seen in gray mechanics' overalls, a symbol of her position on the ship and her ability to transcend gendered roles. In some cases, as in episode five, the overalls have a pink flowered shirt underneath them. When Kaylee attempts to tell Mal and Bester what is wrong with the ship, the men are confused. Unabashedly, Kaylee tells Mal that she saw the problem while having sex; while they still appear at a loss, she coquettishly and patiently shows them the problem as she repairs it. After she solves the problem, Bester angrily questions Kaylee's actions, a statement to which Mal responds, "She fixed it" ("Out of Gas"). Mal then proceeds to respectfully address Kaylee as "Miss" and offer her the engineer's position ("Out of Gas"). While Mal places emphasis on Kaylee's sex in the aforementioned statements, he addresses her as such out of admiration for her mental acuity rather than to demean her.

When Mal asks Kaylee about her ability to repair the ship, she expresses that she understands she is skillful, but is unable to explain how she obtained the knowledge needed to complete the repairs. Kaylee is not being self-deprecating, but rather her youth is reflected here. In fact, after Mal offers her the job, Kaylee informs him that she must approach her parents for permission to take it. According to Kolodny, "By the middle of the nineteenth century, Americans had to struggle to preserve their shared self-image as a nation of independent yeoman farmers. Everywhere there was the inescapable evidence of an increasingly industrial urbanization" (161). As Kaylee races off the ship with her braids bouncing, she is the picture of youth, but not of innocence. Even though she may not be worldly, Kaylee is aware of the realities of planet living. Kaylee symbolizes industrialization, advancement on the frontier; her father, however, who is unable to find employment, is part of the "new class of urban poor" (161). In domestic literature, female writers tended to document the ill effects that urban space and its technology have on society, in particular the impact that they have on the family (162). Significantly, technology is seen as problematic for the pioneer woman because it replaces her, thereby removing the need for her in the frontier society. For *Serenity*'s crew technology drives them to need to make money. For Kaylee, however, technology offers her life a purpose; it aids her in becoming the contemporary frontier woman as it offers her a functional place in her community. When taken away as it is in "Out of Gas" when the ship is irreparable and "Shindig" when she goes to a party on a planet, Kaylee enters a liminal space. She is bewildered as she feels she is no longer an essential part of her community. Once her connection to the ship is reestablished, Kaylee's confidence returns. In reference to Kaylee Whedon writes, "As sweet and cheerful as she was mechanical, she found the opportunity to be chief engineer (a title she used only to herself) on a Firefly-class ship to be beyond her imaginings" ("Brief History"). Kaylee's use of technology facilitates her joining the *Serenity* community.

In the early to mid-nineteenth century, "a number of women spoke out against the shift from the earlier division of labor according to sex to the increasing allotment (or even elimination) of labor according to class" (Kolodny 165). By offering Kaylee the job and subsequently firing Bester, Mal shows that employment positions on the ship are not designated by sex, but by proficiency. In nineteenth-century literary works the warning regarding industrialization and its connection to the displacement of women from the home tended to be for the middle class woman; these women wanted to ensure that they did not lose their importance in their society (165). In "Out of Gas," Mal's recollections of the distant and recent past and the present are revealed. After Mal recalls hiring Kaylee, he next remembers a moment where she is seated bemoaning her inability to keep the ship running. Kaylee stares at a ship part, dreadfully distressed that she is unable to repair the engine, and speaks to Mal offering her apologies for her perceived inadequacies. She is upset because she is unable to hold together the home.

Significantly, earlier in "Out of Gas" and in the order of events, Kaylee and the crew are pictured in the galley for Simon's birthday party. Kaylee is the one that presents Simon with the lit birthday cake that she has prepared for him. Kolodny documents the portrayal of community in domestic fiction, noting that their version of the frontier community was "idealized" and "informed by the domestic ethos in which the values of home and hearth, rather than the market economy, organized the larger social structure" (169). *Serenity*'s community attempts to leave behind the societal structure of the Alliance, thereby taking the opportunity to build their own societal structure on the ship. While on the planet Persephone in "Shindig," Kaylee wishes for a dress to wear to the ball. Like the fairytale this moment resembles, Kaylee's dress permits her access to the party, but its gaudiness and her unrefined behavior make her the subject of ridicule by the women. Kaylee attempts to conform to Alliance societal guidelines and, like Mal, is unsuccessful. She is next pictured at the party surrounded by men regaling them with tales of her mechanical knowledge. Kaylee is not permitted authentic communal acceptance until she is back on board. Dressed in the mechanics' overalls and a flowered tank top, Kaylee skips and sings her way towards her room on *Serenity*. She sits on her bed, turns on the music playing from the party and, staring at the dress hanging on the wall, is gleefully happy. Whether she is in a public or private space on the ship, Kaylee reveals her authentic identity. Throughout the series, the character of Kaylee takes on an updated version of the nineteenth-century novelists' perceived role of the Western woman. It is she that recruits members of the Firefly's community in the pilot episode, namely Shepherd Book and Simon. Later in that episode, the seriousness of the bullet wound draws the community closer together, thereby enabling Mal to defeat the Alliance spy and allowing Simon and River to remain on the ship. When Mal brings up the idea of having passengers on board, Kaylee is very excited whereas other crew members, namely Jayne, are less so. Kaylee expresses her gratitude to Mal, kissing him on the cheek and noting her happiness: "I like to meet new people" ("Serenity"). This moment reflects her youth and her desire to expand the community. Clearly, Kaylee embodies the "home and hearth" concept as she attempts to keep the peace in her community, thereby ensuring that her family stays together (Kolodny 169). In "Trash," Kaylee is involved in the heist to steal a gun, a plan which is hatched around the kitchen table. The integral part of the plan, the method of escaping with the gun, Kaylee imagines and confidently shares with her group. While Kaylee does not permit money to control her lifestyle, she does see it as integral to maintaining the others' happiness. Kaylee has the ability to go from being childlike when she is playing with River in "War Stories" to assisting in repairing an old Alliance ambulance with Wash for another heist in "Ariel." Throughout the series, Kaylee remains the contemporary version of the pioneer woman and the heart of the *Serenity* crew.

In his series, Whedon creates characters that are able to transcend traditional limitations for their gender. Whedon highlights the one condition that must be met in order for the crossing of boundaries to occur—residence on the ship. While on the planets, the characters must adhere to the dominant ideology in the space. When the characters, Mal, Zoe, and Kaylee, land on Alliance planets they have difficulty adjusting to the restrictive societal guidelines that do not exist on *Serenity* in their community. The characters do try to adapt to their limited space, but cannot become accustomed to the falseness of the behavior. As Mal notes to Inara in "Shindig," when she attempts to explain the guidelines of her relationship, "Well, I guess you'd know. It's not my world." Mal correctly identifies the disparaging treatment that an Alliance member shows towards Inara, but his "Wild West" attitude does not suit this space. On board the *Serenity*, however, the obsolete gender guidelines are observed as harmful and, therefore, no longer applied to this community. According to Budgen, "The frontier represents a clean slate, a place removed from civilization; it enables hope of recovery or redemption" (29). For the *Serenity* crew, the ship offers a place of refuge to harmful societal guidelines. When they are utilized, as in the case of Wash, the character is longer permitted to exist in *Serenity*'s community as he is unable to adapt to this new societal structure. While that which exists outside of *Serenity* is dangerous, the ship itself as a domestic space, as a home, offers safety for the crew if they adhere to the liminality of the space. Unfortunately, for their community to survive surrounded by people who remain unchanged (like the Alliance), they must live separate from others floating together in space.

Notes

1. Episode eleven, "Serenity," was intended to be the first episode in the televised series. FOX, however, aired the series out of order and "The Train Job" was aired first. For this essay, the series will be examined in the order in which Whedon intended.
2. It is liminal because the planet has not yet been won by either side of the war.
3. The Alliance reinforces traditional gendered constructs regarding behavior while the Browncoats do not. Female and male Independents are not restricted to public and private spaces in accordance with their respective genders.
4. Only the Tams' past is delineated in the television series and in the *Serenity* film. The viewer obtains a glimpse of the others' past in "Out of Gas"; however, only when they arrive on the *Serenity* to become part of the crew is this witnessed. The *Serenity* comic book

series and the notes that Whedon has included within delve more completely into each character's past.

WORKS CITED

"Ariel." *Firefly*. Episode 9. Writ. Jose Molina. Dir. Allan Kroeker. Fox. 15 Nov. 2002. Twentieth Century Fox, 2003. Hulu. 30 Jan. 2016.
Armitage, Susan. "Through Women's Eyes: A New View of the West." *The Women's West*. Ed. Susan Armitage and Elizabeth Jameson. Norman: University of Oklahoma Press, 1987. Print.
Beadling, Laura L. "The Threat of the 'Good Wife': Feminism, Postfeminism, and Third-Wave Feminism in *Firefly*." *Investigating* Firefly *and* Serenity: *Science Fiction on the Frontier*. Ed. Rhonda V. Wilcox and Tanya R. Cochran. London: I.B. Tauris, 2008. 19–36. PDF.
Bhabha, Homi. *The Location of Culture*. 1994. London: Routledge, 2007. Print.
Budgen, David. "'A Man of Honor in a Den of Thieves': War Veterans in *Firefly* and *Serenity*." *Firefly Revisited: Essays on Joss Whedon's Classic Series*. Ed. Michael Goodrum and Philip Smith. Lanham, MD: Rowman & Littlefield, 2015. 19–33. Print.
Fillion, Nathan. Interview with Nathan Fillion. *Dreamwatch Magazine* 107. 9 Sept. 2003.
Green, Paul. "Firefly." *Encyclopedia of Weird Westerns: Supernatural and Science Fiction Elements in Novels, Pulps, Comics, Films, Television and Games*. 2nd ed. Jefferson, NC: McFarland, 2016. 105–106. Print.
Haldeman, Joe. "Viewpoint: Science Fiction and War." *Isaac Asimov's Science Fiction Magazine* (April 1986). Print.
Kolodny, Annette. *The Land Before Her: Fantasy and Experience of the American Frontiers, 1630–1860*. Chapel Hill: University of North Carolina Press, 1984. Print.
"Out of Gas." *Firefly*. Episode 8. Writ. Tim Minear. Dir. David Solomon. Fox. 25 Oct. 2002. Twentieth Century Fox, 2003. Hulu. 30 Jan. 2016.
"Safe." *Firefly*. Episode 5. Writ. Drew Z. Greenberg. Dir. Michael Grossman. Fox. 8 Nov. 2002. Twentieth Century Fox, 2003. Hulu. 30 Jan. 2016.
"Serenity." *Firefly*. Episode 1. Writ. and Dir. Joss Whedon. Fox. 20 Dec. 2002. Twentieth Century Fox, 2003. Hulu. 30 Jan. 2016.
Serenity. Writ. and Dir. Joss Whedon. Universal Pictures, 2005. Hulu. 6 Feb. 2016.
"Shindig." *Firefly*. Episode 4. Writ. Jane Espenson. Dir. Vern Gillum. Fox. 1 Nov. 2002. Twentieth Century Fox, 2003. Hulu. 30 Jan. 2016.
Slotkin, Richard. *The Fatal Environment: The Myth of the Frontier in the Age of Industrialization 1800–1890*. Norman: University of Oklahoma Press, 1994. Print.
Stableford, Brian. "Science Fiction Before the Genre." *The Cambridge Companion to Science Fiction*. 2002. Ed. Edward James and Farah Mendlesohn. Cambridge: Cambridge University Press, 2009. 15–31. Print.
"Trash." *Firefly*. Episode 11. Writ. Ben Edlund and Jose Molina. Dir. Vern Gillum. Fox. 21 July 2003. Twentieth Century Fox, 2003. Hulu. 30 Jan. 2016.
"War Stories." *Firefly*. Episode 10. Writ. Cheryl Cain. Dir. James Contner. Fox. 6 Dec. 2002. Twentieth Century Fox, 2003. Hulu. 30 Jan. 2016.
Whedon, Joss. "A Brief History of the Universe, Circa 2516 A. D." *Serenity: Firefly Class 03-K64*. Ed. Scott Allie and Sierra Hahn. Milwaukie, OR: Dark Horse Books, 2006. Print.
Whedon, Joss, Brett Matthews (w), and Will Conrad (a). "Those Left Behind." *Serenity: Firefly Class 03-K64, Vol. 1* #1–3 (July–Sept. 2005). Ed. Scott Allie and Sierra Hahn. Milwaukie, OR: Dark Horse, 2006. Print.

Scythe Matters
Performing Object Oriented Ontology on Domestic Space in Buffy the Vampire Slayer

JULIE L. HAWK

> What is left if we aren't the world? Intimacy. We have lost the world but gained a soul—the entities that coexist with us obtrude on our awareness with greater and greater urgency.
> —Timothy Morton, *Hyperobjects*

Critics have largely ignored the scythe in *Buffy the Vampire Slayer* (1997–2003), perhaps assuming that its role as a *deus ex machina* in the last episode delegitimizes it as a critical object in its own right. At most, the scythe gets a passing mention in existing scholarship. For example, Christine Hoffman includes it in the title of her work on the evolution of villainy throughout the series, "Happiness Is a Warm Scythe: The Evolution of Villainy and Weaponry in the Buffyverse," but it is actually only a small piece of her argument. This essay aims to intervene in that gap in scholarship, specifically arguing that the scythe represents far more than the all-too-easy plot device to fix everything at the end of the series run on television. The scythe's important presence in the comic continuation of the narrative, currently comprising seasons eight through ten, only furthers the need for a critical analysis of the scythe as object with object agency. Indeed, the scythe is the first transmedial object in the series, even before any of the characters themselves. As such, the scythe becomes an object of transnarrative space as well as a dynamic character that exhibits both growth and agency. The scythe appeared first in both the seventh season and the concurrently published standalone comic, *Fray*, which takes place sometime in the 23rd century, but clearly and directly connects to the narrative of the show and of the continuation in the comic book "seasons."[1] In addition to its status as a transmedial object, the scythe is an inherently paradoxical object, as it both kills and heals, both divides and unites, and both rips apart spaces and sutures them back together. The scythe's paradoxical powers, I argue, complicate the spaces constructed before its presence. Whereas its construction is firmly rooted in second wave feminism, Willow's spell shares its power, complicating the tidy and essentialized second wave space the Guardians created the scythe to maintain. Further, the scythe at times divides and at times sutures domestic space itself, both on the micro and macro levels (the small space of Buffy's house in season seven on the micro level, for example, and, on the macro level, the world itself in the season nine quest to restore magic). Not only does it cut across domestic space, but it also comes to represent it, defining and redefining roles, gender and otherwise. Domestic space, then, becomes an environment of opposing forces, both of which must be leveraged at different times for different ends. Before discussing the scythe's specific vital materialism within the narrative, I will briefly outline some of the theoretical constructs at play.

I aim, here, to read the Slayer scythe through a vital materialist lens to argue that the scythe is an object through which we might see the ways the narrative both in the television run and in the comics, sets up, complicates, and even troubles domestic space. Graham Harman argues in *The Quadruple Object*,

> While there may be an infinity of objects in the cosmos, they come in only two kinds: the real object that withdraws from all experience, and the sensual object that exists *only* in experience. And along with these we also have two kinds of qualities: the sensual qualities found in experience, and the real ones that Husserl says are accessible intellectually rather than through sensuous intuition [49].

In other words, as humans relating to objects we only ever interact with an object's appearance or effect, not its essential objectness. Levi Bryant and Timothy Morton both put this in terms of translation, Morton insisting that "all entities whatsoever constantly translate other objects into their own terms" ("An Object Oriented Defense of Poetry" 207) and Bryant conceding that while it is true that "all objects translate one another," "the objects that are translated are not irreducible to their translations" (18). An object, then, simply *is*. But it also *appears*, and it is the appearance that we are able to translate into our own terms for our own purposes.

Jane Bennet argues for a more ecologized notion of this translation, seeking "to give voice to a thing-power" (2). She advocates for what she calls a "vital materialism" in her book *Vibrant Matter*, contending that "[w]hile the smallest or simplest body or bit may indeed express a vital impetus, conatus, or *clinamen* an actant never really acts alone. Its efficacy or agency always depends on the collaboration, cooperation, or interactive interference of many bodies and forces" (21). This approach, I should note, differentiates her from Object Oriented Ontologists in that she is combining her sense of "thing power" with a systems theoretical approach, which Object Oriented Ontology (OOO) purists would consider, with no small disdain, "co-relationist." In other words, to theorists like Bryant and Harman, an object's essence should be theorized with no regard to human access or perception of it, nor with concern for how it interacts with other objects. Bennett, however, does not dismiss the processes involved with object ontology, and it is from this vital materialist position that we can best understand the scythe's vitality as an object with its own withdrawn essence that is nevertheless accessible in various kinds of ways to other agents in the story. First, the scythe is available via "translation" by the Slayer as a powerful weapon, and then as an object to be hacked by Willow's magic in order to bestow a greater shared power. Finally, the scythe cuts across space—narrative, dimensional, and domestic—ultimately to suture and heal those spaces. The scythe, then, *appears* as a weapon, but its essence, its real object agency, *is* something entirely other.

"It's not just a tool. It's important"

While the scythe's first moment of importance comes at the end of the television run of the series, it continues to be a crucial object in the Scoobies' arsenal—as weapon, yes, but as much more than that throughout the narrative continuation in the comics. In what follows, I highlight the key plot points in which the scythe is involved, from its introduction at the end of season seven and in the standalone comic *Fray*, through to where the narrative currently stands at the conclusion of season ten before turning to deeper analyses of particular moments in the narrative and thematic concerns within the transmedial text.

Season seven finds Buffy confronted with the First Evil, a force that has no materiality of its own and thus has to use the materiality of others to further its agenda. It does so by manifesting in the (non-material) form of people who have died in order to manipulate others to act in the material world on its behalf. Additionally, the First Evil cultivates its own order of minions consisting of monk-like mute warriors and a priest-like leader, Caleb, played by Nathan Fillion. Caleb, despite Fillion's inspired performance that makes him paradoxically affable, is an unmistakable representation of the patriarchy writ large, assuming all women are whores and yet deriving unmistakable sexual pleasure from his communion with the First Evil, who takes Buffy's form whenever that communion takes place (since Buffy *has* died, even though she also lives, the First *can* take her form). This focus on a patriarchal villain makes the narrative come full circle, as the first season's villain was the ancient vampire known as The Master. Additionally, it makes the feminist ending that much more satisfying. The First has spent the entire season sending its minions to hunt and kill Potential Slayers, all, of course, young women, and many of whom, through Willow's locating spell, have been found and taken in by the Scoobies.

In many ways, the arrival of the scythe in the narrative heals that space, suturing the domestic to the sphere of power that the Slayer inhabits. In the first episode in which the scythe appears, the Scoobies and the Potential Slayers have kicked Buffy out of her own house, and Faith now ostensibly leads them. However, Faith's leadership is far from solid, and the atmosphere is one of chaos, not order. The opening scene, in Buffy's living room, shows a group of people with no solid plan, no cohesion, and a complete failure to enact a feminist ideology among themselves. The arrival of the scythe coincides with Buffy's facing up to her own inner (and metaphorical, in this case) demons and rallying the troops, including Faith, behind her. In the third to last episode of season seven, Buffy, still estranged from the group, finds the weapon they have been searching for, hidden by Caleb while he tries to figure out how to get it out of its hiding place, embedded in stone. The penultimate episode of season seven—and of the television run of the show—begins with Buffy easily pulling the scythe out of the rock, or as Buffy puts it, "King Arthuring it out of the stone," a move that predictably frustrates Caleb and results in a fight ("End of Days"). The scythe is powerful enough to allow Buffy to escape Caleb and return to the Scoobies, and, indeed, to return to—and be welcomed into—her own home. Further, her return with the scythe is the moment that Buffy becomes the leader again. Buffy, not Faith, Willow, or Giles, once again has firm command of the troops.

Before we learn anything about the scythe itself, we learn of its invisibility in the existing scholarship upon which the Scooby gang has always relied, scholarship curated and fiercely guarded by the Watchers Council. Indeed, the scythe's inherent feminist power is underscored by the very fact of its obscurity. They learn only its name, "Mʔ," the last character signifying a glottal stop. As such it is quite difficult to pronounce, and Buffy later notes that she can never remember its name ("The Core, Part I"). Its difficulty in pronunciation, its almost unintelligibility, ties into its secret origins. It is only when Buffy finds the Guardian herself that the scythe's origin is revealed. The Guardian tells Buffy, "We are the last surprise" ("End of Days"). Forged as it was by the ancient female order known as the Guardians and kept hidden from the predecessor to the Watchers Council and the creator of the Slayer, the Shadow Men, the scythe exists outside the patriarchal structures of power and thereby outside of linguistic and discursive structures as well.

The Guardian reveals this information orally, woman to woman, telling her that the weapon was to be protected not just from the First Evil, but also from the Shadow Men and then the Watchers Council. Indeed, Kevin K. Durand argues that these two entities are as much a servant of the First, albeit unwittingly, as is Caleb (par. 2). What Buffy cannot learn from the Guardian, because Caleb kills her first, is how to use the scythe. She gives only this hint: "It's a weapon, but you already have weapons. Use it wisely" ("End of Days"). This bit of information certainly suggests that the Guardians knew that its power goes far beyond its appearance as a weapon. The sharing of the scythe's power is, of course, the *real* last surprise, and it is a fitting feminist end to the television run of the series. The plan, for Willow to use the scythe to grant all the Potential Slayers full Slayer power, according to Giles, "flies in the face of the way every generation has fought evil" ("Chosen"). When describing the plan to the Potentials to let them vote, Buffy says, "What if you could have that power now? In every generation, one Slayer is born because a bunch of men who died thousands of years ago made up that rule. They were powerful men. This woman [pointing to Willow] is more powerful than all of them combined. So I say we change that rule. I say my power should be our power" ("Chosen"). Willow, with a new feminist power, is able, Buffy contends, to "use the essence of the scythe to change our destiny" ("Chosen"). The "our" here is both very specific to the Potentials—if one is born to be a Slayer, when Willow performs her hack, she will be—but it is also descriptive of the world at large. If the patriarchal stranglehold that first the Shadow Men and then the Watchers Council had is now broken, and female power tips the scales, the world will start to look very different indeed. This empowering end to the television run is just the beginning of a new story, a story in which the scales tip thanks to both Willow and the scythe. While the end of the television run is a feel-good moment, the narrative wastes no time in the comic continuation problematizing the events that, at the end of season seven, seem so empowering.

Before the story continues in the comics, however, the groundwork was already laid in the new medium, and the scythe serves as a transmedial bridge that connects the pieces of the narrative together. While season seven aired on television, Whedon also published a miniseries standalone comic, *Fray*, set in the 23rd century, which followed the first Slayer to be called since the 21st century (though when in the 21st century is left unclear), Melakka Fray. Melakka was a thief who had always been a bit unnaturally strong and "good at things," but she did not experience the Slayer dreams. Her male twin, Harth, experienced those instead. When Harth becomes a vampire, or a "lurk," as they are called in this series, he sets about to destroy Melakka, conquer the world, and bring demonic magic back. At roughly the midpoint of the narrative, Urkonn, the demon who serves as Melakka's Watcher, though he is not a member of the Watchers Council, gives her the scythe, telling her it had been lost for centuries. The arrival of the scythe in the story parallels Melakka's acceptance of her Slayer status and the responsibility that status confers. The inclusion of the scythe and the reference of the last Slayer in the 21st century who removed magic from the world, bridges the narrative from the television show to the comic continuation, though it takes reading through season eight and into season nine before the bridge is fully built. This transmediation of the scythe before any of the actual characters cross from the televisual medium to the comic medium gives it a special importance. In other words, *Fray*—and importantly, the scythe—gives readers a reason to follow the narrative into the new medium, for it is clear that the story will continue.

With that transmedial bridge built, season eight opens with the Scooby gang's having grown to include the literal army of Slayers that Willow's spell on the scythe created. In addition, the scythe is closely guarded because other entities desire the power the scythe holds as well, particularly now that it is clear that while it is the Slayer's scythe, others both can and have tapped into its hidden essence. Indeed, the season eight villain, Twilight, makes a bid for the scythe (though we later learn that this not his endgame) when he sends his vampire minions, Kumio and Toru, to retrieve it in order to undo Willow's spell, leaving no Slayers in the world. Twilight tells Buffy, "One Slayer was all right, but all these girls. The world can't contain them, and they will suffer for that.... You have brought about disaster, and it falls to me to contain it" ("A Beautiful Sunset" 18). Twilight's agenda, then, is to restore balance to the world, at least as he sees it.

Once Angel reveals himself as Twilight, Buffy and Angel/Twilight literally create a new dimension through their cosmic sex, and Giles, attempting to explain what is happening, says that Buffy did something no other Slayer had done. He argues that Buffy did not just share the power, but with Willow "and the power of the scythe, she *created* it. She gave the world a new breed. A new evolution" ("Twilight, Chapter Three" 99). Buffy ultimately rejects the new dimension she and Angel created, understanding that so doing would mean the large-scale destruction of the world they would leave behind. Angel/Twilight seems at first to acquiesce, but ultimately turns against her, killing Giles, who, with the scythe in hand, stands between Buffy and Angel/Twilight. At this point, Buffy, fueled by rage and grief, uses the scythe to destroy the Seed of Wonder, the source of all magic, in an effort to undo the damage she and Angel caused by closing off the dimension from which pour thousands of demons. The Seed was the source of all magic in the world, so without it, the only magic left is that inherent to a person or an object. Vampires already sired and Slayers already chosen retain their powers; however, those who require a source for magic, such as witches, are now cut off from that power. The act of destroying the Seed also breaks the scythe in half. The scythe, then, is not only physically broken; it is also cut off from the very source of power that catalyzed the state of affairs in which the world now finds itself. While traces of magic persist in the scythe's blade, it is no longer capable of the kind of magic it once was.

In season nine, the fact that magic is gone from the world predictably causes trouble. Vampires sired after the destruction of the seed are more violent and animalistic because the demon is stuck in some sort of limbo. Worse, Willow discovers that without magic the world will eventually die completely. One of the major plotlines that extends throughout season nine is Willow's quest to restore magic to the world, which necessitates first healing and then utilizing the scythe. The first part of her quest takes Willow from season nine of *Buffy the Vampire Slayer* to season nine of *Angel and Faith* before ultimately landing in her own season nine spin-off, *Willow: Wonderland*. Once again, the scythe becomes the focal point of the transnarrative space. It cuts across space within the narrative (ripping a hole into Quor'toth) and simultaneously unifies the different narratives in the larger season nine arc.

Jane Bennett's notion of "enchanted materialism" is a useful lens through which to read season nine, as in it we learn that, though the destruction of the seed removed magical access, there are still traces left, mostly inside particular objects. Bennett takes on the pervasive persistence of what she calls "disenchantment tales," or myths that modernity is characterized by the loss of enchantment in the world (*Enchantment* 57). Essentially, the tales turn on the notion that the world is too calculable or knowable to produce wonder, or on the notion that the world's calculability comes with an attendant meaninglessness. Bennett argues against these tales, looking for an "enchanted materialism" that locates wonder not just in nature but also in technology and, importantly, in human connection with either or both (*Enchantment* 57). In season nine, Angel is on a quest to resurrect Giles, and has therefore been collecting magical objects that have pieces of Giles' soul in them. The scythe is, as by now we should be accustomed, the most important of those. In a supposedly disenchanted world, in other words, the scythe and a select few other objects still hold wonder. Willow offers the parts of Giles in the scythe to Angel in return for his (and, importantly, Connor's) help in getting to Quor'toth so that she can go from there to a dimension where she can recharge her power and hopefully find a way to bring magic back to the dying world. All of this takes place in the living room of Giles' house, which now belongs to Faith. Willow informs Angel that she needs both the scythe and Connor to get to Quor'toth because "magical items are like batteries—most still have residual energies left in them. The scythe is one of the most powerful," and she can use it to open a rift if she has "'something steeped in the essence of Quor'toth' to serve as a compass" ("Family Reunion, Part I" 10). Connor's role is to allow Willow to cut him with the scythe in a particular pattern while Willow utters the incantation. This ritual allows the portal to Quor'toth to open, despite the lack of magic in the world. Because of the traces of magic within the scythe and because of the repetition of the incantation, another important ingredient in reclaiming an enchanted world, according to Bennett (*Enchantment* 36), Willow is able to cut a rift through dimensions and reach a more enchanted space. From Quor'toth, Willow is able to jump dimensions until she finds one that will allow the scythe to be healed and her magic restored. Importantly, again, the scythe is serving as a narrative and transmedial bridge. Both Willow and the scythe have come from *Buffy the Vampire Slayer* season nine to *Angel and Faith* season nine, and the rest of her quest occurs in *Willow: Wonderland*. While this jump from one narrative space to another is not quite as dramatic as the transmedial jump from television to comics, it reinforces the scythe's power as an object that transcends narrative space.

While on this quest, Willow finds a supercoven inhabited by, among others, the trickster snake-woman witch, Alluwyn, who she had become intimately acquainted with in season eight. This plot point is an Odyssian siren situation, an obstacle to Willow's quest disguised as a paradise. Nevertheless, it results in the crucial healing of the scythe. The ritual to heal the scythe occurs early in Willow's stay at the coven and it takes up five panels, totaling one page. The ritual itself is almost comically corny, but we do learn some crucial information about the scythe from the ceremony. Vulcana, the healer of weapons in the coven says these words: "A weapon blessed as its counterpart Excalibur! *A blade that holds its power even in a magicless world.* A weapon so made can never be broken! A perfect design is eternal!" ("Willow: Wonderland, Part 2" 50, emphasis added). From this short passage, we learn that not only did Buffy "King Arthur it out of the stone," but that the scythe is a literal counterpart to King Arthur's mystical sword. We also learn that the scythe is perfect in design and that once Vulcana mends it, the blade can still wield its power. It will no longer be cut off from magic even when in a world that is so cut off. If the scythe was a *deus ex machina* before, it certainly seems to remain so here.

Season ten shows a significant shift in the role of the scythe within the narrative. This has to do with the shift of prominence, in terms of object-agency, to *Vampyr*, the book of magic, the book that begins each episode of the television series and that Giles leaves Buffy in his will. The book's contents were magically erased with the destruction of the Seed. In season ten, with magic back in the world, the book has to be rewritten, and while there are authors, the book has an agency of its own. The scythe has been so many times so critically important to the plot, but now it takes a supporting role while the book becomes a narrative focal point. This is not to say that the scythe disappears completely; it continues to figure into the story, particularly coming to embody familial relations. For example, when Andrew attempts to resurrect Jonathan by putting his downloaded personality into a new body, the Sculptor offers to create a body in exchange for the scythe. It then becomes a symbol of family, when Andrew manages not to betray the group by accepting the replica from the Sculptor and attempting to pass it off to Buffy as the real thing ("In Pieces on the Ground, Part Three"). This important moment for Andrew demonstrates that he meant his promise to be a loyal part of the family. Similarly, in the crossover with *Angel and Faith*, when Archaeus tries to turn Angel and Spike to his side using their vampire-familial connection, the scythe figures prominently in that battle, at times dominating the frames as almost a stand-in for Buffy herself. This is particularly the case in the battle that results in the near destruction of the artifact Archaeus used, the battle in which Archaeus realizes that the familial bonds that Angel and Spike have made with Buffy and the Scoobies are stronger than he will ever be alone ("Old Demons, Part Three"). Finally, at the very end of the arc of *BtVS* season ten, the scythe comes back to prominence exactly when the Scooby gang begins to heal their internal squabbles and unite as a family once more ("Own It, Part Three"), and it takes a literal seat at the table on the last page of the season ten arc ("Own It, Part Four"). In season ten, then, the scythe becomes, more than ever before, a symbol for family, and it is routinely pictured not just in the familial spaces they inhabit, but also as an actual part of the family itself.

"It's old, and it's strong, and it feels like mine."

Throughout the narrative since the scythe's appearance, a central point of concern has been to whom it belongs, if, indeed, it belongs to anyone. As an object with agency of its own, it "belongs" to different people in different stages of the narrative. When Caleb needs to be dispatched, for example, it belongs to Buffy; when the hellmouth opens and pours out the Turok-Han, it belongs to any Slayer; when the spell is to be cast to share the power or the world needs to regain its magic, it belongs to Willow. Before Buffy learns of its origin from the Guardian, she can feel its power, as can Faith. When Faith holds it in "End of Days," she says, "It's old and it's strong, and it feels like mine." Buffy does not refute her, answering simply, "It belongs to the Slayer." In object oriented ontological terms, then, the essence of the scythe as object is withdrawn from everyone, though the Slayer has a special kind of relationship to it such that they translate each other in particular ways. Only a Slayer could have pulled it from its hiding place. Only a Slayer can wield it with the full power of its primary function as weapon.

In *Fray*, the scythe does not appear until about midway through the narrative, once Melakka Fray is ready for both the powers and the responsibilities of being a Slayer. Urkonn, her frenemy, gives it to her with these words: "I have a gift for you. It is a weapon. Forged eons ago, for the Slayer alone. Lost for centuries. Carry it, for it is your sword and your scepter. Let it proclaim you the hero—and the monster—that you will need to be" ("Chapter Five: The Worst of It"). This passage highlights one of the many paradoxical dualities that inhere in the scythe. To wield it, he implies, the Slayer must be both hero and monster. Further, when she does finally pick up the scythe, her power grows. "Chapter Six" opens with a full page of Melakka holding the scythe, in a clear position of power, and a text bubble reading, "I have something to say." This statement of linguistic power hearkens back to Buffy's well-documented use of banter and language play in her fighting.[2] Accepting Slayer status comes with accepting the power inherent to the female voice, and here, the scythe is crucial in Fray's acceptance of both those things.

Beyond the outward expression of power, the power that only the Slayer can feel, the scythe cloaks a yet more hidden power, the power that Willow is able to hack into with aptitude. Christine Hoffman argues that as Dark Willow, Willow "no longer needs language, because she no longer needs access: She is the magics" (par. 22). Goddess Willow, I argue, does not merely replicate this phenomenon in the reverse, but rather in this instance, Willow approaches the scythe's essence not as a Slayer would—as someone working in tandem with (even in a special relationship with) the tool. For Willow, the scythe is neither weapon nor tool. It is instead an object whose withdrawn access she taps into. This access, OOO theorists might argue, should be impossible. However, Bennett's notion of "distributive agency" is helpful in understanding what is occurring. If we use this idea, we might say, along with Bennett, that "there is not so much a doer (an agent) behind the deed ... as a doing and an effecting by a human-nonhuman assemblage" (*Vibrant Matter* 28). When a Slayer wields the scythe, a phallic and destructive power is the result; when Willow hacks the scythe, she multiplies its power, allowing its essence to be shared by all Potential Slayers. The scythe has a power inherent to it, a power that goes beyond purposive intentions, an agency that sings to the Slayer but bows to the goddess. That is not to say, however, that the scythe chooses Willow permanently. Indeed, the scythe seems to choose whoever needs it most, making it more inherently feminist than its Arthurian counterpart. In season eight, Buffy maintains control of the scythe, though other Slayers also have access to it. Giles takes the scythe from Faith in the epic battle at the end of season eight and attempts to kill Angel/Twilight with it. His plan fails, though, and Buffy uses the scythe to destroy the Seed. In season eight, then, the scythe's most powerful moments are in the hands of Slayers, especially Buffy's. However, its moment of greatest power is also the moment it breaks. At this point in the narrative, it seems as though the scythe has seen its last fight, though we know from the narrative of *Fray* that this cannot be true.

In season nine, the scythe moves between being the Slayer's destructive force to being Willow's constructive force. Both Buffy and Willow come to realize that Willow must take it in order to set right the world after the destruction of the Seed ("Slayer Interrupted"). This quest is documented in the miniseries spinoff, *Willow: Wonderland*. Willow returns with the healed scythe, and at this point it becomes once more a signifier for the Slayer. Indeed, in "Time of Your Life," the crossover with *Fray*, Buffy uses the fact that they both have the scythe to convince Fray that they are both necessarily Slayers. In this issue, Buffy gets transposed in time with a creature from Fray's time, and the visual of Buffy's transposition reveals a hidden aspect of the scythe, pointing once more to the conflict between appearance and essence. The half page visual shows Buffy holding the scythe in a sort of X-ray view, highlighting her organs and veins. The veins do not stop when they hit the scythe. The visual here hints at the notion that the scythe is quite literally an extension of Buffy's own body, and by extension, presumably, all Slayers. This revised view of the scythe as part of the Slayer's body resituates how we envision the spaces the Slayer inhabits as well. In his landmark study of urban spaces, *Postmetropolis*, Edward Soja argues that as we become more "consciously aware of ourselves as intrinsically spatial beings" we realize that "it begins with the body, with the construction and performance of the self, the human subject, as a distinctively spatial entity involved in a complex relation with our surroundings" (6). Buffy's body, and perhaps any Slayer who holds the scythe, is certainly in a "complex relation" to it. The scythe becomes an extension of her body at a level invisible to the naked eye. This fact resituates the scythe, then, as beyond-weapon, beyond-tool, and it resituates Slayer-with-scythe in her immediate surroundings as well. She is both bigger and more powerful by virtue of this bodily extension. Indeed, when Buffy gets to the future, both she and Fray have the scythe, a fact she uses to convince Fray that she is, indeed, also a Slayer and that they are both on the same side ("Time of Your Life, Part 1"). The scythe, then, once again serves as a transnarrative anchor and as a signifier of something much more than a weapon, something that can heal wounded worlds and mark one as chosen.

In season ten, as the scythe shifts in importance as an object, so too the ownership shifts. When the scythe was perceived to be the most powerful object in their possession, it was more closely guarded by the group, and not Buffy alone. In season ten, however, Buffy refers to the scythe as *hers*. As the physical and external representation of her Slayer power, the scythe perhaps signals to Buffy that magic can come again, and as such, she creates a special room for it within her own home. This designated space within her home suggests that Buffy considers the scythe important to the fight but also a member of the family. Despite the fact that the scythe created an army of Slayers, all of whom could use it in exactly the same way Buffy does, Buffy claims it as her own. The scythe comes to represent Buffy's calling as "The Slayer," something Spike often reminds her. Because of the scythe, there is no longer just one (or two) Slayer(s), but Buffy is still the Chosen One, and the scythe's presence seems to affirm this fact, at least for Buffy herself.

The end of season ten highlights the scythe's special relationship to Buffy. Throughout the season, it has been of lesser importance than the book of magic that the Scoobies must rewrite. Their reluctance to believe in themselves to do this task leads to the ascendance of D'Hoffryn and the seeming (and short-lived) death of Xander. Once again, however, the scythe becomes more prominent as Buffy takes more ownership of her own powers. Indeed, the title of this last story arc is "Own It." After defeating D'Hoffryn, the Scoobies must replace the members of the Magic Council that D'Hoffryn murdered. They finally do "own it" and name Buffy, Willow, and Giles to the council, along with Dracula, Riley, and a few others. Before the first meeting of the council, which takes place in a hotel conference room, Buffy is in her own hotel room, a liminal domestic space, with Willow and Spike, nervously discussing the meeting about to take place. The scythe rests by the door of the hotel room, leaning against the wall, its position showing both the nominally relaxed environment of this liminal domestic space and the readiness for action. At a moment's notice, Buffy could have the scythe in hand. The scythe's "body language" in other words, echoes Buffy's own. The next scene shows the members of the council seated at the table, all but Buffy. At one end is Giles, and at the other, an empty chair. The council bickers among themselves, ignoring Giles' attempt to bring them to order with both his call to order and a gavel. From out of frame comes the scythe, landing decisively on the table. Buffy says, "The man said 'order,'" which silences the table ("Own It, Part Five: It's On You" 24/26). The scythe stays lodged in the table, almost resting on Buffy as she tells the council that their mission is to figure all this out without killing each other, adding, "To be honest, I have no idea how its gonna go." The final frame shows her, at last, seated at the head of the table, the scythe firmly in hand—scepter-like—as she says, "But that's life, isn't it?" ("Own It Part Five: It's On You" 24/26). The end of season ten, then, makes clear that Buffy has indeed taken ownership of herself, her mission, her life, and at least insofar as she can, the scythe itself.

"Holy Grail or Holy Hand Grenade"

Regardless of to whom at any specific moment it "belongs," the scythe's essence versus its appearance creates a paradox. To illustrate, when Buffy first finds the scythe and brings it back to her house, headquarters for the fight against the First Evil, she quips, it "Kills strong bodies, three ways" ("End of Days"). The quip is an allusion to Wonder Bread's slogan, "helps build strong bodies twelve ways," and whether Buffy means to slice, dice, and julienne a preacher or stake, behead and bludgeon a vampire, the scythe has multiple ways to kill. The scythe's traditional phallic power is obvious. It is an axe, more than a scythe, at one end, powerful enough to kill the Turok-Han, and a stake for garden variety vampires at the other end. Penetration with intent to kill is built into it at both ends, in other words. For example, Toru, having stolen the scythe from Buffy, uses the stake end to kill Xander's brand new love interest, Renee. This violent act takes place in a full page visual in which the phallic resonance is clear, the stake end of the scythe penetrating her completely ("Wolves at the Gate, Part 3"). The scythe in the wrong hands is used to penetrate, hurt, and kill. Of course, Buffy, too, can and does use the scythe in this way as well, even killing future Dark Willow in this manner. From this angle, then, this weapon, when in Slayer hands, is phallic power belonging to women, a clear second wave feminism. However, its larger power ties into the Wonder Bread allusion, which is more meaningful than it at first appears. That is, ultimately the scythe's power is precisely to *build* strong bodies, those of the potential Slayers, more than it is to *kill* strong bodies. Its essence, then, is more powerful, and more constructive, than its more easily accessible, destructive appearance.

Indeed, the very name of the scythe suggests its paradoxical nature. In addition to the weapon's appearing to be more an axe than a scythe, a scythe's traditional use is to harvest crops, an activity that carries with it both death and life. The crops themselves die in the process, but they are used to further life. Pushing the metaphor further, the scythe has long held a metaphorical role in the cultural imaginary as the tool of the Grim Reaper, which he uses to harvest souls, again carrying with it both death and a new kind of life. Willow calls attention to this death/life paradox when she returns to Buffy, who is now fighting Siphon, the villain of season nine. Willow greets Buffy with these words: "Since I left without properly saying goodbye, I brought you a peace offering ... ironically in the form of an extremely lethal weapon" ("The Watcher" 118). Once again, dualities and paradoxes inhere in the scythe. Not only is the scythe a peace offering in that Willow is making up to Buffy for leaving without saying goodbye, but it is literally the tool by which Willow intends to restore magic, and thus some balance, to the world. She is right, of course, to point out that it is in the form of an extremely lethal weapon. Whenever the narrative asks us to see the scythe as something other than a weapon, it then swiftly reminds us that it is still and also a weapon.

The portrayal of the scythe in domestic settings, particularly in season seven, highlights this tension between its role as a weapon and its role as something that heals and unifies. During the television run, the scythe inhabits domestic spaces as naturally as it does fight scenes. Indeed, aside from the moment Buffy pulls it from its stone hiding place and from the final battle at the end, most of the scenes with the scythe involve the Scoobies, in various rooms in the Summers' home, trying to figure out its special power, holding and caressing it in order to determine what vibrant matter seems to make it almost hum to the Slayer. When Faith is convalescing from the disastrous mission that resulted in her being in the path of an explosion, Buffy brings the scythe to her in Faith's room, which used to be Buffy's mother's room, adding yet another layer of familial resonance for viewers. Faith's initial responses to the scythe, then, are formed from the most intimate space she has, especially considering Faith's troubled relationship with home spaces. This positioning of the scythe points viewers to a nuanced interpretation of its power. While Buffy has always kept her arsenal of weapons in her bedroom, the difference here is the way in which the scythe is shared by the members of the domestic environment. The scythe seems to be from the very outset simply part of the family.

Indeed, the scythe becomes more integral to the narrative than Mr. Pointy ever was. Mr. Pointy, the iconic stake carried first by Kendra, the Slayer called after Buffy's (first) death, and then after Kendra's death by Buffy, represents a feminism that replicates phallic power, providing a tool by which Kendra could bond with her own power. After Kendra gives it to Buffy, with the express purpose of killing Angel, Buffy keeps the stake and eventually has it bronzed in Kendra's memory ("Helpless"). In other words, Mr. Pointy was a precursor in many ways to the familial status of the scythe, but it never really broke out of its role as a pretty simple killing device. This kind of feminism, a second wave version, is a necessary and important step, but it was never the end game. The scythe, on the other hand, represents so much more than a phallic power. It includes the masculine, but does not essentialize it, as does Mr. Pointy. It includes the feminine, but it does not essentialize it, as does the supercoven into which Willow wanders during her transdimensional sojourn. Most importantly, it includes a third space—a space carved out of the domestic but including non-domestic elements, a space that blends, muddles, and complicates masculine and feminine, peace and strife, unity and separation. Looking only at the television series, it is tempting to call the scythe a mere *deus ex machina*. This itself is an argument for transmediation, and indeed, an argument for the transmedial as representative of the importance of complicating the ways in which we think about space. Just as the scythe can cut through dimensions inside the narrative, it cuts through media outside the narrative. The scythe's ability to connect bodily to the Slayer in ways that are invisible to us and its ability to both rupture and suture spaces, both domestic and hostile, provides an anchor, but also perhaps a compass by which we might navigate these seemingly disparate spaces.

"At times, only separation can bring about unity"

Ultimately, the tension of the inherent paradox of the scythe's appearance versus its essence points to the intricately entwined coexistence of two opposing forces. Rather than in a dialogic relationship, though, I contend that these opposing forces exist in a harmonic tension, always vibrating with the other's force. In the scythe's initial appearance at the end of the television run, Willow hacks its appearance as weapon to get to its essence as a unifier. The sharing of the power is, after all, a kind of unification, though not, as we see in the comic continuation, one without problems.

This harmonic tension is perhaps most clear at the end of Willow's quest to restore magic to the world. The penultimate issue of *Willow: Wonderland* begins with Willow finally realizing she needs to leave the addictive paradise of the coven. Alluwyn appears on the opening page handing Willow the scythe. Included in the panel are only the scythe, the mermaid's hand, and the text bubble: "The strength of the supercoven comes from joining together, not cutting apart" "Willow: Wonderland, Part 4" 80). The visual makes clear that she is referring to the scythe and the use to which Willow wants to put it. As she says this, however, Willow, still reeling from the dream in which Marrak has tried to make her understand that she is being sucked into the supercoven and away from her task, has a flashback to the moment she first hacked the scythe and shared the Slayer power to all potentials. The visual conveys this information to the reader, as it shows white-haired willow saying, as she does in that final season seven episode, "Oh ... my ... Goddess" ("Willow: Wonderland, Part 4" 80). This begins Willow's process of understanding how to restore magic to the world, an understanding that unfolds throughout the rest of this story arc. In the final issue, Marrak, now revealed as a magically disguised Rack from season six, steals the scythe from Willow. She says, "No! You can't..." He cuts her off with this: "Use it as well as you? No ... but I can use it well enough" ("Willow: Wonderland, Part 5" 106). Willow, then, while not a Slayer, seems to have an ownership of the scythe at least comparable to Buffy's. As she wrests the scythe away from Rack, she says to him, "real power isn't something you steal. It's something you *earn*. And once you do ... it comes to you from everywhere." The "it" here refers to "real power," but she says this as the scythe flies back to her hands, conflating the object itself with the abstract concept of power. Real power, embodied here by the scythe, is something that only the worthy can wield. Moreover, what qualifies one as "worthy" is a willing recognition of and respect for the agency of the power one wishes to wield. Real power/the scythe is figured here as a gift from Magic as an entity to Willow for completing her quest by eliminating the selfish reasons for it. The magical embodiment gives Willow the scythe with these words: "At times, only separation can bring about unity ... and we must be destroyed to be made whole" ("Willow: Wonderland, Part 5" 122). The accompanying visual makes clear that this almost trite adage applies quite directly to the scythe. The scythe has already been broken, and it has already been healed. Now Willow must apply the metaphor of the scythe to magic itself and return to the world with both her own magic and the scythe restored. She must share the power with others instead of keeping it for herself. The scythe, then, returns to a version of its use in its initial appearance in season seven; it returns to building strong bodies rather than killing them.

This theme of unity through a period of separation appears again in season ten, though not as directly tied to the scythe as in season nine. Instead, in season ten, this theme manifests in the literal relationships among the human characters. The Scoobies weather several internal squabbles related to the best methods by which to fight those trying to rewrite the book of magic for their own ends. In addition, they become literally separated when Dawn and Xander are stuck in another dimension in order to seal a rift between worlds (using Dawn's Key powers that manifest in other dimensions). Dawn and Xander eventually find their own way back to their dimension, returning in the penultimate issue of the season, just as D'Hoffryn has revealed his plan and the Scoobies unite to fight him. This eventual reuniting of everyone includes, importantly, the scythe itself. Buffy even makes mention of its potential to kill D'Hoffryn, though her first attempt to do so fails ("Own It Part Four"). As the season closes, the scythe has a literal seat at the council table, making it not just part of the family, but part of the power structure surrounding the rewriting of the book of magic.

The scythe's importance to the narrative goes far beyond its appearance as a *deus ex machina* on the television series, and indeed, far beyond its appearance as a weapon. It is more nuanced—and more vulnerable—than a *deus ex machina*. More than a weapon and more than a tool, the scythe becomes an extension of the Slayer family, both in terms of those called to be Slayers and those in the extended family of the Scoobies. It cuts across space and time, both within the narrative and without. It both disrupts narratives and sutures them together. It both kills and heals, destroying the seed of magic and then restoring it. The sycthe's presence complicates the notion of domestic space in ways that signify and parallel the human characters. In the beginning of its arc, it entered Buffy's home space as a welcome signifier of violence. The scythe, in other words, was a tool of death, but for the Scoobies, it meant survival, and for the Potential Slayers, it meant destiny. At the end of season ten, it stands at the ready with Buffy. Buffy does not own the scythe, but she does at last own her own power and agency—both within her own domestic space and within the new spaces of power she is forging with the council. By her side in this new ownership of power are both her friends and the scythe, all in an ecology of agency and power.

Notes

1. The comic book continuation maintains the structure of television in that the large narrative arcs are contained within seasons, each of which have between twenty and thirty individual issues. The individual issues, then, are analogous to episodes. The structure diverges a bit from the television series in that the title *Angel and Faith* follows the seasons of *Buffy the Vampire Slayer*, and not the seasons that would exist were it to follow the television series *Angel*. This fact is probably influenced by the various entities that own the rights to the *Angel* series in addition to the fact that the storyline of *Angel and Faith* dovetails with the storyline of *Buffy the Vampire Slayer*. The standalone series within season nine, *Willow: Wonderland* also fits within this particular storyworld and its season-based structure.

2. For more on the intersections of language and power in the Buffyverse, see Michael Adams *Slayer Slang: A Buffy the Vampire Slayer Lexicon*; Karen Eeileen Overbey and Lahney Preston-Matto's "Staking in Tongues: Speech Act as Weapon in *Buffy*"; and *Slayage* 5.4 (May 2006) Special Issue, "Beyond Slayer Slang: Pragmatics, Discourse, and Style," guest edited by Michael Adams (Indiana University).

Works Cited

Adams, Michael, ed. *Slayage: The Online Journal of Whedon Studies* 5.4, Special Issue, "Beyond Slayer Slang: Pragmatics, Discourse, and Style." May 2006. Web.
_____. *Slayer Slang: A Buffy the Vampire Slayer Lexicon*. New York: Oxford University Press, 2003. Print.
Bennett, Jane. *The Enchantment of Modern Life: Attachments, Crossings, and Ethics*. Princeton: Princeton University Press, 2001. Print.
_____. *Vibrant Matter: A Political Ecology of Things*. Durham: Duke University Press, 2010. Print.
Bryant, Levi R. *The Democracy of Objects*. Ann Arbor: Open Humanities Press, 2011. Web.
Chambliss, Andrew (w), Georges Jeanty (p). "The Core: Part I." *Buffy the Vampire Slayer Season Nine* #32 (May 2013). Part 1 [of 5]. Milwaukie, OR: Dark Horse Comics. Print.
Chambliss, Andrew (w), Karl Moline (p). "Slayer Interrupted." #5 (Jan. 2012). *Buffy the Vampire Slayer Season Nine, Vol. 1: Freefall* #1–5 (Sept. 2011–Jan. 2012). Ed. Scott Allie and Sierra Hahn. Milwaukie, OR: Dark Horse Comics. Print.
Chambliss, Andrew (w), Karl Moline (p)." The Watcher." #20 (April 2013). *Buffy the Vampire Slayer Season Nine, Vol. 4: Welcome to the Team* #16–20. (Dec. 2012–April 2013). Ed. Scott Allie and Sierra Hahn. Milwaukie, OR: Dark Horse Comics. Print.
"Chosen." *Buffy the Vampire Slayer Collector's Set*. Season 7. Episode 22. Writ. Joss Whedon. Dir. Joss Whedon. UPN. 20 May 2003. Twentieth Century Fox, 2006. DVD.
Durand, Kevin K. "'Are You Ready to Finish This?' The Battle Against the Patriarchal Forces of Darkness." *Slayage: The Online Journal of Whedon Studies* 7.4 (Summer 2009): n. pag. Web. 20 April 2016.
"End of Days." *Buffy the Vampire Slayer Collector's Set*. Season 7. Episode 21. Writ. Douglas Petrie and Jane Espenson. Dir. Marita Grabiak. UPN. 13 May 2003. Twentieth Century Fox, 2006. DVD.
Gage, Christos (w), and Rebekah Isaacs (p). "Family Reunion, Part 1." *Angel and Faith* #11 (June 2012), Part 1 [of 4]. Milwaukie, OR: Dark Horse Comics. Print.
Gage, Christos (w), and Rebekah Isaacs (p). "Old Demons, Part Three." *Buffy the Vampire Slayer Season Ten* #18 (Aug. 2015), Part 3 [of 3]. Milwaukie, OR: Dark Horse Comics. E-text.

_____. "Own It, Part Three: Taking Ownership." *Buffy the Vampire Slayer Season Ten* #28 (June 2016), Part 3 [of 5]. Milwaukie, OR: Dark Horse Comics. E-text.

_____. "Own It, Part Four: Vengeance." *Buffy the Vampire Slayer Season Ten* #29 (July 2016), Part 4 [of 5]. Milwaukie, OR: Dark Horse Comics. E-text.

_____. "Own It, Part Five: It's On You." *Buffy the Vampire Slayer Season Ten* #30. (Aug. 2016), Part 5 [of 5]. Milwaukie: Dark Horse Comics. E-text.

Goddard, Drew (w), and Georges Jeanty (p). "Wolves at the Gate, Part 3." *Buffy the Vampire Slayer Season Eight* #14. (May 2008), Part 3 [of 4]. Milwaukie, OR: Dark Horse Comics. Print.

Gage, Christos (w), and Megan Levens (p). "In Pieces on the Ground, Part Three." *Buffy the Vampire Slayer Season Ten* #23 (Jan. 2016), Part 3 [of 5]. Milwaukie, OR: Dark Horse Comics. E-text.

Harman, Graham. *The Quadruple Object* Alresford, Hants, UK, 2011. isites.harvard.edu. E-book.

"Helpless." *Buffy the Vampire Slayer Collector's Set*. Season 3. Episode 12. Dir. James A. Contner. Writ. David Fury. The WB. 19 Jan. 1999. Twentieth Century Fox, 2006. DVD.

Hoffman, Christine." Happiness Is a Warm Scythe: The Evolution of Villainy and Weaponry in the Buffyverse." *Slayage: The Online Journal of Whedon Studies* 7.3 (Spring 2009): n. pag. Web. 20 AprIL 2016.

Meltzer, Brad (w), and Georges Jeanty (p). "Twilight, Chapter Three: Them F#©%ing (Plus the True History of the Universe)." *Buffy the Vampire Slayer Season Eight* #34 (April 2010), Part 3 [of 4]. Milwaukie, OR: Dark Horse Comics. Print.

Morton, Timothy. *Hyperobjects: Philosophy and Ecology After the End of the World*. Minneapolis: University of Minnesota Press, 2013. Print.

_____. "An Object-Oriented Defense of Poetry." *New Literary History* 43.2 (Spring 2012): 205–224. Print.

Overbey, Karen Eileen, and Lahney Preston-Matto. "Staking in Tongues: Speech Act as Weapon in *Buffy*." *Fighting the Forces: What's at Stake in* Buffy the Vampire Slayer. Ed. Rhonda Wilcox and David Lavery. Lanham, MD: Rowman & Littlefield, 2002. 73–84. Print.

Parker, Jeff (w), and Brian Ching (p). "Willow: Wonderland, Part 2." #2 (Dec. 2012). *Willow: Wonderland* #1–5 (Nov. 2012–March 2013). Ed. Scott Allie. Milwaukie, OR: Dark Horse Comics. Print.

Parker, Jeff, Christos Gage (w), and Brian Ching (p). "Willow: Wonderland, Part 4." #4 (Feb. 2013). *Willow: Wonderland* #1–5 (Nov. 2012–March 2013). Ed. Scott Allie. Milwaukie, OR: Dark Horse Comics. Print.

_____. "Willow: Wonderland, Part 5." #5 (March 2013) *Willow: Wonderland* #1–5 (Nov. 2012–March 2013). Ed. Scott Allie. Milwaukie, OR: Dark Horse Comics. Print.

Soja, Edward. *Postmetropolis: Critical Studies of Cities and Regions*. Oxford: Blackwell, 2000. Print.

"Touched." *Buffy the Vampire Slayer Collector's Set*. Season 7. Episode 20. Writ. Rebecca Rand Kirshner. Dir. David Solomon. UPN. 6 May 2003. Twentieth Century Fox, 2006. DVD.

Whedon, Joss (w), Georges Jeanty (p). "A Beautiful Sunset." #11 (Feb. 2008) *Buffy the Vampire Slayer Season Eight, Vol. 3: Wolves at the Gate* #11–15. (Feb.–June 2008). Ed. Scott Allie and Sierra Hahn. Milwaukie, OR: Dark Horse Comics. Print.

Whedon, Joss (w), Karl Moline (p). "Time of Your Life, Part 1." *Buffy the Vampire Slayer Season Eight* #16. (June 2008), Part 1 [of 4]. Milwaukie, OR: Dark Horse Comics. Print.

Whedon, Joss (w), Karl Moline (p), Andy Owens (i). "Chapter Five: The Worst of It." #5 (Dec. 2001). *Fray* #1–8 (June 2001–Aug. 2003). Ed. Matt Dryer, Michael Carriglitto, and Adam Gallardo. Milwaukie, OR: Dark Horse Comics, 2003. Print.

_____. "Chapter Six: Alarums." #6 (March 2002). *Fray* #1–8 (June 2001–Aug. 2003). Ed. Matt Dryer, Michael Carriglitto, and Adam Gallardo. Milwaukie, OR: Dark Horse Comics, 2003. Print.

Wilcox, Rhonda, and David Lavery, ed. *Fighting the Forces: What's at Stake in* Buffy the Vampire Slayer. Lanham, MD: Rowman & Littlefield, 2002. Print.

Deliver Us from Evil
Demons, Feminism and Rhetorical Spaces in Buffy the Vampire Slayer

Victoria Willis

In *Buffy the Vampire Slayer* (1997–2003), the home is used as a site of feminist subversion. Buffy, from the first episode, is strongly connected to her home. She has just moved into her new house with her mother, and when we first meet Buffy, she is waking up from a dream, her bedroom still filled with boxes and evidence of her recent move. Buffy's home is something she and her mother construct together, creating a space that is theirs, and, later, Dawn's as well. With the loss of her mother, Joyce, Buffy has to reconstruct what home means for her and Dawn, frequently literally, as she has to repair the damages from fighting demons in her living room. Buffy opens her home to the Scoobies, and after her own death, Willow and Tara move in to take care of Dawn and the Summers' house. When Buffy is brought back to life, Dawn takes her home, and her ability to pick up her domestic routine is part of what the Scoobies use to measure her recovery from death. Later, in season seven, she opens her home to the Potentials, providing them with both shelter and training. In "Empty Places," when the Potentials and Scoobies vote for a change of leadership, they do so by asking Buffy to leave her home, underscoring the significance of the home to Buffy as a source of strength. She wanders into a stranger's home, and spends one night there with Spike, finding strength in herself, with his encouragement, before she is able to retrieve the scythe from Caleb.

The home may be where Buffy's heart is, but more importantly, it is where her voice is. By using her home, a traditionally feminine space, to find and use her voice to deliver speeches, particularly in season seven, Buffy subverts heteronormative gender roles, eventually empowering women and changing the world. The locations and delivery of public speaking in *Buffy the Vampire Slayer* create and demonstrate a feminist re-vision of rhetorical practices. Public speaking, for these purposes, is defined as a spoken address, on a specific topic, to an audience that consists of more than five members. In season three, the episodes "The Wish," "The Prom," and "Graduation Day Part II" contain public speaking events where the speakers engage in traditional rhetorical practices. In each of these instances, the speakers are male. All of the male orators, who engage in traditional rhetorical speaking and delivery, from traditionally masculine spaces like podiums or stages, are evil (or become evil-ish). In the Buffy-verse, traditional rhetoric, and particularly traditional delivery, is significant because traditional rhetorical practices are historically embedded with hegemonic masculinity, requiring speakers to perform hegemonic and idealized masculine roles. Buffy's speeches, on the other hand, are what Nan Johnson terms "parlor rhetoric" (*Gender* 17). Buffy does not speak from a stage, but from her living room or kitchen. She also speaks and fights in the cemetery, another traditionally feminine space. Buffy creates a feminist rhetoric, changing the practice of rhetoric from a traditionally masculine model in masculine locations to a model of rhetoric where women can speak without adhering to traditional speaking norms and masculine performances. Buffy changes rhetoric so that women can find their voices, redefining the ideal orator into a good, and powerful, woman, speaking well.

Rhetorical Spaces and Delivery

The rhetoric and principles of domesticity were taught and passed on to women much like the rhetoric and principles of public speaking and civic duty were taught and passed on to men. In classical rhetoric, Quintilian defined delivery as "A good man speaking well" (*Education* 2.15.1–2). Delivery is how a speech or a spoken address is conveyed to an audience: the tone of the voice, the movement of the hands, the position of the feet, and the expressions on the face. Delivery evolved throughout the classical tradition to include the clothes and the appearance of the orator. For Aristotle, delivery focused on the voice (3.1.4). Cicero expanded Aristotle's focus on the voice to include bodily expressions as well, writing that delivery "must be regulated by the movement of the body, by gesture, by facial expression, and by inflecting and varying the voice" (1.18). And in Quintilian's *The Orator's Education*, delivery consisted of both voice and gesture (11.3.14). Some rhetorical guides, like the *Rhetorica ad Herennium*, described delivery in exhaustive detail. The *Rhetorica ad Herennium* divides delivery into Voice Quality and Physical

Movement, and then further breaking down each category into subcategories and sub-subcategories that are described at length, with examples and admonitions for each (3.11.19–3.13.23). The unknown author of the *Rhetorica ad Herennium* took every care to painstakingly describe, prescribe, and categorize the mechanics of speaking in any given situation for the orator because delivery needed to be tightly regulated and controlled; delivery was the performance, not just of a speech, but of the speaker himself.

Delivery, according to Cicero and Quintilian, conveyed the character of the orator. How an orator spoke was just as important, if not sometimes more important, than what he said. In order to perfect his own delivery, Demosthenes was said to have practiced speaking during storms, gesturing into the wind and articulating around several round stones that he placed in his mouth. (Cicero 1.114–115). For Quintilian, delivery began even before an orator spoke. An audience would judge an orator based on his appearance before he even began speaking, drawing conclusions about his character and his attentions based on his posture, his facial expressions, his clothing (11.3.156–159). Quintilian assumed that anyone trained in oratory would have only the best of intentions; an orator, after all, was a *good* man, speaking well.

In ancient Greece and Rome, women were excluded from rhetoric because they were not allowed to speak in public. Women had no legal rights and no civic duties; their only duties were domestic, and they were the property of their husbands. Because women were not public figures, epitaphs taken from tombstone inscriptions provide the clearest pictures of ancient Greek and Roman women; these examples demonstrate how women's worth was tied to their domestic talents:

> She loved her husband in her heart. She bore two sons, one of whom she left on earth, the other beneath it. She was pleasant to talk with, and she walked with grace. She kept the house and worked in wool. That is all. You may go [Lefkowitz and Fant 133].

> My wife, who died before me, chaste in body, my one and only, a loving woman who possessed my heart, she lived as a faithful wife to a faithful husband with affection equal to my own, since she never let avarice keep her from her duty [Lefkowitz and Fant 134].

A women's place was in the home. The Greeks and Romans believed that nature had a "natural" order—the physical world had inherent properties and characteristics that constructed it, and so the social world also was constructed from innate characteristics. For the Romans, for example, men were naturally, or innately, superior to women, and women who proved themselves to be extraordinary in some fashion, were women whose natural, innate woman-ness was augmented or superlative. Men's innate maleness made them suited for public life and authority, women's innate femaleness made them suited for taking care of the home and raising children.

The innate goodness of women was rooted in the domestic. A good woman was just as good as any other good woman; it was more important to praise their values rather than the women themselves, so that the domestic values of good women might continue on, even if individual women perished. Another epitaph explained:

> For these reasons praise for all good women is simple and similar, since their native goodness and the trust they have maintained do not require a diversity of words. Sufficient is the fact that they have all done the same good deeds with the fine reputation they deserve, and since it is hard to find new forms of praise for a woman, since their lives fluctuate with less diversity, by necessity we pay tribute to the values they hold in common, so that nothing may be lost from fair precepts and harm what remains [Lefkowitz and Fant 136].

These inscriptions not only describe the essentializing aspects of Roman belief and societal structure, but they also serve to rhetorically reinforce and prescribe domestic roles for women. Each inscription is a form of epideictic speech, praising these women for their natural and womanly qualities, while positioning them in subservient positions to their husbands. These women earned praise for loyalty, domestic work, and obedience to men, in other words, for excelling within the established framework for women. These epideictic epitaphs reinforce the location of women in the home and also exclude and silence women from public life.

Because women were seen as innately inferior to men and virtuous only within the context of the home, Roman marriage law reinforced the domestic position of women by continuing to deprive them of agency. Marriage laws demonstrate how women were regulated by Roman custom:

> The chief purpose of marriage in upper class Roman society was the procreation of children to guarantee the continuation of the family line. Thus a wife who had already borne enough children to one husband could be conceded to a close loyal friend. One advantage of this was that sons born of the same mother, as half-brothers, would find it easier to act as allies in the fierce political struggles of ancient Rome.... According to both law and custom a pregnant woman could not enter into a second marriage until the child in her womb had been born into her legitimate husband's home [Fraschetti 103].

In this example, women have no voice or agency within the process—the men involved make the decision to concede and accept the concession. Additionally, the wife-transfer benefits not only her spouses, who are able to strengthen their loyalties and allegiances through the concession, but also the sons who are born to both marriages. Because the woman is doing her duty, and using her womanly virtues—bearing children and keeping house—she is regulated by law and custom into a position without agency or voice. For the Romans, it is only natural that a woman be treated as a transferable piece of domestic property, because innately, she has the qualities of property—her greatest virtue lies in her use and contribution to men.

Women could speak in the home, for the benefit of others, without agency for themselves while men were taught to speak publicly, for the benefit of themselves and their country. Public and private gender performances were embedded into the rhetoric of public speaking. In *Roman Eloquence*, Gualtiero Calboli and William Dominik observe: "For rhetoric, like any other field of activity, is constructed socially, politically, and cognitively in ways that reflect, express and extend—through its rules, structures, processes and values—the culture that produces it" (11). In Rome, this aspect of rhetoric manifested itself by creating a structure that reified culture norms and practices, including practices of exclusions and silencings where women were confined to the home. To some extent, this function of rhetoric was recognized in Rome. For example, Quintilian states, "Language is based on reason, antiquity, authority, and custom.... Custom, however, is the surest preceptor in speaking: we must use phraseology, like money, which has the public stamp" (49). Rhetorical texts, such as the *Ad Herennium*, focus on producing a student capable of public addresses, a mode of discourse unavailable for many subjects of Rome. The instruction in rhetoric, and where delivery occurred, is important because the sphere of influence became divided into the public life of the podium for men, and the private, domestic life of the home for women. The teaching of rhetoric consistently draws on the ancient rhetorical roots of Greece and Rome, continuing to reinforce, and sometimes subvert, this divide, well into the early 1900s, to the extent that this division continues to manifest in rhetorical practices to the present day.

Evil Men Speaking Well

When Quintilian outlined his theories of rhetoric, he embedded gender ideals by giving examples of examples of masculine and effeminate speaking. He argued that the manly and virtuous was desirable, and the womanly and effeminate was undesirable. In *On the Teaching of Speaking and Writing*, Quintilian states:

> Let his [the student's] mode of reading aloud, however, be manly above all, uniting gravity with a certain degree of sweetness. Let not his reading of the poets be like that of prose, for it is verse, and the poets say that they sing. Yet let it not degenerate into sing-song, or be rendered effeminate with unnatural softness [64].

Quintilian later states explicitly that he does not want his student "to be broken to the shrillness of a woman's voice," indicating that women's voices are not only undesirable and unsuitable for rhetoric, but also implying that women should be silent (81). Quintilian reinforces the male privilege to speak, and consigns women to silence. Rhetoric, then, becomes not only a tool for persuasion and speaking, but also a tool for reconstructing and reinforcing heteronormative, patriarchal privilege. And for Quintilian, the ideal orator demonstrates manliness and goodness; he is the "good man, speaking well."

In *Buffy the Vampire Slayer*, the only orators who speak from podium or a stage, the only speakers who deliver traditional public addresses, are all male, white, and presumably straight and middle/upper class. But they are hardly good men. In fact, all of them are, in some form or another, demons. Their ability to deliver their speeches, and their ease and proficiency with public speaking, is directly correctly to how evil each of them are. The more evil the man, the more demonic he is, the better he speaks. In *BtVS*, the ideal orator turns Quintilian's definition upside-down. The ideal orator, steeped in traditionally masculine rhetoric, is an evil man, speaking well.

In "Graduation Day, Part II," Mayor Richard Wilkins, III gives a speech to the graduating class of Sunnydale High. He stands behind a podium, on a platform, in front of the audience of graduating seniors, their parents, and various representatives from the high school and town. He has note cards even though, as he mentioned earlier to his vampire minions, he has worked on this speech for over a hundred years. And he certainly seems to have practiced enough to time it well. Although he does not manage to get to the part about civic responsibility, the Mayor begins his ascension after proclaiming, "Today is about change. Graduation doesn't just mean your circumstances change, it means you do. You ascend to a higher level. Nothing will ever be the same. Nothing." And then he turns into a giant snake demon and is killed by the joint efforts of the class of '99.

Season three is rife with speeches. Earlier in the season, in "The Wish," Cordelia wishes that Buffy had never come to Sunnydale. Anya, a vengeance demon, grants her wish and creates an alternate universe where Sunnydale is overridden with vampires who are ruled by the Master. The Master, in his efforts to advance vampire society, opens The Factory, where humans are systematically drained of their blood on an assembly line. Standing on a platform, the Master gives a speech to an audience of vampires and caged humans concerning progress and the superiority of the vampire race. The opening ceremony continues as a human is pulled from the cage and placed on the assembly line. As the Master toasts his audience with a goblet of fresh blood, the Slayer and Angel, her ally—the vampire with a soul, attack, and are both killed. The Master snaps Buffy's neck just as Giles destroys Anya's power source and restores the normal Buffy-verse (in which the Master is dead).

One of the only speeches in season three that does not end (immediately) in death is Jonathan's speech in "The Prom." Standing on the stage, after awkwardly adjusting the microphone, Jonathan prefaces his speech by saying,

"We have one more award to give out. Is Buffy Summers here tonight? Did she ... um.... This is actually a new category. First time ever. I guess there were a lot of write in ballots and the prom committee asked me to read this." He is clearly not a practiced speaker. But from a folded up piece of paper he reads his speech, concluding with, "Most of the people here have been saved by you. Or helped by you at one time or another. We're proud to say that the class of '99 has the lowest mortality rate of any graduating class in Sunnydale history. And we know that at least part of that is because of you. So the senior class offers its thanks and gives you, uh ... this." Then Jonathan pulls out the sparkly umbrella and adds, "It's from all of us. And it has written here, Buffy Summers—Class Protector" and hands it to Buffy.

These three speeches, delivered by the Mayor, the Master, and Jonathan, are all traditionally delivered speeches. During each of these three speeches in season three, the speaker stands on a stage or at a podium—the traditional location for the delivery of a speech. The speakers all appear to be familiar with public speaking conventions and the rules of delivery: appropriate dress, voice inflection, and gesture. Although the Mayor and Jonathan both have their speeches written out, the Mayor maintains better eye contact with his audience and reads naturally, not relying on his notes. Jonathan reads directly from the paper, rather like a student giving a presentation. The Master, on the other hand, appears to speak completely extemporaneously, giving the impression that he is a more accomplished public speaker than either Jonathan or the Mayor. The location is what these speeches have in common: regardless of the speaker's facility with delivery, each speech is delivered in a traditional, public rhetorical space. But these are not Quintilian's orators; these are not good men, speaking well. Each speaker's facility with public speaking falls on a spectrum that correlates with his evil-ness. The Mayor becomes a demon, the Master is a demon, and Jonathan, well, Jonathan will turn temporarily into a fake demon with sparkly wings and boxing shorts ("Life Serial").

Out of the three orators, the Mayor falls in the middle. He has a villain moniker, "The Mayor," and a human name, "Richard Wilkins, III," showing that he falls somewhere between human and demon. He has been practicing evil as a human, getting ready for his demon debut, but he does not get to do much evil as a demon—he gets to eat Principal Schneider, chase Buffy, and explode ("Graduation Day, Part II"). His evil doing equates to his speech giving; he has been practicing and preparing, but he does not quite get to finish. He speaks well, but still needs note cards, which compromises his gestures. His inability to achieve oratory perfection is similar to his inability to achieve his demonic conquest of Sunnydale.

The Master, on the other hand, is a master orator. He is also the most accomplished evildoer of the three. As a vampire, he is so old, and so powerful, that his demonic visage is visible at all times—he is unquestionably a demon with little to no humanity left. In Cordelia's alternate universe, the Master succeeds in breaking free of his temporal prison and conquering Sunnydale. When he opens The Factory, he speaks extemporaneously and is naturally eloquent. He projects his ethos as Master with his body language, his confident voice and posture. He rallies his vampire audience, speaking passionately as he proclaims the dawn of a new age ("The Wish"). The Master as orator is also the Master as victor—if Buffy had not defeated him in season one, Sunnydale would have fallen. The Master's power is such that, in this alternate universe, he kills Buffy.

And Jonathan, finally, is the least practiced, and least evil, orator of the three. He is clearly not comfortable on stage, and when he is not reading from his notes, his voice is hesitant and unsure. He has to awkwardly adjust the microphone to his height. When he begins speaking, he fidgets and appears vaguely anxious. Jonathan seems to know what he should be doing, but is not able to do it fluidly. Jonathan's speech, which was written by the prom committee, is the only speech that is not self-serving; he is praising someone else. He is more invested in giving the award to Buffy than he is in the speaking itself ("The Prom"). In evil doing, Jonathan has a similar pattern of investment; he is not as interested in being evil as he is in the rewards. He enjoys being a member of the Trio but has no wish to harm Buffy or engage in seriously evil acts. He protests several of the more evil plans, leading to Warren and Andrew conspiring to kick him out of the Trio ("Entropy"). However, despite his rather mild evil-ness, Jonathan will eventually die as well, when Andrew kills him and sacrifices him to the First Evil.

All of these demonic(-ish) orators deliver their speeches in traditional, public spaces that have historically operated to exclude women speakers. Only men had complete access to public oratory until the mid–1800s, and then, women's access was strictly controlled and regulated. Women's domain continued to be the home, and the Seneca Fall Convention of 1848 marked the turning point where women began to organize openly to fight for equal rights, including the right to speak, to participate in public life, and to vote. However, women continued to be marginalized and silenced, and forced to return to the home. Andrew, the formerly evil member of the Trio from season six, gives us an example of the way that women have been excluded from rhetoric in "Storyteller," when he attempts to create a video documentary of Buffy's efforts to save the world. Andrew's documentary, however, is a hodgepodge of narcissistic fantasy, exaggeration, and assumption. When Buffy begins to give a speech in her kitchen to the potential slayers about the importance of preparing for the upcoming war, Andrew, who is filming, turns the camera away from Buffy, commenting that her speeches are long, and kind of boring. He turns the camera on himself and begins to tell the audience of his documentary (and the audience of *BtVS*) his own story about his quest for redemption and his membership in the Trio. He pauses once to see if Buffy's speech is over, and then continues his story. Although Buffy can be heard talking in the background, almost the entirety of her speech is overwritten by Andrew and excluded from his film.

The example of Buffy's speech in "Storyteller" demonstrates how women have been written out of the rhetorical canon. As Nan Johnson points out in *Gender and Rhetorical Space in American Life, 1866–1910*, rhetorical space has been traditionally constructed as masculine. Women were written out of the rhetorical canon in the early 20th century because their speaking occurred in non-traditional spaces and locations, like the parlor. Johnson concludes, "When early canon authors chose to privilege only the rhetorical spaces controlled by statesmen, they erased not only the voices of women who helped to shape American political culture, but also the significance of the rhetorical spaces in which most Americans heard words that changed their views and lives" (171). As women began to speak in the domestic spaces available to them, they continued to be excluded from rhetorical tradition. Buffy's speech occurs in her kitchen, which is certainly a non-traditional location. She does not speak from a stage or use a podium; her delivery space is domestic. Andrew attempts to exclude and silence her, trying to overwrite Buffy's delivery by moving the camera and telling his own story. He fails to recognize Buffy's rhetorical space as legitimate and uses a video camera to attempt to create his own narrative by overwriting hers, effectively silencing her in his fantasy documentary.

The First Evil and the First Slayer

The history of the Slayer is the history of servitude, of a woman chosen and violated by a demon against her will, literally disrupting her humanity and forcing her to answer to a council of men, the Watchers. Betty Rizzo, in "Male Oratory and Female Prate: 'Then Hush and Be an Angel Quite,'" explains, "Courtiers and domestic servants, women and children, working people, and subservients of every order were directed only to speak when spoken to" (23). The Slayer is the servant of the Watchers, who repeatedly try to dictate her actions and control her voice. The *Tento di Cruciamentum*, the "test" that Buffy is given by the council when she turns 18 in "Helpless," removes her Slayer powers so that she can fight a battle against a vampire, while powerless, in order to prove to the Council of Watchers that her resourcefulness and intelligence match her Slayer powers. Quentin Travers, the head of the Council, tells Buffy that she passed the test, but fires Giles as Buffy's Watcher because he helped her. The test reasserts the Council's authority over the Slayer, making her strength appear less hers and reducing her agency. At the end of the episode, Travers congratulates Buffy, and she replies with a caustic "Bite me." Her comment situates Travers on the side of the vampires and demons, the side of evil men. Buffy, even after having been reduced to a powerless tool of the Watchers, refuses to remain silent.

In her article, Betty Rizzo continues, "And as women's repression in general was contingent on their keeping silence, their speech became a forerunner of revolution" (24). From the first episode, "Welcome to the Hellmouth," Buffy's speech is revolutionary. She talks in slang, she and the soon-to-be Scoobies make up words, and their mode of speaking is infectious. She interrupts Giles and mocks him, undermining his speech with her own. When Giles tells her, "Because you are the Slayer. The one girl in all the world with the strength and skill to hunt the vampires..." Buffy interrupts him, saying, "and stop the spread of their evil blah blah blah, I've heard it, okay?" ("Welcome to the Hellmouth"). By the second episode, Giles breaks from his own speech patterns when Buffy interrupts him again when he begins to explain the role of the Slayer to the Willow and Xander. Abandoning his previous, formal speech, Giles instead says, "Alright. The Slayer hunts vampires, Buffy is a Slayer, don't tell anyone" ("The Harvest"). From the beginning of the series, Buffy is not afraid to speak, even if her identity and her actions are kept secret, private, and, in a sense, silenced.

The history of the Slayer is a history of silence. In "Restless," at the end of season four, Buffy meets the First Slayer in a dream. Buffy, the First Slayer, and Tara stand in the desert, and Buffy wonders why Tara is there. Tara says, "Someone has to speak for her." Buffy rejoins, "Let her speak for herself. That's what's done in polite circles." While partly dream speech, "polite circles" is also a nod to the rules and constraints of language and public speaking, both rhetorical rules and conduct manuals. The First Slayer has no delivery or speaking conventions because she has no place or space in which to speak, no stage, no parlor, no rhetorical location. She has no home. Her only space is the sacred space of the desert—a place of death. When Tara continues to speak for the First Slayer, Buffy insists that the First Slayer speak for herself. Tara replies, "I have no speech. No name. I live in the action of death, the blood cry, the penetrating wound. I am destruction. Absolute. Alone." The First Slayer is without speech, silent, and only able to talk through an intermediary. She tells Buffy, through Tara, that her purpose is to fight alone, that "the Slayer does not walk in this world." Buffy argues that she does, and she and the First Slayer fight, until Buffy wakes up. Before she wakes up, finally, Buffy stops being polite; she stops following the rules of civil conduct. She tells the First Slayer, "Are you quite finished?" when the First Slayer attempts to keep fighting. "You're really going to have to get over the whole primal power thing," Buffy says, no longer keeping her slang in check, before she goes on to criticize the First Slayer's hair.

In season seven, the season when Buffy first begins giving speeches, she opens the emergency Slayer kit in "Get It Done" and is transported to the past, to the Shadow Men who gave the First Slayer her powers, robbed her of speech, and silenced her in servitude. They chain Buffy to the ground and offer her more power in the form of another violation: a demon spirit forcing its way into her soul. When Buffy argues with them, one of the Shadow Men says, "The First Slayer did not talk so much." Eventually, Buffy breaks free from her chains and says to them "You think I came all this way to get knocked up by some demon dust? I can't fight this. I know that now. But you guys? You're just men. Just the men who did this to her. Whoever that girl was before she was the First Slayer.... You violated that girl, made her kill for you because you're weak, you're pathetic, and you obviously have nothing to show me." Buffy refuses to be silenced, and yet they silence her anyway, by showing her a vision of the Turok-Han in the Hellmouth, waiting for battle.

This conflict of speech and power is at the heart of season seven, which has the most speeches because it is the season that is most overtly feminist. Buffy declares war on the First Evil, a Big Bad whose only power is speech, who cannot touch, who cannot physically manifest, and who convinces Chloe, a Potential, to commit suicide merely by staying up all night and talking to her ("Get It Done"). The First Evil commands the hive-like Bringers, but cannot actually bring. The First can infuse Caleb with power, but cannot use that power itself ("End of Days"). The First's power is the first Power, the power of the word. The First can appear like anyone, can persuade with its appearance and speech, can be in any place, at any time, blurring the boundaries of public and private. The agents of the First, the Turok-Han and the Bringers, are all silent; the use of speech is reserved for the First, with the exception of Caleb. Caleb, the only man able to be the First's vessel, uses speech like weapon. In "Dirty Girls," the First, while reenacting Caleb's previous murders, tells him, "All these girls. They followed you willingly." Caleb replies, "I only told them the truth." The audience never finds out how many women Caleb has murdered, or how many Potentials the First manages to have killed before Buffy starts to train them. But Caleb, the Bringers, and the First attack and destroy women, specifically. And by killing women, they silence them.

Rizzo states, "Strictures against public speaking, which consistently indicated that speech was understood as power, were directed at women and at men of the lower social orders, in whom oratory was regarded as an unseemly distraction from their useful but silent vocations" (31). In "Lessons," the first episode of season seven, the First Evil gives a speech to Spike (and the viewing audience) while morphing into the Big Bads of all the previous seasons of *BtVS* in reverse order. At the conclusion of the speech, the First, as the Master, the most evil and effective orator, says, "It's not about right. It's not about wrong," before it transforms into Buffy and asserts, "It's about power." It is no accident that season seven has more speeches than any other season of *BtVS*. Public speaking *is* about power, and Buffy's subversion and assertion of rhetoric is her claim to power, and integral to her defeat of the First.

Buffy creates power by speaking in her home. Her speeches are made possible by her domesticity, her house, her family, her woman-ness. All those things typically disparaged as weak and female, Buffy uses to become strong, and to make other women strong.

The entire series of *Buffy the Vampire Slayer* leads up to this final battle for power, this battle between silence and speech, private and public. Throughout the series, regardless of what space she is in, Buffy is not afraid to speak, and to speak with her own voice. She delivers zingers when she slays. When she dies, Willow tries to program Buffybot to pun, unsuccessfully ("Bargaining, Part I"). Language is Buffy's playground. And she rebels against the slayer traditions, from firing the Watchers Council to rejecting the Shadow Men's offer of more power. She slays, and talks, her own way. But when she begins to deliver speeches, Buffy not only claims her right to oratory, she subverts the traditional oratorical tradition, effectively changing it.

The Parlor and the Grave

As women claimed the right to speak, they began to write about women's place in education and oratory. In *Strictures on the Modern System of Female Education*, Hannah More wrote, "A lady studies, not that she may qualify herself to become an orator, but to act" (qtd. in Rizzo 46). Up to this point, Buffy's actions have saved the world, again and again. Her own epitaph reads, "She saved the world. A Lot" ("The Gift"). But all of her actions have gone towards saving the world's status quo as well, and the world remained patriarchal, heteronormative, racially biased, and classist. It is not until Buffy begins delivering speeches that she is able to do more than merely save the world; she is able to change it.

In "Bring on the Night," Buffy gives a speech in her dining room, declaring war on the First Evil and calling the first arriving Potentials an army. Despite her defeat at the hands (or claws, rather) of the Turok-Han, she declares, "There's only one thing more powerful than evil. And that's us." This speech, delivered in her dining room, is important because Buffy has moved from privately speaking to publically orating. She has encroached into masculine territory yet again by engaging in "parlor rhetoric," and speaking to an audience composed primarily of women within her home (Johnson *Gender* 17). Rizzo discusses the power of speaking before an audience when she examines women's oratorical societies in the mid–1800s, saying, "And the female societies offered women not only a genuine opportunity to speak, but, more importantly ... a claim of a women's right to speak, a claim supported by the endorsement and applause of audiences" (43). In *BtVS*, the female society that gives her the right to speak, the platform to speak, and the audience to hear her words is the Potential Slayers.

The Potential Slayers do not have the powers of the Slayers, and they are frightened and intimidated by their weaker bodies, particularly once the Turok-Han begin to hunt them. Jordynn Jack points out, "One of the primary symbolic resources for masculine domination rests on the antithetical logics that continually figure men's bodies as strong and women's bodies as weak" (290). Buffy reverses this, having a stronger body than human men, and most demons, and she proves it in "Showtime" with a stunning display of visual rhetoric. She orates, to the Turok-Han, and her audience of Potentials "I always find a way. I'm the thing that monsters have nightmares about. And right now, you and me are gonna show 'em why. It's time. Welcome to Thunderdome," before she defeats the Turok-Han. In addition to being über-vamps, the Turok-Han are also über-masculine; all of the visual signifiers of gender for the Turok-Han indicate that they are male. After Buffy defeats one of the Turok-Han in "Showtime," she tells the Potentials, "See? Dust. Just like the rest of them. I don't know what's coming next, but I do know it's going to be just like this. Hard. Painful. But in the end it's going to be us. If we all do our parts, believe it, we'll be the ones left standing. Here endeth the lesson." Buffy's speech, part visual display, part spoken oration, is crucial because it also demonstrates her claim of rhetorical space. Elizabethada A. Wright, in "Rhetorical Spaces in Memorial Places: The Cemetery as a Rhetorical Memory Place/Space," states, "Women were allocated a domestic rhetorical space, men all other" (53). The construction site of the future library is neither. It is a liminal space, a partially built public space, neither domestic nor finished. Wright continues, "Not only must a rhetor choose the appropriate moment, but s/he must choose the appropriate place" (53). The choice of the appropriate place, and moment, is a key element of Buffy's speech in "Showtime." When we see that the fight and the speech have both been orchestrated for the Potentials, we see the telepathic discussion where Xander thinks, "I know just the place." The place is important because it allows for Buffy's visual argument, her defeat of the Turok-Han. As Wright states, "Rhetorical space, then, can deny truths by translating the truth's discourse into something more appropriate to the rhetorical space. Thus, in creating rhetoric, a rhetor must consider where the discourse is delivered as much as s/he must consider any other element of invention. Without the proper rhetorical space, all discourse can be moot" (53). The construction site of the library is as radically nontraditional as her living room, and, much like the construction of a library (where knowledge is power), Buffy is constructing her own rhetorical power.

Without the defeat of the Turok-Han, it does not matter what else Buffy says. Her delivery is what matters here, and her delivery is her battle with the Turok-Han.

In "Potential," she gives a speech about slaying to the Potentials in a crypt, another crucial, and surprisingly domestic, location for Buffy. As Buffy fights a vampire in the crypt, she delivers her speech with the same precision as her blows:

> The question is never "what do you think," it's always "what do you know?" You gotta know it. If you don't, if you make one mistake, it takes just one vampire to kill you. So you've got to know you can take him. Know your environment. Know what's around you, and know how to use it. In the hands of a slayer, everything is a potential weapon, if you know how to see it. When you're fighting, you have to know yourself, your brain, your body. Know how to stay calm, centered. Every move is important, every blow's got to be part of your plan 'cause you make that one mistake, and it's over. You're not the slayer. You're not a potential. You're dead. What do you know? Right now, the only thing you know for sure is you got me ["Potential"].

Then she and Spike close the doors of the crypt and leave the Potentials with the vampire, forcing them to fight the vampire on their own, in a crypt, in a cemetery. The location is crucial for this speech, because cemeteries are Buffy's bread and butter. The Potentials need to learn to use the power that one of them will inherit, but even without that power, they are not, as Buffy argues, helpless. They are still powerful even without Slayer powers, even without Buffy. Just because they are "only" women, does not mean they cannot fight.

The cemetery, the crypt, is a particularly significant location for this speech. As Elizabethada A. Wright argues, "the cemetery is able to act a public rhetorical space for those excluded from most other public rhetorical spaces, in particular women" (52). The cemetery, she claims, "is both unique and ordinary, and it is this paradox, the essence of a heterotopia, that makes the cemetery a particularly important rhetorical memory space" (Wright 52). Buffy is not speaking from a podium or stage, but she is not speaking from a construction site, either. She is no longer building her rhetoric power, but learning use it and make it her own. She is now in a liminal space, one that is already uniquely hers by virtue of being the Slayer. She patrols the cemetery regularly, she studies there for her SATs, she meets Angel there for ~~dates~~ patrolling. The cemetery is her home away from home.

However, like the home, the cemetery is a feminine space. Wright discusses the femininity of the cemetery and compares the rhetoric of the cemetery to the parlor rhetoric discussed by Nan Johnson:

> Because the cemetery is perceived as a symbolic space representing the ideals consistent with femininity, the memorial to Louisa Mills [whose grave became known as the Mill Girl Monument] is in an appropriate space. However, because the cemetery

> is a heterotopia—representing, contesting, and inverting—it can convey messages that contradi'ct the norms of femininity. In the cemetery, individual women—who achieved nothing' other than raising their families, building homes, doing daily chores, and helping to build a country—are remembered while they are forgotten in all other public memory spaces. Like the parlor that granted women's discourse legitimacy, the cemetery delivers the rhetorical goods, singing praises to many people, including women of all races and classe [Wright 56–57].

The cemetery, in other words, offers the same sort of rhetorical opportunity that the parlor does. Women can be women and speaking agents at the same time. For Buffy, the cemetery is another room in her house, a room of her own (quite literally, since in "The Weight of the World," her mother's grave is in a bedroom in her house). The cemetery is an extension of the home, of the domestic, in *BtVS*. The only time the First Slayer manages to speak is to tell Buffy, "Death is your gift" ("Intervention"). If death is her gift, then speech is her gift and rhetoric is her gift. Her cemetery occupation gives her the ability to widen the parlor's boundaries. The death of traditional oratory is what is at stake for Buffy's oratory. The First Slayer could not speak, but Buffy, with the power of all the women who came before her, has found her voice. And her voice is powerful. Consider, for example, "Hush," where a "scream from the princess" kills the Gentlemen. Shrieking rhetoric was disdained, and was yet another tactic used to keep women from speaking in public. But Buffy turns this around, saving Sunnydale from the Gentlemen not only through the power of her voice, but through the very qualities of her voice that traditional rhetoric attempted to feminize, vilify, and silence.

Buffy re-visions rhetorical spaces and delivery while speaking with a feminine *ethos* that the male orators in the Buffy-verse all lack. In "Storyteller," Andrew can only over-write Buffy's speech through the lens of the camera; he cannot overwrite her speech without his camera creating an entirely different frame for his narrative. His attempt to exclude Buffy's rhetoric fails, and demonstrates that Andrew is the one who is excluded from the domestic community that Buffy and the Potentials create. Although Andrew attempts to exclude Buffy's rhetorical space in the same way women's rhetorical spaces have historically been excluded, his use of a camera to exclude Buffy's rhetoric demonstrates that Andrew cannot participate (yet) in the rhetoric of the Buffy-verse, because Andrew speaks a fantasy rhetoric. He fantasizes about power through evil and being evil, glorifying himself and his own power. Evil is the only way he can see to access power; Andrew fancies himself an evil man, speaking well.

The space he attempts to overwrite is the kitchen, which is another significant domestic location. The kitchen is traditionally a female space, and while women have written about being captive in the kitchen, many other women found the kitchen to be a space of female empowerment. Angela

Meah, in "Reconceptualizing Power and Gendered Subjectivities in Domestic Cooking Spaces," writes, "Indeed, many of these women reported that appropriation of the kitchen provided them with a space through which they could express their identities and exercise agency within the survival politics of extended neighbourhood [sic] and kinship networks, particularly female in-laws" (676). Like the parlor and the cemetery, the kitchen is a space where women could speak, hear and be heard by other women.

None of Buffy's speeches occur in traditional rhetorical spaces. But because Buffy delivers her speeches in non-traditional rhetorical spaces, and spaces which are frequently traditionally associated with women or femininity, such as her living room, dining room, and kitchen, Buffy is able to speak. And she speaks well. Her voice is strong, well-sustained, and clearly projected. Her gestures and expressions are appropriate. Her posture is straight and determined. And her eye contact is unbreakable. Buffy's parlor rhetoric is what allows her to deliver her speeches in a way that it is impossible for her to be silenced or excluded. Buffy is able to speak because she creates a feminist rhetoric that alters traditional rhetorical models. It is no accident that her final speech in "Chosen" is delivered in her living room, the modern day parlor. In that speech, the culminating speech in *BtVS* that effectively sums up the series' progression, Buffy asks:

> So here's the part where you make a choice. What if you could have that power ... now? In every generation, one slayer is born ... because a bunch of men who died thousands of years ago made up that rule. They were powerful men. This woman [pointing at Willow] is more powerful than all of them combined. So I say we change the rule. I say my power ... should be our power. Tomorrow, Willow will use the essence of the scythe to change our destiny. From now on, every girl in the world who might be a slayer ... will be a slayer. Every girl who could have the power ... will have the power ... can stand up, will stand up. Slayers ... every one of us. Make your choice. Are you ready to be strong?

Buffy chooses her home as her rhetorical space, emphasizing that her rhetoric is a feminist, woman-centered rhetoric. She uses her domestic space as a point from which to create power and enter the rest of the world—much like men do. And she makes sure that other women are able to choose that power for themselves. Power, in *BtVS*, is not about disavowing one's femininity in order to enter masculine spaces. It is about claiming the power from feminine, domestic spaces, from things that have been deemed particularly female-centric, and using that power to subvert masculine spaces. Only orators who speak from domestic and feminine spaces are able to enact change in *BtVS*.

Cemeteries are the bridge between public and private spaces. They are spaces open to anyone, but the plots must be privately purchased. Gravestones and memorials are private expressions that are publicly available to view by anyone (Wright 61). And both men and women are memorialized, putting women's work and men's work on the same level (Wright 63). Cemeteries are an equalizer—for all of the attempts of cemeteries to marginalize the poor or the non-white, all subjects continue to be on display, together. The only way to truly exclude someone from the cemetery is not to bury them in it. When she tells Riley what a Slayer is, in "Doomed," Buffy explains, "I'm the Slayer. Slay-er. Chosen One. She-who-hangs-out-a-lot-in-cemeteries? You're kidding. Ask around. Look it up: Slayer, comma the." The cemetery is an integral part of who she is and what she does. For some, dying is also referred to as "going home," a trope that emphasizes the importance of home as a place of origin, of roots, of stepping-stones to the rest of the world. Buffy's gift is death, she herself has died twice, and she kills the undead. She is, in many ways, death to the dead, particularly when she wields her scythe, which contains the untapped power used to turn the Potentials to Slayers. Buffy has gone proverbially home, she sends demons "home" (which is probably less heavenly), and she shelters and provides headquarters to the Scoobies, and later the Potentials, in her literal home. Only those with the power of home, only women who speak from their roots, are able to use their rhetorical spaces to create a feminist rhetoric. Even the scythe, whose name is a sound, a glottal stop, which is used to end speech rather than create it, is a weapon used for silencing the demons around her. Traditional rhetoric is demonized in the Buffy-verse; Buffy changes the world through her creation of a feminist rhetoric into a place where women have the power to stand up and speak.

Conclusion

In *Our Beacon Light, Devoted to Employment, Education, and Society* (1889), B.R. Cowen proclaims, "It is as a mother that woman's most signal triumphs are achieved. The home is her kingdom, the domain of her greatest and most lasting influence" (qtd. in Johnson "Reigning" 225). For Buffy, this is true. Her greatest triumph is as the mother to all the Potentials, the Slayer from which all other Slayers are born. In a subversively feminist parenthood, Buffy and Willow, together, using the powers of the Slayer and the magic of witchcraft, give birth to the Slayers, who are no longer Chosen, but who are Choosers, agents in their ability to be strong. Cowen's conduct manuals make the argument that "any seeds of influence women plant had best be sown close to home" (Johnson "Reigning" 231). Buffy draws her powers of speech from her home, using those powers to persuade within her home. She turns rhetoric upside, and subverts the rhetorical tradition by redefining it.

In "Remapping Rhetorical Territory," Cheryl Glenn argues that in order to effectively construct a history of rhetoric that includes marginalized subjects, such as women, we must also re-conceive rhetoric itself. It is not enough, she claims, to re-situate women within a rhetoric that is a masculine construction; we must also re-conceptualize what rhetoric is and what rhetoric means (293–294). Simply including marginalized subjects into the dominant discourse fails to question the discourse itself, whereas an effective re-mapping shakes the dominant conception of rhetoric and the historical map of rhetoric (294). In other words, rhetoric needs to be redefined to include the ways in which marginalized subjects speak, in their own voices, and in their own words. Jordynn Jack, in "Acts of Institution: Embodying Feminist Rhetorical Methodologies in Space and Time," states, "Just as women rhetors have had to reinvent rhetorical strategies in order to speak effectively, feminist rhetoricians have had to reinvent rhetorical methodologies in order to research nontraditional subjects" (287). *Buffy the Vampire Slayer* is important as a rhetorical text because it remaps rhetoric, creating a universe where men who speak well, within the masculine oratorical tradition that excluded women, are evil and demonic. Speakers who speak outside of the "normal," masculine rhetorical paradigm, speakers entrenched in domesticity and feminine spaces, not only have the ability to speak, they have the choice to speak, and that choice grants them agency and power.

Domestic space is the only viable oratorical space available in the Buffyverse; speaking anywhere else, using traditional, masculine delivery, leads to permanent death. Johnson points out, "conduct manuals told women again and again that their voices were powerful ones only in the home" (Johnson 225), and this is true in the Buffy-verse, where only by speaking in the home, by using her female, domestic, rhetorical space, is Buffy able to change the world. Domestic space, feminine space, is chosen in *BtVS* for its power of feministic rhetoric. Women choose rhetoric, they choose power, and they choose to be strong. Speech *is* power, as season seven makes clear, and Buffy uses this power to break apart gender roles. She gives women not just power of their own, but the *choice* to have their power, markedly unlike the First Slayer, who was silenced by the power that was forced upon her and turned into a subservient tool to the Shadow Men and Watchers. No longer a silent Slayer, Buffy becomes the ultimate master, the master of rhetoric, using the power of her language, grounded in the power of her home, to change the world.

Works Cited

Aristotle. *On Rhetoric: A Theory of Civic Discourse*. Trans. George A. Kennedy. Oxford: Oxford University Press, 1991. Print.
"Bargaining, Part I." *Buffy the Vampire Slayer: The Complete Sixth Season*. Episode 1. Writ. Marti Noxon. Dir. David Grossman. UPN. 2 Oct. 2001. Twentieth Century Fox, 2004. DVD.
"Bring on the Night." *Buffy the Vampire Slayer: The Complete Seventh Season*. Episode 10. Writ. Marti Noxon and Douglas Petrie. Dir. David Grossman. UPN. 17 Dec. 2002. Twentieth Century Fox, 2004. DVD.

Calboli, Guiltiero, and William J. Dominik. "Introduction: The Roman *Suada*." *Roman Eloquence: Rhetoric in Society and Literature*. Ed. William J. Dominik. London: Routledge, 1997. Web. 4 May 2016.

"Chosen." *Buffy the Vampire Slayer: The Complete Seventh Season*. Episode 22. Writ. and Dir. Joss Whedon. UPN. 20 May 2003. Twentieth Century Fox, 2004. DVD.

Cicero. *On the Ideal Orator (De Oratore)*. Trans. James M. and Jakob Wisse May. New York: Oxford University Press, 2001. Print.

"Dirty Girls." *Buffy the Vampire Slayer: The Complete Seventh Season*. Episode 18. Writ. Drew Goddard. Dir. David Solomon. UPN. 15 Apr 2003. Twentieth Century Fox, 2004. DVD.

"Doomed." *Buffy the Vampire Slayer: The Complete Fourth Season*. Episode 11. Writ. Marti Noxon, David Fury, and Jane Espenson. Dir. James A. Contner. The WB. 18 Jan. 2000. Twentieth Century Fox, 2003. DVD.

"Empty Places." *Buffy the Vampire Slayer: The Complete Seventh Season*. Episode 19. Writ. Drew Z. Greenberg. Dir. James A. Contner. UPN. 29 Apr 2003. Twentieth Century Fox, 2004. DVD.

"End of Days." *Buffy the Vampire Slayer: The Complete Seventh Season*. Episode 21. Writ. Douglas Petrie and Jane Espenson. Dir. Marita Grabiak. UPN. 13 May 2003. Twentieth Century Fox, 2004. DVD.

"Entropy." *Buffy the Vampire Slayer: The Complete Sixth Season*. Episode 18. Writ. Drew Z. Greenberg. Dir. James A. Contner. UPN. 30, April 2002. Twentieth Century Fox, 2004. DVD.

Fraschetti, Augusto." Livia the Politician." *Roman Women*. Ed. Augusto Fraschetti. Trans. Linda Lappin. Chicago: University of Chicago Press, 2001. Print.

"Get It Done." *Buffy the Vampire Slayer: The Complete Seventh Season*. Episode 15. Writ. and Dir. Douglas Petrie. UPN. 18 Feb. 2003. Twentieth Century Fox, 2004. DVD.

"The Gift." *Buffy the Vampire Slayer: The Complete Fifth Season*. Episode 22. Writ. and Dir. Joss Whedon. The WB. 22 May 2001. Twentieth Century Fox, 2003. DVD.

Glenn, Cheryl. "Remapping Rhetorical Territory." *Rhetoric Review* 13.2 (1995): 287–303. Web. 4 May 2016.

"Graduation Day, Part II." *Buffy the Vampire Slayer: The Complete Third Season*. Episode 22. Writ. and Dir. Joss Whedon. The WB. 13 July 1999. Twentieth Century Fox, 2003. DVD.

"The Harvest." *Buffy the Vampire Slayer: The Complete First Season*. Episode 2. Writ. Joss Whedon. Dir. John T. Kretchmer. The WB. 10 March 1997. Twentieth Century Fox, 2002. DVD.

"Helpless." *Buffy the Vampire Slayer: The Complete Third Season*. Episode 12. Writ. David Fury. Dir. James A. Contner. The WB. 19 Jan. 1999. Twentieth Century Fox, 2003. DVD.

"Hush." *Buffy the Vampire Slayer: The Complete Fourth Season*. Episode 10. Writ. and Dir. Joss Whedon. The WB. 14 Dec. 1999. Twentieth Century Fox, 2003. DVD.

"Intervention." *Buffy the Vampire Slayer: The Complete Fifth Season*. Episode 18. Writ. Jane Espenson. Dir. Michael Gershman. The WB. 24 April 2001. Twentieth Century Fox, 2003. DVD.

Jack, Jordynn." Acts of Institution: Embodying Feminist Rhetorical Methodologies in Space and Time." *Rhetoric Review* 28.3 (2009): 285–303. Web. 4 May 2016.

Johnson, Nan. *Gender and Rhetorical Space in American Life, 1866–1910*. Carbondale: Southern Illinois University Press, 2002. Print.

_____. "Reigning in the Court of Silence: Women and Rhetorical Space in Postbellum America." *Philosophy and Rhetoric* 33.3 (2000): 221–242. Web. 4 May 2016.

Lefkowitz, Mary R., and Maureen B. Fant. *Women's Life in Greece and Rome*. Baltimore: Johns Hopkins University Press, 1982. Print.

"Lessons." *Buffy the Vampire Slayer: The Complete Seventh Season*. Episode 1. Writ. Joss Whedon. Dir. David Solomon. UPN. 24 Sept. 2002. Twentieth Century, 2004. DVD.

"Life Serial." *Buffy the Vampire Slayer: The Complete Sixth Season*. Episode 5. Writ. David Fury and Jane Espenson. Dir. Nick Marck. UPN. 23 Oct. 2001. Twentieth Century Fox, 2004. DVD.

Meah, Angela. "Reconceptualizing Power and Gendered Subjectivities in Domestic Cooking Spaces." *Progress in Human Geography* 38.5 (2014): 671–690. Web. 4 May 2016.

"Potential." *Buffy the Vampire Slayer: The Complete Seventh Season.* Episode 12. Writ. Rebecca Rand Kirshner. Dir. James A. Contner. UPN. 21 Jan. 2003. Twentieth Century Fox, 2004. DVD.
"The Prom." *Buffy the Vampire Slayer: The Complete Third Season.* Episode 20. Writ. Marti Noxon. Dir. David Solomon. The WB. 11 May 1999. Twentieth Century Fox, 2003. DVD.
Quintilian. *On the Teaching and Speaking of Writing.* Ed. James J. Murphy. Carbondale: Southern Illinois University Press, 1987. Print.
_____. *The Orator's Education: Books 1-2.* Vol. 1. Trans. Donald A. Russell. Loeb Classical Library. Ed. Jeffrey Henderson. Cambridge: Harvard University Press, 2001. Print.
_____. *The Orator's Education: Books 11-12.* Vol. 5. Trans. Donald A. Russell. Loeb Classical Library. Ed. Jeffrey Henderson. Cambridge: Harvard University Press, 2001. Print.
"Restless." *Buffy the Vampire Slayer: The Complete Fourth Season.* Episode 22. Writ. and Dir. Joss Whedon. The WB. 23 May 2000. Twentieth Century Fox, 2003. DVD.
Rizzo, Betty. "Male Oratory and Female Prate: 'Then Hush and Be an Angel Quite.'" *Eighteenth-Century Life* 29.1 (2005): 23-49. Web. 4 May 2016.
"Showtime." *Buffy the Vampire Slayer: The Complete Seventh Season.* Episode 11. Writ. David Fury. Dir. Michael Grossman. UPN. 7 Jan. 2003. Twentieth Century, 2004. DVD.
"Storyteller." *Buffy the Vampire Slayer: The Complete Seventh Season.* Episode 16. Writ. Jane Espenson. Dir. Marita Grabiak. UPN. 25 Feb. 2003. Twentieth Century Fox, 2004. DVD.
Unknown. [Cicero]. *Rhetorica Ad Herennium.* Trans. Harry Caplan. Loeb Classical Library. Ed. Jeffrey Henderson. Cambridge: Harvard University Press, 2004. Print.
"The Weight of the World." *Buffy the Vampire Slayer: The Complete Fifth Season.* Episode 21. Writ. Douglas Petrie. Dir. David Solomon. The WB. 15 May 2001. Twentieth Century Fox, 2003. DVD.
"Welcome to the Hellmouth." *Buffy the Vampire Slayer: The Complete First Season.* Episode 1. Writ. Joss Whedon. Dir. Charles Martin Smith. The WB. 10 March 1997. Twentieth Century Fox, 2002. DVD.
"The Wish." *Buffy the Vampire Slayer: The Complete Third Season.* Episode 9. Writ. Marti Noxon. Dir. David Greenwalt. The WB. 8 Dec. 1998. Twentieth Century Fox, 2003. DVD.
Wright, Elizabethada A." Rhetorical Spaces in Memorial Places: The Cemetery as a Rhetorical Memory Place/Space." *Rhetoric Society Quarterly* 35.4 (2005): 51-81. Web. 4 May 2016.

Militarization of the Domestic Space
Positioning Buffy as a Post-Feminist Heroine through the Lens of Choice Feminism

Karen Walsh

Buffy's struggle to balance slaying, paid work, and personal life as a woman in her early 20s parallels the post-feminist woman's desire to "lean in" or, at the very best, the struggle it takes to maintain all three. In the Buffy-verse, space, particularly the domestic space, often defines femininity. In the first season of the television show, Buffy's traditional femininity is most often enacted in the private, domestic spaces. In public spaces, and particularly in public government-owned spaces, she performs her Slayer-self. In this manner, the narrative through most of *Buffy the Vampire Slayer*'s televised series (1997–2003) is one that separates both her personal and professional selves. This narrative is one that tracks the first and second waves of feminism in which women focused predominantly on their rights to perform in the public space. The comics, particularly seasons nine and ten, however, showcase an increased use of the domestic space as a base of militarized Slayer operations. This evolution of the domestic space mirrors the third wave, or post-feminist, narrative that women can "have it all." The post-feminist narrative increasingly focuses on the integration of personal and professional, or in Buffy's case family, romance, and Slayage. As such, the use of the domestic space cannot be separated from Buffy's journey as a post-feminist heroine.

Increased militarization of Buffy's domestic space parallels the post-feminist narrative that women working from home balances professional, parental, and personal duties thereby creating the myth of "having it all."

Stephanie Genz in her article "Singled Out: Postfeminism's 'New Woman' and the Dilemma of Having It All" defines the post-feminist woman (PFW) as having "been the subject of considerable debate and ... described as an antifeminist backlasher, a sexually assertive 'do-me feminist,' a prowoman pseudo-feminist and a feminine Girlie feminist" (98). Buffy's representation in seasons nine and ten places her firmly within this post-feminist narrative by defining her Slayer and romantic journeys through her choices. These choices do not occur in a vacuum. They are made in various spaces. Therefore, space, both public and domestic, impacts how Buffy is crafted into a post-feminist heroine.

The militarization of the domestic space redefined Buffy's post-feminist experience. The use of space in *BtVS* tracks Buffy's maturity and feminist journey. As Buffy becomes more comfortable with her ability to co-negotiate the personal and the professional (i.e., "having it all"), she incorporates military planning into the home, the Buffyverse equivalent of working from home like non–Slayer post-feminists. The evolving militarization of the domestic space in seasons nine and ten hybridize the home into a personal and professional space paralleling Buffy's choices to identify with her leadership and nurturing roles placing the domestic space as an important component in Buffy's post-feminist narrative.

The Demilitarized Home: Neo-Domesticity and Buffy the Unsatisfied Post-Feminist Heroine

The post–Seed narratives of seasons nine and ten transition Buffy's domestic space into a hybrid personal/professional space through increased militarization of the domestic space that comes with a sense of confusion and chaos symbolizing the post-feminist experience. The segregation of slayage and private life in early season nine creates a sense of chaos and shows how Buffy's life lacks balance. This dichotomy of space reflects the dichotomy of self that Buffy experiences. Therefore, the spatial distinction shows Buffy's struggle as a post-feminist heroine to redefine herself in a new world. In much the same way, the post-feminist narratives in society and literature also surround the need to redefine what feminism means.

Recent research documenting the post-feminist narrative incorporates discussion of socio-normative changes leading to a sense of chaos and confusion. In the context of the Buffyverse, season seven's "Chosen" creates a structural change in the Slayer mythos but does not rewrite the feminist storyline to address the post-feminist narratives. Buffy tells the Potentials, "So here's the part where you make a choice. What if you could have that power? In every generation, one Slayer is born because a bunch of men who died thousands of years ago made up that rule ... so I say we change the rule. I say my power be should be our power" (Whedon). As with much of television-era Buffy, this speech is about the traditional second-wave feminism in which women retake power from men to make it their own. Therefore, the domestic space in which Buffy delivers this speech fits the second-wave feminist narrative of using the domestic space as a seat of power to overcome a male dominated world.

The destruction of magic arising out of the Twilight narrative in season eight, however, forces a seismic shift in the overall socio-normative structure. Erasing magic repositions it outside its traditional patriarchal history meaning that Buffy has to work within a new power structure. Instead of the pre-defined norm of being "the only girl in the all the world to fight" the vampires who can only walk the world at night, she is now one of many who are forced to fight zompires who survive daylight. Similarly, the domestic space which had previously been militarized is now split. In the same way, Buffy is split. Without magic and without the responsibility of being the sole Slayer, she begins to negotiate her new role within the Buffyverse. She attempts to return to the old model of separating personal and professional which causes a sense of dichotomized self and space. In "Individualized Femininity and Feminist Politics of Choice," Shelley Budgeon references Beck and Beck-Gernsheim's 2002 writings: "Theorists who have developed the reflexive modernization thesis assert that during the latter part of the 20th century structural changes in key sectors of society, including the family, education and work, and the legal system, significantly altered norms circumscribing femininity" (310). Buffy's continued split between her personal life and professional life represents this reflexive nature. Buffy attempts to work within public or quasi-public slayage groups, such as Kennedy's security group Deepscan. However, she has a hard time both working within the external world's new framework and recognizing that, in a world without magic, she and the demons are equally trapped. For this reason, she finds it hard to work for Deepscan and in the end walks away from the public slaying sphere. This sense of chaos and confusion regarding her role as a Slayer, which replicates her role as a young woman in society, begins to shift the focus of her slaying activities towards her domestic space.

Simultaneously, as Buffy attempts to find her way through this new chaotic world without magic, she also longs for the same hetero-normative home and boyfriend for which other post-feminist heroines search. In many ways, therefore, Buffy can be analogized to other traditionally "chick lit" heroines such as Bridget Jones or popular television shows of the same era such as *Ally McBeal*. Genz's discusses the "friction between Bridget's ideal, balanced persona and her chaotic, genuine self, depicting the singleton's journey through self-doubt to the understanding that 'realness' is the only guarantee for happiness" (114). In season nine, Buffy faces both external and internal dilemmas that lead to her self-doubt which are represented by the space in which they occur. In the same way that Buffy has been heralded as a "strong feminist character," she has equally been created in the mold of the traditional stereotype of the "dumb blonde" interested in only clothes and boys. As Buffy has matured, however, this post-feminist narrative matches Alison Horbury's discussion of Ally McBeal in her book *Post-feminist Impasses in Popular Heroine Television: The Persephone Complex*. Horbury incorporates the works of Mosely and Read, Heywood, McRobbie, and Gorton, writing:

> [Ally] is unapologetically preoccupied with "feminine" pursuits such as love, romance, gossip and obsessive concerns about how to catch a husband ... she uses her emotions to confront problems in the workplace ... and she frequently mirror gazes obsessing over her bodily attributes as they signify her feminine identity. Ally nevertheless embodies feminist achievements: she is Ivy League educated, employed in what was traditionally a male dominated professions, is financially independent, and enjoys a liberal sexual life [47–48].

Buffy continues this tradition by negotiating her personal desires of achieving a heterosexual relationship and being a leader in an otherwise male-dominated slaying "business." Buffy has been characterized as a girl interested in the mundane intricacies of femininity such as clothes and hair while also being a woman who can lead others and accept responsibility. Moreover, Buffy's domestic space is one in which she is unable to own her slayerness. She faces roommates unsure of whether to evict her for her slaying which reinforces her fear of being able to incorporate a personal and work life in a meaningful way. The traditional, non-militarized domestic space here represents Buffy's internal chaos in dealing with the unknown. Home should be a place of comfort, but for Buffy, it is a place where she needs to hide her truest self.

Moreover, a new type of vampire, a "zompire" that is stronger and more feral than those prior to the loss of magic, redefines Buffy's literal battle strategies. These changes lead to an external and existential chaos that impacts her sense of confidence. At the end of "Freefall" and into the beginning of "On Your Own," Buffy takes a pregnancy test and needs to determine whether to keep a baby or have an abortion ("Freefall" #3, "Slayer, Interrupted," "On Your Own, Part One"). During this emotional chaos, Buffy also learns that Spike is still in love with her. At this point during "On Your Own, Part One," she tells him, "You know I'm terrible at everything that doesn't involve slaying. I'm not well rounded. I have lots of corners. And most of them are pointy" (Chambliss 48/4–52). Buffy's self-doubt regarding her ability to control her personal life parallels the post-feminist struggle. However, her domestic and public space dichotomy represents Buffy feelings of being incapable of successfully incorporating an external and internal life. Buffy's inability to be well-rounded and her assertion of pointy corners, evoking her adeptness at staking vampires, incorporates within her narrative the sense of one dimensionality so often associated with the segregation of the public and private spaces.

For Buffy, the domestic space acts as a metaphor for the struggle between Buffy's two identities. In "Apart (of Me), Part One," Spike notes to what appears to be an intoxicated Buffy, "You're a god-awful mess, Slayer, in more ways than one—but may you feel no pain til morn" (Chambliss 62/1). This sense of bemusement and adoration shows that he loves her despite—or even because—of her messy, chaotic self. In much the same way, Genz notes, "Negotiating the conflicting demands of heterosexual romance and professional achievement, feminine embodiment and feminist agency, the postfeminist singleton occupies a multivalent and paradoxical space between dualities as she creates a new subjective stance that complicates female identity rather than defining it" (115). In "Freefall," Buffy's roommates are not officially aware of her slaying activities. As such, her professional achievements are not incorporated into this space. In the scene in which Spike calls her a mess, she is hosting a party at her new apartment. This duality leads to both duplicity and confusion. Similar to the early seasons of *BtVS*, Buffy finds herself concealing her Slayer self from the people with whom she lives evidenced by her roommates learning about her Slayer identity from the news in "Freefall, Part Three" (Chambliss 91/1–4). The segregation of personal and professional, represented by the domestic and public spaces, complicates her ability to create a united identity for herself. Therefore, until she can incorporate the slaying activities into the domestic space, she inhabits a partitioned, chaotic identity.

This chaotic struggle within the hetero-normative tradition continues through the Buffybot narrative wherein Buffy's body is safely placed in a neodomestic narrative while her mind remains in a robot. The search for her authentic self becomes the focus of "Apart (of Me)" (#8–10). Buffy's conflicted desires embody much of Lauren Gillingham's discussion of neodomesticity in her article "Of Bombs, Baking and Blahniks," where she writes,

> Currently feminism's privileged sign of apocalyptic decline, neodomesticity serves as the locus of much handwringing about the demise of feminist struggle in the early twenty-first century. The idea that women today might return to the very home that our foremothers worked so hard to spring us from appears, to some, an unmitigated betrayal. From the perspective of apocalyptic theories of feminist history, domesticity functions as the always reliable index of women's oppression [26].

Buffy's inability to reconcile her "strong female character," defined by physical strength and low emotional quotient, with her desire to be living the traditional idyllic existence causes most of the narrative conflict. Her desire for the traditional domestic space therefore represents the chaotic struggle of straddling two identities. The domestic space and longing for the traditional, upper-middle class suburban domestic space acts as an allegory for Buffy's desire to be a whole *self*.

The domestic spatial representation of this disconnect between traditional and post-modern feminism is clearest in the textual and artistic narratives of "On Your Own, Parts One-Two." When BuffyBot Buffy (Buffy's mind trapped in the robot self) sees BodyBuffy (Buffy's body with an Andrew induced brain), her mind admits a sense of astonishment. Despite admitting that this would not be her ideal, she acknowledges in "Apart (of Me), Part One," "My kitchen is awesome" (Chambliss 74/1). Fellow Slayer Simone, on the following page of the same arc, incorporates the post-feminist tension of the neo-domestic narrative saying, "I'm gonna liberate you from this Betty Crocker bull$%$@" (76/3). This dichotomous approach to neo-domesticity continues in "Apart (of Me), Part Two" when Buffy tells Spike that "he [Andrew] gave me the kind of life I couldn't create myself" (Chambliss and Allie 81/3), while on the next page Simone screams at Buffy, "You gave it all up to be a yuppie hausfrau. Disgusting" (82/4). Despite both characters rejecting neo-domesticity, Buffy's is a bittersweet, personal choice while Simone's is a generalized disdain. Simone's vitriol regarding the domestic space and what it embodies evokes the sense of traditional feminism's fight against the larger external patriarchal society. Buffy's rejection of the space comes with a sense of wanting to incorporate both the domestic as well as the professional into her life but feeling that this is impossible. The story of "On Your Own" narratively acts as a discourse on the tensions within feminism's divergent views of domesticity and the domestic space. Since Buffy continues to find her domestic and militarized selves as separate entities that must be enacted in separate spaces, she is unable to engage in unified sense of self and stays in a chaotic limbo.

The visual narratives provide greater insight into Buffy's internal chaos and highlights the feminist tensions that neo-domesticity and the domestic space represent. "On Your Own" visually focuses on the domestic space, which foreshadows their increasing militarization. In "Apart (of Me), Part One," BodyBuffy accidentally snaps a wooden spoon in half while mixing batter (Chambliss 67/1-2). In the next panel, she holds the broken handle like a stake, continuing the narrative that Buffy cannot escape slaying or the militarization of her domestic spaces. The juxtaposition of the weaponization of the spoon in the suburban domestic space parallels the juxtaposition of Buffy's feminine and fighter identities making the home a metaphor.

After finding out that her body and brain have been separated, BuffyBot moves into Spike's bug spaceship to protect the fragile robot exterior housing her brain. The private spaces of the bug spaceship and the upper-middle class suburban kitchen further the parallel of space and self. This inability to separate the home from the war is perfectly encapsulated by two panels in "Apart (of Me), Part One" (Allie and Chambliss 73/4–5). The top panel shows Body-Buffy living the "normal" domestic life while the bottom panel shows the Buffybot on Spike's spaceship. Despite the private nature of the spaceship, it is not a traditional "domestic space." After all, it is a spaceship filled with gigantic talking bugs. The top image is larger than the bottom, giving it physical prominence, and pictures Buffy wearing an apron and oven mitts while placing a baking pan in the oven. This represents the normal that Buffy has been seeking since she was Chosen. The complex composition of the visual text with its contrasting colors and textures furthers the sense of cognitive tension and chaos.

The visual prominence of the suburban home setting indicates domestic space's importance to Buffy's desired sense of identity. The fact that her whole body is showcased not only highlights the part of BodyBuffy that is living this life but unifies the image and gives a sense of the whole person. The bottom image, representing where Buffy's mind is, shows only her head. The faded colors of the domestic space's image indicate Buffy's inability to attain this domestic dream. Moreover, the contrast with the BuffyBot's disappointed, sad look gives the visual narrative that while Buffy may want this idyllic lifestyle, her domestic space will never be this socio-normative. These contrasts both in space and in visual representation of the spaces and characters parallel the inner sense of chaos Buffy feels. The post-feminist narrative of choice revolves around incorporating Buffy's full self into the domestic space. As the BuffyBot bemoans in "Apart (of Me), Part Three," "I'll never have a life like that" BodyBuffy reassures her, "You will have it someday. But it won't mean anything unless you get it for yourself" (Chambliss and Allie 123/4–6). This positions the segregation of the domestic space from Buffy's slaying in the first arc of season nine as representative of the importance of choice as the way from chaos to order in the post-feminist narrative. When Buffy can choose where and how to enact her Slayer-self, she militarizes the domestic space. In unifying these two senses of self, she brings order to the chaos of her life. Therefore, the domestic space becomes representative of Buffy's post-feminist journey.

The Evolution of Buffy, the Post-Feminist Heroine: The Hybridization of the Domestic and Public Space

Buffy's lack of designated domestic space to engage in personal and slaying conversations demonstrates how space continues to represent Buffy's post-feminist evolution. Once Buffy finally accepts her identity as The Slayer, she begins to not only accept that her version of domesticity will be militarized, but she also begins to use that space for private conversations. The ownership of the domestic space incorporates her "work" and her "personal." Budgeon explains this framing of choice: "By positively evaluating women's choices as evidence of women's exercise of freedom the troubled relationship between femininity and feminism is seemingly resolved. Feminist dis-identification allows women to practice femininity according to the logic of postfeminism, that is, as the product of individually empowered choice guided by an ethic of self-fulfilment" (306). Post-feminist discourse focuses on choice in order to incorporate women's varying lifestyles. Buffy's choices, in terms of her ability to coordinate her personal and professional lives, inherently rely on this feminist narrative. Her choice to identify as a Slayer, after working with Kennedy's Deepscan and rejecting the private contractor life, means that she begins to incorporate her home into that sense of identity. Although in "Welcome to the Team, Part Four" her roommates know that she is the Slayer, she feels forced to sneak Koh and Illryia into the house telling them, "Sorry, the roomies don't like me to bring my work home" (Chambliss 86/3). Sneaking through the window like a teenager undermines her ownership of the domestic space and therefore indicates a continued sense of nomadic chaos. Only when she finally matures as an independent Slayer-woman will she be able to fully militarize her domestic space and choose to incorporate her whole self into her living space.

The transition from the quasi-public space to a Scooby-controlled domestic space occurs in the final arc of season nine, "The Core." This transition begins to normalize the otherwise disjunct and chaotic use of space that has come to represent Buffy's lack of cohesive post-feminist identity. "The Core" begins in Andrew's apartment with the original Scoobies working together and bringing out the book, *Vampyr*, for the first time since Giles' death. Despite moving into a private space controlled by a Scooby, similar to the shared apartment building in season ten, Buffy has not claimed a domestic space as her own, signifying an incomplete transition to full maturity. With Dawn in danger (must be Tuesday) because of Buffy's decision to destroy the Seed of Wonder (from now on referred to as "The Seed") that animates the Key, the Slayer embraces the post-feminist opportunity that she was not given earlier. Unlike season five, when her desire to save Dawn is intertwined with her responsibilities to the save the world, her focus here is on saving her sister, with the re-magickification of the world a possible bonus. Instead of choosing her professional Slayer life over family (or in conjunction with family), Buffy tells D'Hoffryn, in "The Core, Part Three," "Sorry, my sister comes first. I'll help if I can, but I'm sure you'll manage without me. My sister won't" (Cambliss 60/3). This final shift signifies maturity for Buffy in negotiating the hybridized life of the post-feminist woman. Moreover, the rebirth of magic that occurs at the end of season nine sets the stage for the normative changes that occur in season ten, changes that will allow Buffy to fully incorporate her multivaried identities. Buffy's re-evaluation of her purpose in the midst of this chaotic socio-normative shift symbolizes feminism's shift from its traditional second wave into choice. Buffy's choices, therefore, define both her actions and her spaces. The majority of season nine places Buffy in the public realm. Although her roommates accept her abilities, her apartment is not her base of operations. As such, her inability to militarize her domestic space suggests that she continues to engage in a bifurcated sense of self. Once again, space becomes the visual cue to Buffy's sense of owning her own postfeminist narrative. The lack of home base for Buffy leaves her ungrounded despite her confidence in her choices. Season ten, however, moves this narrative forward by incorporating a new living situation as well as by using that domestic space to embody Buffy's new sense of cohesion between her Slayer self and her private self.

Socio-Normative Shifts in the Buffyverse: The Militarized Domestic Space as a Metaphor for the Lean-In Movement

The socionormative shift caused by the blank *Vampyr* book in season ten engages post-feminist narratives of grassroots mobilization and choice as the Scoobies militarize their shared domestic space which redefine the role of the home in the Buffyverse. The Buffyverse created its own socionormative behaviors as part of its mythos. Therefore, when discussing socionormative shifts within the Buffyverse, "socio-normative" refers to norms accepted within the Buffyverse. For the twenty-four years since the *BtVS* movie, Buffy has lived in a mythology of norms involving vampires who burn in sunlight and a *Vampyr* book that sets the rules of magic. Most important in terms of socio-normative shifts within the Buffyverse is the evolution of the Slayer essence. Traditionally viewed as a feminine force, the essence of the Slayer, the power itself, enacts choice now that it is no longer bound by the former conditions. In "New Rules, Part Two," Giles reads the *Vampyr* book change:

> "No longer is but one chosen. The power *itself* becomes the chosen one.... And the one who chooses." The implication is that the combined spiritual force of all past slayers, most often embodied in visions by the primitive—has more agency than it once did. Men still cannot be slayers outright. Billy does not share your strength or speed. But the essence of the slayers has clearly accepted him as an ally [Gage 40/4].

This change embodies the evolution of feminism itself through the discussion of choice. No longer bound by patriarchal rules of magic, it has a greater power to choose. Instead of being focused in a single person, defined and guided by men, the Slayer essence, similar to other post-feminist narratives, now chooses to whom it grants power whether that be Slayer or ally. Anita Harris, in "Mind the Gap," explains the importance of this socionormative shift within the Buffyverse:

> Importantly, however, all of these activities have strong continuities with earlier feminist political traditions, practices and performances, even while they are enacted under new social conditions. Individual and grassroots practices have come to the fore in times when public spaces for connection and action have diminished and young women are increasingly obliged to take personal responsibility for their own choices and life chances [478].

The Slayer essence is a metaphor for these types of choice narratives. By choosing the Slayers and their allies, the essence acts upon individuals from within, giving them a sense of purpose, which then creates a grassroots movement of empowerment. Without the historical *Vampyr* book, the lack of regulated patriarchal authority creates a power structure that focuses less on the external forces dictating and more on the internal forces choosing. By rewriting the very essence of the Slayer mythology, season ten represents a major shift similar to those seen in modern day feminist narratives. The use of space, particularly the dichotomy of public versus domestic, then becomes more integral to understanding how the recent narratives use the home as a metaphor. The militarized domestic space as a post-feminist space, therefore, represents Buffy's wholeness within this new social norm in the same way that post-feminist women can choose to work from home as a consequence of the technological changes that create remote work opportunities.

Initially, season ten narratively echoes the chaos of space and society from earlier seasons. The spaces in which Buffy's post-feminist interactions occur illustrate her negotiation of the new norms created. Season ten immediately tackles the socio-normative shift that bringing magic back to the world caused. Unlike season nine, which began to hint at the Slayer being outdated, the erasure of the *Vampyr* lore forces a matured Buffy to reinvent herself and her role. The role of Slayer, much like that of feminism, is no longer viewed as obsolete. Gillingham, addressing this notion of outdated feminism, claims, "By focusing on feminism in the present as 'failed,' 'exhausted,' or 'obsolete,' then, we refuse to recognize that women's political needs of the present and future may not resemble or even coincide with those of the second wave, which defined itself largely through the construction and deployment of an activist female subjectivity" (24). Seeing feminism, or its Buffyverse representative the Slayer, as outdated ignores the ability of these responsive institutions to evolve. In season ten, this youthful swagger is represented by Vicki the Vampire, an external force who, by virtue of being a vampire, is specifically excluded from the notion of the home unless specifically invited. During their first battle in "New Rules, Part Two," Vicki brags, "News flash. It's never going your way again. You're the past. We're the future. Lucky for you, we're still figuring out exactly what that means. You and your nostalgia act had your chance. I think we known how that went. What little I remember of biology class, you either adapt or you die. And I only see one of us changing." Buffy responds incredulously, "Did she just call me old?" (Gage 34/2–4–35/1) Buffy, much like the old school feminism, is represented as being entrenched and invested in the old rules. Importantly, Vicki is outdoors and in sunlight showing the vampiric evolution and the shifting norms within the Buffyverse. Since magic is different, the methods of killing vampires has changed. Using a public space to engage this dialogue of socio-normative changes in the Buffyverse reinforces the dynamic that space plays in the narrative. Buffy's continued negotiation of new rules and new norms in the public sphere tracks the chaotic environment. Until Buffy can fully integrate all of her activities in her own domestic space, she can only partially enact her post-feminism. As the Scoobies begin to learn how to negotiate the new rules of magic, Buffy evolves into a representation of third wave feminism by focusing on the choice to embrace this new norm, specifically evidenced through a greater focus on the home space.

This new emphasis on the domestic space makes the home the nucleus of the Scoobies' militaristic activities. Buffy's evolution as a representation of post-feminist discourse is tied to the location of the *Vampyr* book and the rewriting rules of magic. Season ten's immediate focus on the action within the domestic space of "New Rules, Part Two" shifts the spatial narrative from public to private. The season opens with "San Francisco. Xander and Dawn's Apartment" (Gage 42/1). The dialogue moves directly into "So Giles" and a barrage of questions that focus on battle planning, "How do we find the new Big Bad? Should I shake somebody down?" (Gage 42/2) This introduction parallels the high school seasons and highlights the importance of location change from public space (a school library) to domestic space (an apartment). In the earlier seasons, Buffy and the Scoobies were tied to the antiquated system of spells passed down through the Watchers Council, as well as to the public spaces and quasi-public spaces where they were allowed to meet. Their youth in the earlier seasons meant that they did not have owned spaces and were forces to congregate in places such as the high school library or the Magic Shop. These incorporated a sense of patriarchal ownership. From the start, therefore, season ten's focus on the home as the location of Scooby planning refocuses the domestic space within the militarized context. This distancing from the traditional spaces and authority figures highlights "a sense that ideas such as structures (patriarchy), unequally positioned social groups (women, men) and organized responses to these circumstances (the women's movement) no longer have the purchase they once had" (Harris 477). The traditional feminist models of activism evidenced by protests and organizing against an external force no longer matter to many young feminists. Similarly, Buffy's struggles are as much internal and interpersonal as they are demonic. Additionally, Harris notes, "many young women continue to pursue a feminist agenda through and around narratives of choice and individualization, conditions of de-collectivization and globalization, a pervasive media culture and the emergence of new information and communication technologies" (477). Season ten positions Buffy as a post-feminist heroine by reinventing her world so that demons are no longer hidden, acting as an allegory for globalization, while simultaneously creating narrative tension from Buffy's internal world and her choices. The *Vampyr* book is no longer housed in the traditionally male dominated public, or quasi-public, spaces. Further, with the book blank, Buffy no longer needs to follow the precedents set by those earlier patriarchal generations. Storing the *Vampyr* book in the home focuses the domestic space as the central location for changing social norms. Since the people most affected by the book's rules are now writing them, the narrative reinforces the importance of individualism and choice. Even more important, by housing the book within their living space, the Scoobies accept the risk accompanying potential attacks. The domestic space therefore becomes the central location for both changing norms and the battles associated with protecting those changes.

This redefinition of self and space parallels the recent change in women's economic roles. E-commerce opportunities such as Etsy and telecommuting provide opportunities for women's economic stability while shifting between the roles of mother and worker. As women increasingly "lean in" with these new home-based outlets for commercial success, the traditional feminist goal of domestically external economic and social equality integrates with domestic space. Therefore, Buffy's evolving focus from a public space to a domestic space acts as a metaphor for these socionormative shifts—as the rewriting of the *Vampyr* book indicates. In "New Rules, Part Five," Buffy and D'Hoffryn discuss power and choice:

> D'HOFFRYN: We have the requisite experience, and wisdom to share the laws of the new era. We shall gladly relieve you of your burden.
> BUFFY: Y'know what? No. I don't think I want a vengeance demon making the rules or *any* of the whack jobs you hang out with.
> D'HOFFRYN: You have just admitted you do not trust yourself with the responsibility.
> BUFFY: I don't. But y'know who I *do* trust: Us. *All* of us. Together. I want the best people I know doing this. And lucky me—here they all are. We've got this. If you think you can *take* the book from us, you're welcome to try [Gage and Brendon 118/3–5].

As Buffy and D'Hoffryn argue in Xander's apartment, the location of the ideological battle has shifted away from the public spaces defined by the male demon who epitomizes the patriarchy. As such, this disagreement is positioned as the first "battle" that occurs in a Scooby domestic space. By taking control from D'Hoffryn, Buffy reinforces her power as both Slayer and mentor merging the personal and professional. Moreover, choosing who controls the new rules of magic positions Buffy as a post-feminist example of the choice narratives in the shifting social norms.

As Buffy becomes more confident in her ability to control the *Vampyr* book as well as her personal and professional lives, she invites these activities into her domestic space. This redefinition of her domestic space showcases Buffy's choices as well as the changes in the normative structure. Buffy's confidence is evident in her pushback against D'Hoffryn in "I Wish, Part Two," when she tells him, "We discussed this. The bigger the rule change, the bigger the potential complications, right? We can't push it too far or we get pushed back" (Gage and Brendon 33/3). Asserting her youthful, female authority over a centuries-old, male-gendered demon places Buffy clearly at the center of this changing dynamic and as the one in control of it. In fact, Buffy's authority arises out her confidence in her abilities as both Slayer and woman. As Buffy and Willow discuss their career choices in their bedrooms, Willow prepares for a job interview. Simultaneously, in "Day Off (Or Harmony in My Head)," various mystical creatures await the women in their living room to engage in arbitration/mediation of issues concerning the new rules of magic.

> BUFFY: I could [have chosen to work with the Supernatural Crimes Unit]. I have. But the work's spotty. Spike doesn't have to buy groceries, and his wardrobe hasn't changed since 1974. It's fine. I chose the freelancer's life. I knew it would be a challenge. It's the other stuff I wasn't banking on. Are they still here?
> WILLOW: The leprechaun's drunk, at eight am. He's annoyed the Lucky Cat into a murderous rage. Dawn's running out of pots and pans to put under Cedric the Slime Man.
> BUFFY: We should really go out there. Ugh. Monsters, okay, but I never thought I'd have to deal with lobbyists. Does this annoy you as much as it does me? [Gage 03/5–6–104/1].

This arc reinforces the changing dynamic of the domestic space by noting that demon arbitrations take place in the apartment that Willow and Buffy share while also incorporating Buffy's new sense of determination and self-confidence. The use of the apartment to engage in the creation of these new social norms means the women are choosing to use the domestic space for a professional as well as a personal purpose. Moreover, despite the lack of formal "warlike" aspects, these negotiations perform as a militarization of the home because they act similarly to a peace accord after a war. By incorporating the professional activities into the socio-normative shift of rewriting the *Vampyr* book, Buffy recreates the domestic space as a hybrid space.

Choosing to enact these post-feminist activities within a female dominated domestic space also overrides the conditions that heretofore had limited Slayer power. Budgeon reminds her readers, "Socio-structural conditions continue to limit choices available to many women and shape differential access to resources—economic, political, cultural, emotional—needed if they are to avail themselves of those on offer" (308). By removing the limiting conditions of tradition and rewriting the *Vampyr* book while using the domestic space as a meeting place, Buffy rewrites the socio-structural condition and takes full ownership of the space while reworking it as a base of operations. By the fourth volume of season ten, "Old Demons," Buffy has matured into herself and has thrown off her past. Bringing Angel into the narrative of season ten incorporates a particular choice narrative. Buffy's history with Angel is constructed in limitations. Their inability to have a meaningful relationship crippled her emotionally throughout the early seasons. In addition, the Twilight prophecy limited her decisions and led to the current new magic scenario. Therefore, by taking control and effectively shutting Angel out of the battle planning in "Old Demons, Part Two," she removes the socio-cultural limitations she has faced up to this point:

> ANGEL: Both spell casters on one team? Isn't that kind of...
> BUFFY: I don't wanna split up our magic dudes. Whether you find the artifact or the Big Bad, it'll take all the mojo we've got to deal with the situation.
> ANGEL: So this has nothing to do with you not trusting me. Wanting me around people who can take me down if I lose control.
> BUFFY: Did that enter into my thinking? Yeah. You telling me I'm wrong?
> ANGEL: Let's just go [Gage 36/2–5].

By taking control from Angel in this situation, Buffy normalizes her power and leadership. With one question, Buffy undermines Angel's power in the conversation moving him into a subservient position. Moreover, since planning the battle takes place in domestic space, Buffy must proactively choose to invite Angel to help. The narrative positions Buffy as a post-feminist heroine by focusing on her choices as and shapes the story as one that overcomes traditional limitations through its shifting of the power dynamic when Buffy invites Angel into her domestic space but gives him neither physical nor emotional authority.

Season ten predominantly focuses on change and choice. As Buffy and the Scoobies settle into their shared domestic space, they also take control of the *Vampyr* book and the decisions necessary to ensure that the rewriting of the book is done appropriately. With the book housed in the domestic space, the home evolves from purely personal to a hybrid personal/professional location. Since the book also acts as a vehicle for socio-normative change within the Buffyverse, this places the domestic space at the center of that evolution. In order to ensure the safety of these changes, Buffy and the

Scoobies not only must plan their battle strategies from their home but also protect their home from invasion. The choices that Buffy and the Scoobies make will ultimately inform the changes in the norms of magic. Acting as a grassroots movement that takes place within the home, the Scoobies transform a passive living space to an active location for change. By incorporating these militarized activities into the domestic space, the Scoobies redefine the home as a place of activism for social change in the same way that third wave feminists have used the home as a space to gain social and economic equality. However, the incorporation of slayage into the home space only partly addresses Buffy's search for her authentic post-feminist self. Buffy still remains a young woman who seeks romantic fulfillment as well.

Having It All: Romance, Relationships and the Militarized Domestic Space

In order for the post-feminist heroine to effectively "have it all," she must also negotiate a successful, stable, romantic relationship. Space again plays a large role in signifying Buffy's level of success at enacting her full post-feminist self. Buffy's sense of integration between her Slayer self and personal self is evident by the locations in which these romantic interactions and discussions about romance occur. As Buffy's romantic encounters move from public to private to personal locations, her relationship with Spike in the militarized domestic space symbolizes her successful integration of the personal and the professional. In season ten, Buffy not only settles into her acceptance of being a professional Slayer, but she also seeks to stabilize her love life. The first half of season ten focuses on Buffy's desire to have a successful, normal romantic relationship. This positions her within the fictional narratives that depict the post-feminist woman as struggling to balance all aspects of her life. Her level of success in these relationships mirrors the location in which the interactions occur. The romantic comedy aspect to this section of the series highlights "the most challenging and controversial depictions of postfeminism's project to 'have it all' [which] consider the PFW's struggle to integrate 'it all' into her life and combine her job aspirations and material success with her desire for a rewarding home life, her feminist beliefs in agency and independence with the pleasures of feminine adornment and heterosexual romance" (Genz 98). Now that Buffy has officially made peace with her professional role as Slayer, she seeks romance. As Buffy attempts speed dating in "Love Dares You, Part One," she finds that she is somewhat of a celebrity in the vampire community as two vampires try to woo her. Buffy walks between them, ripping out their accidentally entwined nipple rings, saying, "That's it. I'm done. For future reference—I like my vampires with a little more soul and a little less *Portlandia*. Oh relax. You'll heal in like two seconds" (Gage and Brendon 9/6). This failed relationship adventure takes place in a public space showing that her emotional engagement is low. Despite having a relatively "normal" life at this point—she lives with friends independently and has a stable work commitment—she is unable to foster a romantic connection. The disconnect between private life and public space reinforces the chaotic nature of the post-feminist heroine's life in the same way that the disconnect between work and home symbolized it.

Buffy's relationship with Spike in "New Rules, Part One" still suffers from the after effects of the season seven sexual assault, further complicating her ability to engage in a successful romance with him. She knows that because of Spike's past as both vampire and assailant, her feelings go against feminist narrative. As Buffy ruminates, "The super-hot but oh-so-wrong affair. The awful place I was in when it happened. All the ways we hurt each other.... It's all good now. This is exactly what I wanted" (Gage 13/1–3). The character tries to talk herself into believing that friendship is better than romantic relationship. This trope of friendship instead of romance is one often found in romantic comedy pieces (consider Rachel in *Friends* or Penny in *The Big Bang Theory*). In this sense, Buffy's job, which requires her to work with Spike, combined with the additional relationship history narratively hinders her ability to "have it all." "New Rules, Part One" furthers this cross purposes narrative as Spike pulls her up onto the back of the van, with his arm around her waist, and asks, "All right?" Buffy responds, "Couldn't be better." However, the image hints at romantic intimacy. They face each other close proximity as though they are about to kiss. Then, the final line of the panel and page reminds the reader of their status as Buffy says, "Yay for maturity" (Gage 13/4). Despite the weight of the emotional narrative, all of these actions occur in a public space, the street on the back of a van. The physical distance from her own private space then becomes a metaphor for the emotional distance.

Incorporating Buffy's slayage into the domestic space unites her professional self with her personal self. Buffy now has the flexibility to be Slayer, sister, friend, and lover without feeling divided. However, season ten creates a sense both spatially and emotionally that this unification is difficult to attain. The romantic comedy aspects of the narrative serve to reinforce some of the negative stereotypes for these types of post-feminist characters. Genz notes, "Backlash texts try to convince their female readers/viewers of the impossibility and undesirability of being Superwomen as, in the attempt to juggle job and family, boardroom and babies, they jeopardize their feminine appeal and sign up to an exhausting existence filled with pain and guilt" (105). When reading season ten as a backlash text, Buffy's failed attempts at romance and her frustration at these failures has greater power. Buffy, the attractive woman, cannot attract a healthy relationship because of her job as Slayer. She is forced into a narrative where she feels she has to choose between enacting her Slayer self or being in a content emotional relationship. Genz continues, "The stigmatization of working womanhood is particularly castigatory and deprecatory in the case of single women who dare to diverge from homely femininity in search of a career" (ibid.). Buffy's failed romance with Dowling reinforces the tension that comes from the desire to have a healthy relationship while recognizing that she has a difficult time balancing the personal and the professional in order to be the "superwoman" she expects (or is expected) to be. The dangers of slaying act as representative physical dangers in ways that the non-superheroine post-feminist woman would have in more abstract socio-economic ways. In "New Rules, Part Two," Buffy faces the typical post-feminist dichotomy of work and romance:

> BUFFY: I have a pattern. Normal people, even tough ones, who know the world I move in, tend to get crushed by my life. And I can't protect them, no matter how much I want to. That's why.... I don't think we should take things any further. I'm sorry.
> DOWLING: Okay.
> BUFFY: Okay'?
> DOWLING: I appreciate you telling me now, before we got ... you know, attached.... We'll probably be working together a lot. You're right—it's better this way [Gage 47/2–5].

Having to choose work over a relationship and having to admit that she is a chaotic mess whose life "crushes" others, Buffy is firmly positioned in the post-feminist narrative as being broken in a way similar to characters such as Bridget Jones, Rachel, and Penny. Despite Buffy initiating the emotional distancing, she finds herself upset over Dowling's agreeableness. Buffy has approached Dowling in his home to speak with him emotionally. This sense of using the private space separates this interaction from her previous romantic conversations. For the first time, she is engaging in an emotionally fraught conversation in a private space; however, she has no ownership over the space which indicates that she is still only partially emotionally engaged. Not having a conversation like this in her own domestic space distances Buffy from these interpersonal connections both emotionally and spatially.

In cases where Buffy does engage in emotional conversations in her domestic space, they are rarely with romantic interests. Instead, her friends are the only ones privy to her private spaces and emotions, albeit not at the same time. As Buffy and Willow swoop around the air in San Francisco in "New Rules, Part Three," they discuss their personal lives:

> BUFFY: (sigh) We're hopeless, are we? It's just not fair to expect anyone to put up with our crazy-pants lives.
> WILLOW: Probably, yeah....

BUFFY: We might actually be ok, huh? Horny and frustrated but okay [Gage and Brendon 67/3–5].

In this scene, Buffy and Willow bemoan their singleton lives in a water-cooler style conversation. The line "horny and frustrated" intends to evoke the sense of humor often associated with romantic comedies. Simultaneously, the public location of this discussion furthers their private lives from the home and reinforces the sense of chaos that this segregation causes the post-feminist heroine. As long as their romances are disconnected from or in conflict with their demon fighting selves, they will not be able to fully integrate both sides of their lives. When the narrative allows Buffy to incorporate her private nurturing self into her professional slayer self, the character reads as an emotionally content, complex whole person as opposed to a polarized individual unable to reconcile her dual desires. As she incorporates these two aspects of her personality into one, both the militarized actions and the romantic activities can take place in the domestic space, making the home a metaphor for the fulfilled post-feminist experience.

The first two-thirds of season ten often appear handwringing in terms of Buffy's self-doubt. Her continual concerns regarding her inability to engage in a healthy relationship appear to undermine her power as a Slayer. However, one of the most interesting aspects of her desire to fight against her feelings for Spike is their violent history. As Genz notes,

> the PFW lacks a harmonious inner wholeness or balance and she is troubled by her fate as a "Superwoman" who strives to incorporate her careerism and her need for hearth/husband, her heterosexual femininity and her potentially desexualizing feminist agenda. She faces the dilemma of "having it all" as she endeavors to reconcile her experiences of being female, feminine, and feminist without falling apart or having to abandon one integral part of her existence. She is simultaneously frustrated and elated by her contradictoriness and hybridity, wrestling with self-doubt and despair as well as celebrating hope and confidence [98–99].

The Buffy-Spike relationship narrative and its problematic aspects creates a unique negotiation of the choice feminism discussions. On one level, Spike is a terrible choice of partner since his vampiric nature represents everything that her Slayer heritage fights against. Moreover, within a feminist context, his sexual assault in season seven is troubling in a larger, societal way. Therefore, Buffy doubts her ability to have a relationship—specifically one with Spike—and loses confidence in her own sensuality. For narrative reasons that implicate both trust and emotional distance, the majority of Buffy and Spike's early relationship discussions occur in public places that hinder emotional intimacy to represent these issues. Despite Buffy and Spike living across the hall from one another, Buffy continually chooses to engage in these unsuccessful conversations in open areas. Walking down the street one night after she has terminated any potential relationship with Dowling, Buffy bemoans her singleton status. In "New Rules, Part Two," Buffy and Spike start to hint at discussing their past.

> BUFFY: So what does that mean for me? Are my only relationship choices being alone, hurting the people I care about, or massive train wrecks of dysfunction? I didn't mean it like that. We were both in horrible places. You didn't have a *soul* and you can't really call what we had a relationship.
> SPIKE: No argument. That microbrew's getting lonely. Reckon I'll stop 'round the pub....
> BUFFY: Face it summers, the closes you'll ever get to a healthy relationship is visiting Xander and Dawn [Gage and Brendon 48/2–5–49/1].

This doubt regarding her ability to succeed romantically incorporates the discussions of the post-feminist heroine's inability to have a balanced personal and professional life. Buffy despairs over her options in terms of either hurting her loves or being in dysfunctional relationships. Buffy rewrites that portion of their narrative by simultaneously acknowledging her unhealthy emotional state during that point in their relationship while also distancing it from being an emotionally invested relationship. In doing so, she creates an opening to remove the contradictory nature of their relationship. As Buffy engages in this intimate conversation, the story evidences the emotional distance by having it occur while walking through the very public streets of San Francisco. This indicates that she continues to be unable to integrate her truly private self into these conversations. The domestic space remains a location of unfulfilled self and is therefore absent. Focusing on the public space to the exclusion of the domestic space narratively reinforces the sense of discontent Buffy feels and her chaotic post-feminist experience.

The post-feminist heroine's struggles focus on private-sphere issues that implicate domesticity. Therefore, the location of Buffy's romantic interactions and emotional conversations is important in connecting her to the home. Harris argues,

> young women are grappling to name and act upon enduring feminist concerns, particularly those that coalesce around amorphous and apparently "private sphere" issues such as heterosexual relationships, violence and childcare rather than the vote or the right to work. Further, dominant ideas about girls' potential and opportunity make it difficult to articulate continuing inequity [476].

Buffy and Spike's relationship coalesces various aspects of the private sphere. Spike's relationship as caregiver to Dawn incorporates the sense of childcare with which women grapple. His violence towards Buffy, as well as their heterosexual relationship, encompasses modern feminist discussions of sexuality alluding to lines between abuse and sadomasochism. Unlike Buffy having to fight against the Mayor or the Initiative, her internal struggle over her feelings for Spike place her as a post-feminist heroine rather than the traditional feminist heroine she was during earlier seasons of the television show. The setting is intended to create an emotional metaphor where Buffy and Spike discuss the season seven sexual assault. When they finally address it meaningfully in "Return to Sunnydale, Part One," they do so in the remnants of his abandoned Sunnydale crypt:

> SPIKE: Slayer, I ... I'm sorry. For ... well, all of it, really.
> BUFFY: Spike, I didn't mean *you* were...
> SPIKE: No. Let's not tiptoe around it. When I think of what I did to you, after you ended things between us—What I tried to—
> BUFFY: Listen to me. *You didn't have a soul.* I can't hold what *that guy* did against you any more than I could blame Angel for Angelus spending a hundred years slaughtering nuns. I'm not excusing what you—what he did. But it shouldn't matter now. You're a totally different person. In a lot of ways, so am I. I was in a terrible place back then. Willow had just resurrected me. Being pulled out of ... heaven, or wherever I was.... It was a kind of pain I still can't put into words. I damn sure couldn't face it at the time. I couldn't be mad at my friends. They brought me back because they loved me. So I just hated myself. And did whatever I could to punish myself. To sink as low as I felt [Gage, "I Wish" #8, 74/1–5–75/1–2].

The location of this conversation is important to their ability to grapple with the issues of violence and their burgeoning relationship. Despite having formerly been Spike's domestic space, the crypt is now a quasi-public space, abandoned and no longer under private control. As they are there to hunt a demon, their slaying activities and the emotional conversation momentarily converts the crypt into a quasi-militarized space. Despite being a nontraditional "domestic" space, the hybridized nature of the crypt marks it as a place of transition. For the first time, Buffy is willing to be emotionally honest with her romantic interest. Therefore, although neither traditionally public nor traditionally domestic, the space reinforces the narrative that Buffy's post-feminist romance cannot be traditional. The domestic nature of the crypt shifts the narrative towards integration.

Moreover, this conversation underlies the tension around choice feminism in terms of sex. In this crypt scene, Buffy explains her choices regarding sex to Spike and also to the reader. Her choices regarding her body are defined in a way that also normalizes her decision to use violent, emotionally empty sex as a tonic for emotional problems. Choice feminism accepts this, however, the relationship's existence as a feminist text requires some positioning to make it socially acceptable for readers. Spike needs to apologize for his assault in order for readers to be willing to accept Buffy's post-feminist decision to be in a relationship with her former attacker. Since this conversation occurs in a quasi-public, quasi-militarized space, the location acts as a transition from failed relationships to successful relationship that incorporates all aspects of Buffy's identity.

Ultimately, clarifying their relationship in terms of their history means that Spike can be an acceptable happy ending for Buffy. Buffy needs someone like Spike precisely because of her chaotic life. The life that would endanger someone like Dowling is an exaggeration of the type of discombobulation often depicted humorously in other post-feminist works. Buffy's exaggerated "realness" therefore represents that of a Bridget Jones style post-feminist heroine. Genz refers to an excerpt from Bridget Jones' Diary to explain, "Bridget is wanted and desired, not despite but because of her imperfections and her persistent failure to remake herself in another image, as thinner, more poised, more intellectual.... Bridget's lack of control proves to be her most loveable trait and thus, she is rewarded for being chaotic, for being 'no good at anything. Not men. Not social skills. Not work. Nothing'" (115). Similarly, Spike loves Buffy because of her imperfections, not despite them. Buffy is a singleton in the city whose romantic mishaps are often outcomes of her disorganized, chaotic life. Spike recognizes that Buffy is, to an extent, an overwrought mess. In "Love Dares You, Part One" Xander explains to Spike, regarding Buffy's response to Spike's rejection of a relationship, "From where I'm standing, it seems she rather courageously broke out of her pattern of dysfunction to reach out to you. And at her moment of greatest vulnerability, you slapped her down. Confirming her worst deep-seated fears about male abandonment" (35). The Slayer is dysfunctional and vulnerable in the style of the post-feminist heroine. Despite having saved the world, a lot, she is still emotionally a twentysomething trying to attain personal and professional success. This dysfunctional, chaotic personal life typified in many post-feminist narratives is represented visually and spatially by Buffy's inability to incorporate her romantic life into her domestic space. By creating distance between the private home and the private emotions, the narrative reinforces the sense of post-feminist chaos and inability to fully "have it all."

Until she is clearly content with her decision to be with Spike romantically as well as professionally, she does not discuss her emotions within the domestic space. The domestic space therefore remains militarized, but not private for her. In "Love Dares You, Part Two," Buffy attempts to distance herself from Spike emotionally:

> BUFFY: I was being impulsive and stupid.... And I know "just friends" is supposed to be a bad thing, but there's nothing "just" about it. You mean *so much* to me, Spike. You're one of the few people in this world I can count on. Not just to be there for me, but to be honest with me. Like you were at the cemetery. I mean, do you know how many guys would've used that as an excuse for a roll in the hay, and only brought up the complications after? What I'm trying to say is, I love what we have. It's taken a lot to get here. And it would've been stupid and thoughtless to risk that by rushing into something. So, I'm sorry. You did the right thing. And thanks.
>
> SPIKE: Pretty speech, Slayer. Every word you said is true and right. Just one problem. I'm in love with you [Gage and Brendon 45/2–5–46/1–5].

Buffy spews self-doubt much like the typical bumbling romantic comedy heroine found in other post-feminist works. Buffy's use of words like "impulsive and stupid" and her reiteration that "it would've been stupid and thoughtless" highlight the self-effacing quality of the speech. Therefore, it is unsurprising that she engages Spike in this extremely personal conversation in a public space that continues to reinforce her emotional distance. This separation of home and work continues despite the physically intimate nature of their relationship. Their first sexual experience after admitting their deeper feelings occurs in Xander and Spike's apartment. By continuing to separate Buffy's militarized domestic space from her relationship with Spike, Buffy continues to separate both aspects of her personality. Despite the fact that Buffy and Spike consummate their relationship physically, they have not yet emotionally consummated it. It is only in "Old Demons, Part One" that Buffy finally acknowledges her emotional commitment to Spike within the militarized domestic space. As the Scoobies begin to prepare to fight another battle, they decide to call in Angel. Given Buffy and Angel's history, Spike begins feeling emotionally threatened. For the first time since they agreed to have a relationship, Buffy approaches Spike emotionally within her own domestic space. She tells him, "I said no. And walked away. Angel is part of my past. Who I am now.... *You're* part of that. Him showing up isn't going to change anything" (Gage and Brendon 10/3–4). Not only does Buffy engage in an emotional conversation with Spike in her domestic space for the first time, she does so in order to reassure him. Buffy's choice to reveal her emotional depth to Spike is done not in response to Spike's attestations of love but from within herself. This choice to engage emotionally mingles with the militarized domestic space that is strewn with books and weapons. Additionally, when Buffy asks Spike to speak privately with her, one hand grasps a sword. Of the seven panels that narrate this conversation, four contain weapons in them and two are images of Buffy kissing or preparing to kiss Spike. This integration of weaponry and romance brings Buffy and Spike's relationship to emotionally new level of intimacy by placing it within the militarized domestic space. Simultaneously acknowledging both her weaponized Slayer self and the romantically intimate self finally integrates all aspects of Buffy's identity, proving through the use of the militarized domestic space that she can have it all as a post-feminist heroine.

By finally combining her emotional/private self with her work/slaying self, as represented by her ability to engage in a private conversation in the militarized domestic space, she normalizes her romantic relationships within the structure of her work. As Gillingham notes, "Domesticity in the twenty-first century isn't new but neither is it identical to its past iterations. Recognizing the historical contingency of domesticity, as well as that of feminism, the female subject, and the rhetoric of choice, offers a way of contesting an ahistoricized present (epitomized by the apocalyptic)" (29). By enacting her domesticity in this hybridized and militarized way, Buffy creates a new iteration that mirrors modern women's ability to choose how to engage in their homes. Bringing the personal and the professional into a single space and removing the sense of chaos that comes with the changing social norms, Buffy's use of the domestic space represents the larger feminist narrative of choice. Now Buffy is able to be partner, friend, sister, and Slayer by integrating both self and space.

Works Cited

Allie, Scott, Andrew Chambliss (w), Georges Jeanty, Cliff Richards (p), Andy Owens, and Vines (i). "On Your Own." *Buffy the Vampire Slayer Season Nine, Vol. 2* #6–10 (Feb.–June 2012). Ed. Scott Allie and Sierra Hahn. Milwaukie, OR: Dark Horse, 2012. Print.

Budgeon, Shelley. "Individualized Femininity and Feminist Politics of Choice." *European Journal of Women's Studies* 22.3 (2015): 303–318. Web. 21 March 2016.

Chambliss, Andrew, Jane Espenson, Drew Greenberg (w), Georges Jeanty, Ben Dewey, Karl Moline (p), Nathan Massengil, and Andy Owns (i). "Guarded." *Buffy the Vampire Slayer Season Nine, Vol. 3* #11–15 (July–Nov. 2012). Ed. Scott Allie and Sierra Hahn. Milwaukie, OR: Dark Horse Books, 2013. Print.

Chambliss, Andrew, Jane Espenson (w), Georges Jeanty, Karl Moline (p), Andy Owens, Karl Story, and Dexter Vines (i). "The Core." *Buffy the Vampire Slayer Season Nine, Vol. 5* #21–25 (May–Sept. 2013). Ed. Scott Allie and Sierra Hahn. Milwaukie, OR: Dark Horse Books, 2014. Print.

Chambliss, Andrew, Jane Espenson, Joss Whedon (w), Georges Jeanty, Karl Moline (p), Andy Owens, and Dexter Vines (i). "Freefall." *Buffy the Vampire Slayer Season Nine, Vol. 1* #1–5 (Sept. 2011–Jan. 2012). Ed. Scott Allie and Sierra Hahn. Milwaukie, OR: Dark Horse Books, 2012. Print.

Chambliss, Andrew (w), Georges Jeanty, Karl Moline (p), Andy Owens, and Dexter Vines (i). "Welcome to the Team." *Buffy the Vampire Slayer Season Nine, Vol. 4* #16–20 (Dec.–April 2013). Ed. Scott Allie and Sierra Hahn. Milwaukie, OR: Dark Horse Books, 2013. Print.

"Chosen." *Buffy the Vampire Slayer: The Complete Seventh Season*. Episode 22. Writ. and Dir. Joss Whedon. UPN. 20 May 2003. Twentieth Century Fox, 2004. DVD.

Gage, Christos, Nicholas Brendon (w), Richard Corben, Rebekah Isaacs, Cliff Richards, Karl Moline (p), Richard Corben, Rebekah Isaacs, Andy Owens (i). "I Wish." *Buffy the Vampire Slayer Season Ten, Vol. 2* #6–10 (Aug.–Dec. 2014). Ed. Scott Allie and Sierra Hahn. Milwaukie: OR: Dark Horse Books, 2015. Print.

Gage, Christos, Nicholas Brendon (w), Rebekah Isaacs (a). "New Rules." *Buffy the Vampire Slayer Season Ten, Vol. 1* #1–5 (March–July 2014). Ed. Scott Allie. Milwaukie, OR: Dark Horse Books, 2014. Print.

Gage, Christos, Nicholas Brendon (w), Rebekah Isaacs, and Megan Levens (a). "Love Dares You." *Buffy the Vampire Slayer Season Ten, Vol. 3*. #11–15 (Jan.–May 2015). Ed. Sierra Hahn. Milwaukie, OR: Dark Horse Books, 2015. Print.

Gage, Christos, Nicholas Brendon (w), Rebekah Isaacs, and Megan Levens (a). "Old Demons." *Buffy the Vampire Slayer Season Ten, Vol. 4* #16–20 (June–Oct. 2015). Ed. Sierra Hahn and Jim Gibbons. Milwaukie, OR: Dark Horse, 2015. Print.

Genz, Stephanie. "Singled Out: Postfeminism's 'New Woman' and the Dilemma of Having It All." *The Journal of Popular Culture* 43.1 (2010): 97–119. Web. 22 Dec. 2015.

Gillingham, Lauren, et al. "Of Bombs, Baking, and Blahniks." *English Studies in Canada* 31.2–3 (2005): 22–30. Web. 21 March 2016.

Harris, Anita. "Mind the Gap." *Australian Feminist Studies* 25.66 (2010): 475–484. *Academic Search Premier*. Web. 22 Dec. 2015.

Horbury, Alison. *Post-feminist Impasses in Popular Heroine Television: The Persephone Complex*. Houndsmills: Palgrave MacMillan, 2015. Print.

Classrooms, Classrooms Everywhere, but Not to Slay or Think
The Domestic Learning Environments of Buffy the Vampire Slayer

MELANIE A. JENSEN
and KYLE WILLIAM BISHOP

While Joss Whedon's cult classic *Buffy the Vampire Slayer* (1997–2003) primarily tells the story of a young woman and her destiny to combat the forces of darkness, the series also concerns itself fundamentally with teaching and learning, on both personal and institutional levels. Indeed, the first scene of the pilot episode, "Welcome to the Hellmouth," takes place within the halls of Sunnydale High School, establishing the significant setting of the series' first three seasons. However, all kinds of instruction—both formal and familiar—take place over the course of the show's seven seasons, and the sites of that instruction vary among different locations, some decidedly more effective than others. From libraries to classrooms, from gymnasiums to small businesses, from cemeteries to homes, the spaces of learning featured in *BtVS* offer models of how best to approach and design similar learning environments in real-world situations.

One of the most important factors that determines a student's ability to learn is the physical environment in which that instruction takes place. Ana Luz, of the Bartlett School of Architecture, calls an educational approach with this kind of spatial awareness "built pedagogy," which she describes as "the ability of space to define how one learns, teaches, acts or responds." These environs and settings, which address the physical concerns of a material real *space*, are also key learning *places*, which must be understood in terms of "emotional and ideological conception[s]" (Luz). According to psychologist Ken A. Graetz, "Environments that produce positive emotional states can be expected to facilitate learning and the development of place attachment." One way to achieve these "positive emotional states," while simultaneously respecting the appropriate locations for structured learning, comes from merging the institutional with the domestic, the formal with the familiar.[1] By finding ways to domesticate otherwise sterile learning environments, students can be more at ease, more attached to their educational spaces, and thus more likely to succeed at learning.

During the first three seasons of *BtVS*, Giles effectively provides Buffy with just this type of "built pedagogy" via the fundamentally liminal "domestic learning environment" of the Sunnydale High School library. Barbara McLean, in her study of domestic teaching spaces, reminds us how, traditionally, while the home is the domain of women,[2] the library has always been the one domestic space reserved for men (94).[3] Thus Giles, the (initially) stuffy British educator and keeper of knowledge, locates Buffy's learning within an environment both traditionally pedagogical (as part of the school complex) and comfortably domestic (of the masculine home). Later in the series, the location of his mentoring and instruction shifts first to his apartment (for much of season four) and then to the Magic Box store (in seasons five and six), spaces that prove less conducive to learning because the former is *too* domestic and the latter lacks the comforts of home. Furthermore, in season four, Buffy fails to thrive in the decidedly undomestic learning environment of the U. C. Sunnydale campus, but by season seven, she finds her ideal pedagogical space—this time as the teacher rather than the student—by converting her own home, McLean's domestic "domain" of women, into a kind of boarding school for a host of potential Slayers.

In other words, *BtVS* can be read and understood as an exploration of pedagogical learning spaces, from the less conducive *places* of material form and function to the more effective *spaces* that hybridize the institutional and the domestic for emotional health and wellbeing that represent extremes upon the spectrum.[4] Enterprising educators can thus learn much from the series and its dramatized "built pedagogy," not only from the lessons of Giles and Buffy as effective teachers, mentors, and students, but also from their depicted locations of instruction. For students to learn best, their institutional environments must contain elements of the domestic—from libraries and homes—a fusion more readily realized in public school, where teachers enjoy a certain "ownership" and ability to customize their spaces—the "rooms of their own." Traditionally, the younger the students, the more domestic the learning spaces. For example, many kindergarten classrooms are stocked with sleeping materials for nap time, food for snack time, and even a bathroom inside the classroom. As students age, their classrooms become less domestic, particularly when they begin changing rooms throughout the day to engage with a variety of teachers in a variety of spaces, as seen in most junior high and high schools. By the time students encounter the learning spaces of higher education, they find classrooms not directly "owned" by any one faculty member; faculty may domesticate their offices, but their classrooms tend to be fully institutional rather than domestic. *BtVS* encourages educators of all kinds and at all levels—public schools, institutions of higher education, and even home schools—to develop the best kinds of hybrid institutional-domestic learning spaces, spaces developed by teachers and students alike to maximize learning potential.

The Library as Domestic Pedagogical Space

Over the course of the series' first three seasons, Sunnydale High School takes priority over any other location depicted in the series (although cemeteries are perhaps a close second[5]). From the opening scene of the premiere episode, the school is the first location the audience is introduced to and the first with which they establish a connection. The trope is a familiar one: A boy leads a girl into a dark place he is acquainted with in what appears to be an attempt to gain potential primal pleasure. Of course, what happens next is known to anyone who has viewed the show before, but the fact that this boy decided to take this girl (later identified as the vampire Darla) to his school, a place where he admits he is no longer attending, is a fascinating decision. In doing so he is sending several implicit messages. The first is that this place is preferable to his home. Second, in taking Darla to the school and informing us he *used* to be a student there, he is establishing that he is familiar enough with this place that he feels a sense of control over the space, and, thus, a sense of control over her. Yet this decision is also decidedly unsurprising, considering that high school students spend a sizable portion of their formative years in school. At school, many students create deep friendships that take priority over family, consequently creating a "home away from home" where students eat, socialize, learn, and even sleep—much to the chagrin of their teachers. Sunnydale High even has lockers that allow students a space to put their belongings, a space to decorate, a space to call their own, no matter how small. All of these factors coalesce to create a "domestic" space within the larger construct of the institutional—and thus traditional—learning environment. However, with the death of the boy in the school by the fangs of Darla, Whedon makes perfectly clear that not only do boys *not* run the school, this is also *not* a place that promises the preconceived belief of safety. After all, high school is hell.

While Whedon has stated that the driving focus of the first few seasons of *BtVS* was the literalization of this metaphor,[6] he also created one of the most effectively domesticized learning spaces in the series in the form of the Sunnydale High library. In terms of educational relationships (student/teacher, mentee/mentor, Slayer/Watcher, whichever dyad is the most appropriate at any given moment), Buffy and Giles are easily one of the most important relationships depicted in the series, particularly in the earlier seasons.[7] And, significantly, the school library is the place where this pair first meets. Before that even happens, however, viewers get the sense that the *rest* of Sunnydale High is a pretty lackluster place as far as teaching and learning goes. For example, although Principal Flutie initially promises Buffy a "fresh start" by ripping up her permanent record in the pilot episode, "Welcome to the Hellmouth," he quickly dismisses his new-age administrative facade when confronted with the true severity of her academic transgressions, awkwardly taping the paper back together in front of her. The pedagogical model of high school initially demonstrated in the series is even less impressive: Buffy's very first class—history—features a stereotyped boring and monotone teacher who asks leading questions with no real expectation of receiving the right answers—or *any* answers. The students are totally disinterested, going through the motions of writing notes, perhaps, but never once engaging verbally with the instructor. Even though the classroom is seemingly well decorated and equipped with the standard materials and technology for the time, the environment is otherwise sterile, largely because the instructor fails to engage beyond a superficial level.

This negative portrayal of the U.S. public school system extends to the Sunnydale High library as well, albeit only in "Welcome to the Hellmouth." When Buffy first enters the physical space of the library, the vast hall seems to be deserted, and the foreboding, frightening Gothic space is poorly lit with harsh shadows and dusty beams of sunlight. The central tables are sparse and only vaguely illuminated by sickly yellow lamps. Giles' introduction is hardly warm and comforting either. He attempts to dissuade Buffy from her current mission of finding a history textbook in favor of a hefty, ancient tome with only the word "Vampyre" embossed on its cover, representing the "textbook" of the course in "slaying" that Buffy has been enrolled in despite her wish to escape her supernatural destiny. Furthermore, Giles' dress, accent, and myopic focus on the occult repel Buffy, causing her to reject the book proffered by her new guardian, thus effectively rejecting Giles efforts to "educate" Buffy.

Of course, in the grand tradition of Joseph Campbell's oft-cited "Hero's Journey," Buffy comes to accept her "call to adventure" and embraces—albeit reluctantly—the guidance of her mentoring Watcher, a guardianship established as inextricably linked with the physical space of the library.[8] Furthermore, thanks to the harrowing events of "Welcome to the Hellmouth," new friends Willow and Xander have become privy to Buffy's secret identity, and, as such, Giles initiates what will become known by fans as the "Scooby Gang" in the series' second episode, "The Harvest." This almost formal creation of the series' community—a "community of good" reminiscent of the one at the center of Bram Stoker's *Dracula* (Waller 35)—takes place naturally around the library's central table, the symbolic hearth of the library's domestic space. In stark contrast to the series' first episode, this table is now warm and inviting, covered by books and newspapers, a computer (upon which Willow will work much "magic" over the next few seasons), and—perhaps most tellingly—Giles' coffee cup.

Despite Lorna Jowett's assertion that the library is little more than a "workplace," the library has now transformed into much more of a "domestic space," not only because of the changes in lighting and decor, but also because of this formation of a community. On the one hand, Giles works to foster for Buffy what pedagogical theorist Ken Bain calls a "natural critical learning environment," a space in which students can think critically, examine evidence, improve themselves, and ask insightful questions (99). On the other, Buffy, Willow, and Xander have converted the library into a kind of "home," one in which they are most trusted and where they can be most honest. They are part of something bigger, part of a kind of ersatz family. Indeed, the library is much more home-like for Buffy than her new house, as her bedroom is still, at this point in the series, filled with unpacked boxes—hardly the comfortable trappings of home.[9] Before Joyce knows Buffy is the Slayer, the library continues to be more domestic for Buffy than the house in which she lives because only in the library can she be completely open and honest about who she is. Giles provides her with this safe space, a hybrid, liminal space resting somewhere between the formal, institutional educational setting of the school and the loving, nurturing setting that should be associated with one's home.

Furthermore, Giles quickly learns traditional pedagogical methods will not work with Buffy.[10] Though this process is ongoing and he is not always perfect at it, Giles is engaged in what Lori Gee calls "human-centered design," a set of pedagogical guidelines concerning learning spaces that "build on the premise that learning happens in many ways and that the design possibilities supporting learning are equally numerous." Gee emphasizes how the most effective learning spaces fulfill a variety of required student needs, including their basic *human* needs—both physical *and* psychological comfort—while facilitating a variety of learning and teaching styles. For example, Buffy and her friends seem to enjoy 24/7 access to the library, regularly conducting research after hours or even staying there all night long,[11] and, beginning with "The Pack," Giles also allows Buffy to conduct her physical and combat training in the library, turning the space into a kind of lab or gym—as *she* needs it to be. Another positive result of human-centered design is the creation of a space that affords students a balance between community and solitude (Gee). Indeed, the library, as we have shown, provides Buffy with what Kim Kirkpatrick calls Buffy's "support group," but the relatively isolated space lets Buffy get away from the other students as well, to spend time alone researching, training, or recuperating. In fact, when two unsuspecting students drop in to check out library books in "Passion," Giles is visibly surprised to see them and demands to know what they want.

In the series' third episode, "Witch," Buffy is granted access to Giles' private office, a space within the space of the library that is decidedly (and understandably) domestic because it serves as his home away from home. This "subspace" includes Giles' desk, paintings and photographs, a cluttered bulletin board, mysterious trinkets from around the world, the means of preparing food, and, of course, a tea service.[12] Furthermore, because Buffy is dying from the vengeance spell cast by former cheerleader and local witch Catherine Madison, Giles is not only educating her about what has happened and what the Scoobies must do to save her, but he is also caring for her—placing a cool towel on her forehead, checking her pulse rate, and otherwise trying to make her comfortable. Part of the "domestic space" of education must include the domesticity of parental care and concern, a level of familial intimacy that replicates the way children were educated centuries ago. In 1524, for example, Martin Luther supported the idea of compulsory education because he wanted all parishioners to be able to read the Bible for themselves. This ideology traveled across the ocean to the American colonies, where Puritanical leaders wanted their citizens to be able to read and write as well. Indeed, John Winthrop strongly encouraged his Puritanical settlers to imbue the New World with "a deeply domestic and familial set of values" (Anderson 17).[13] In later years, in fact, it became the legal responsibility of parents either to teach their children these skills or to hire someone to teach for them. As the United States stepped away from this idea of "homeschooling" and adopted a more public school system, it was stripped of much of the domestic aspect, but this idea remained intrinsically tied to the belief that part of raising children is educating them. While this kind of "parental care" manifests repeatedly throughout the series, this moment in "Witch" is the first instance when viewers see Giles as a father figure for Buffy, one who replaces her absent real father. Ideally, physical care and emotional understanding and support must be essential components of domestic and institutional education.

As Winston Churchill reminded his nation while rebuilding England after the World War II bombings, "We shape our buildings, and afterwards our buildings shape us." We see this ideal develop over the course of *BtVS*' first three seasons as Giles (re)builds the library space as a teacher, Buffy and the Scoobies develop it as learners, and the space itself shapes them all into better teachers *and* learners. Jane McGregor argues that "space is literally *made* through our interactions" (354), and one of the things that makes the Sunnydale High School library such a unique and effective living-and-learning space are the interactions between it and those who regularly occupy it. Additionally, as education specialist Dianne Mulcahy claims—building upon Ian Buchanan's assertion that "occupation constructs space"—occupation also "constructs identity" (Mulcahy 58). In other words, the library is not a "true" educational space until the Scoobies fill it, just as a regular classroom is just a room if no students occupy that space. Identities and spaces are intertwined: as the teacher makes the space, the space makes the teacher; the space makes the students, but the students also make the space. Mulcahy further argues, "Spatiality is primarily to be seen not in terms of a backdrop against which action takes place, but rather in terms of activity or practice. Space is 'done': constituted through action, for example acts of occupancy and appropriation" (58). The Scoobies, through their increased occupancy of the library, begin to transform it, to make it into the kind of space that is most conducive for their own learning (bringing in computers, having food delivered there, etc.). Their influence, perhaps more than anything, makes the library a hybrid space, both formal and familiar, what Mulcahy calls an "'in-between space' created by learners themselves" (65).

Once the students have transformed the library's form and function to their pedagogical needs, the space becomes additionally formative for all of the Scoobies because Giles offers each of them the second most basic level of need, according to Abraham Maslow's famous "Hierarchy of Needs," by providing each member of the group security of the body. Yet while the library usually provides the Scoobies with protection, no place, public or private, is truly safe in *BtVS*, as viewers repeatedly see different spaces fail. The library, however, is something special. Again, Luz makes the distinction between space and place: the former is the material reality and the latter acts as an emotional and ideological conception, but the library functions as both. We must note, however, that Giles does violate Buffy's safety (and, more importantly, her trust) when he egregiously drugs Buffy in the library on the orders of the Watchers Council in the episode "Helpless." A large part of Giles' failure, at least from a pedagogical perspective, is reverting back to the "traditional" practices that he has proven time and time again do not work for Buffy and her educational needs.[14] His resistance to the plan is evident, and, though he does go through with the drugging, he ultimately stands by his student and protects her and her needs. After all, teachers learn through failure, just as students do.

Despite his occasional failures and missteps, Giles, as an educator, is mostly successful in his efforts to create this space in which the Scoobies can learn and grow. However, at least during the first three seasons of the show, Giles is a victim of an illness that plagues many educators: they seem to exist only at school. (A common experience is the uncomfortable grocery store encounter with one's teacher.) The audience does not see Giles' "true" domestic space until partway through the second season; again, it would be strange to think of him outside his "natural" habitat of the school. Although many students are impacted daily by their teachers without ever seeing the homes of their educators, this viewing of his home crosses the line between regular student/teacher relations and cements his role as a nurturing father figure not only for Buffy but also for all of the Scoobies. Giles is allowed more freedom as an educator because while he is a school employee, he does not appear to have courses that he is teaching or any teacher assistants to manage. Rather, he teaches "slaying," and, although initially hesitant for his student load to triple, with the addition of Willow and Xander to his roster, he ultimately sees the benefit of diversifying the student body to facilitate a better learning community for Buffy to thrive in, creating a space for a problem-based learning (PBL) module. Although hardly an argument that Buffy's learning group sets her apart as a Slayer and makes her successful, the relationship between the library and the group allows this learning community to gestate more than they would without a safe incubating space.

In other words, what Buffy and all of the Scoobies need most is a safe space where they can learn and grow. Mulcahy explains the concept of PBL in relation to student teachers, which Buffy effectively is for the majority of the series, learning from others—such as Giles, Wesley, and the rest of the Watchers Council—what is effective and, more importantly, what is ineffective. Buffy remains largely in the role of student teacher until she becomes, essentially, her own Watcher, with varied success, and then takes on the role of a Watcher for the Potentials in season seven (as we will discuss below). This exposure to PBL allows Buffy to qualify for a variation of a method found effective with other student teachers. What makes the library throughout the first three seasons special is what Mulcahy explains as the primary benefit of PBL: "It provides an immediate opportunity to 'apply' and practice what has been learned elsewhere" (56). As mentioned above, the Scoobies pour over books to find information about demons that they encounter, and Buffy does much of her physical training in the school library rather a gym. Information and training gained in the library is then taken and applied in the "real world," usually the streets and cemeteries of Sunnydale. However, the library is a more gratifying space for PBL because actual problems, not just simulations, confront our students there. Students are attacked, arrested, ambushed, poisoned, possessed, and transformed; and yet, the Scoobies frequently use it as their home base, their meeting place. It is their headquarters, a fact so concrete and well known that even their enemies exploit this information after luring the Scoobies to the library to capture or injure members of the Scooby Gang, as the vampires do at the beginning of season two in "When She Was Bad." While this attack could have been scripted for practical reasons—because the school is a public place that cannot easily have the same restriction that homes in the series enjoy—it is nevertheless important because the Scoobies continue to meet in the library time and time again. Not only is it a central location, it is their domesticized learning space where they feel at home, where the information about what they are fighting lives, where their mentor (practically) lives, and—perhaps *most* importantly— where the physical weapons live.

The death of this hybrid institutional-domestic space becomes quite literal in "Graduation Day: Part 2" when the Scoobies are forced to set aside their beloved library in order to destroy the demonic mayor of Sunnydale (Harry Groener). Replacing books with bombs, so to speak, the learning community of Slaying sacrifices their space and struggles for the rest of the series to find a space that is as effective as the Sunnydale High library, a sacrifice that foreshadows their inevitable transition from school children to adults. As students somewhat naturally progress from educational spaces that are more domestic than formal (as in kindergarten and grade school) to those that are more professional and traditional (as in high school and college), Buffy and her friends must make a similar journey. However, because young people transition from the spaces of the institutional school system into the spaces of their professional and personal lives—decidedly *adult* lives—Buffy's journey takes her from student to teacher, from Slayer to quasi-Watcher, and the touchstone moments of her maturation can be tracked through the spaces in which she learns (and teaches) along the way.

Life After the Library: Post High School Years

With the destruction of Sunnydale High School, Buffy's formal education and training as a Slayer are negatively disrupted by dislocation. Not only has she lost the official pedagogical influence of Giles—who has, by this point in the series, lost both his job as Watcher *and* as school librarian—she has also lost her most influential learning spaces. U.C. Sunnydale is quickly ruled out as a replacement living-learning community as its primary focus is the institutionalization of education, a formalized space that lacks the personalized attention of the public school spaces, not to mention the absence of Giles and Xander on campus. The first episode of season four, "The Freshman," quickly establishes that college is big, that college is crowded, and that college is *not* a nurturing environment. Buffy is all on her own, wandering almost aimlessly across campus, gathering colorful flyers that falsely offer the promise of new communities. Within the buildings, the spaces of U.C. Sunnydale have no sense of the domestic at all; in fact, even the domestic spaces of the dorms are more "institutional" than "domestic," with a sterile, one-size-fits-all, pragmatic design and purely functional furnishings. The hallways loom over Buffy, and even the college library is coldly architectural; beautiful and awe-inspiring, yes, but with no sense of warmth or love. It is just a space for finding information, not really for "learning." Buffy first classroom experience is presented like a scene from a nightmare—the popular culture professor is horrible and verbally abusive, Buffy is publicly embarrassed by having wandered into the wrong class, and the auditorium space is unadorned, dull, and poorly lit. Professor Walsh's classroom is not any better, and she comes across as stern and impersonal with crossed arms and dark clothes; she is all business with no nurturing instincts. Buchanan reminds us that "space exists only as it is inhabited: it is created by the act of occupancy," and the spaces Buffy encounters at U. C. Sunnydale are never occupied in a way that facilitates her learning.

Of course, Giles *does* remain an active (and interactive) part of Buffy's life, continuing, in a somewhat limited capacity, as her teacher and mentor throughout season four. However, his attempts to use his townhome as a space for "built pedagogy" largely fail. Giles' place starts to develop into a domestic space where research and learning take place in "Fear Itself," but as Buffy and Willow are firmly entrenched at the university at this point in the season, only Giles and Xander—the outsiders—are shown doing any kind of academic work and research there. Tellingly, Giles' messes up his scholarly efforts, failing to realize the fear demon Buffy must defeat in the episode was represented "actual size" in the illustration in his book. With "Pangs," the Scooby Gang comes back together as a community at Giles' townhouse for the first time in the season. At this point, the space finally comes to represent a more balanced synthesis of the institutional and the domestic: Willow brings books and they conduct research together, but their interactions are also fundamentally familial, thanks to their shared celebration of Thanksgiving. Not only do they unite as a family, but they also bicker and fight and work through some of the issues that have been subtly and gradually dividing them all season. Once again, though, they do a poor job with the research, as they completely miss the goal of the Shumash warriors and the threat posed to Buffy directly. In fact, none of Giles' instruction or the Scoobies' research proves very effective during season four, largely because Buffy and her community have yet to develop an effective institutional-domestic space to replace the lost library.[15]

With seasons five and six, the Scoobies largely move their base of operations to The Magic Box, a mystic supply and curios shop that Giles purchases and manages (with the sometimes confounding assistance of Anya); however, this liminal location also fails as a hybrid institutional-domestic learning space because it must share its educational function with the needs of a money-making venture. Giles decides to buy The Magic Shop in "Real Me," notably just the second episode of the fifth season, and, in so doing, he establishes a new place for the Scoobies to work, research, learn, and even train. It represents something of an institutional-domestic space in much the same way the library had been, sharing both a familiar and a formal function, but the focus here is on retail rather than education. Nonetheless, as the Scoobies begin to spend most of their down time—along with their work time, their study time, and their training time—in The Magic Box, it becomes the center of their research, mostly because Giles appears to have relocated all of his books there. While it becomes a liminal and hybrid space in ways that perhaps outstrip the library, it is much less domestic than the library was: Giles has no space analogous to his personalized office, and the Scoobies do not eat or sleep there. The analogous nature of the shop-as-library becomes overt in "No Place Like Home," however, when Xander asks Buffy, "Did you ever think in a million years you would miss the high school library?" when she is trying to research in books amidst the bustle of a crowded retail outlet. Of course, this change in location can also be simply a reflection of their shift in life: the Scoobies are no longer adolescents, worried primarily about going to school and passing their classes, but adults, which means going to work and making money. The Magic Box is thus a liminal professional space, as well as a pedagogical space, a combination that shows the tension of higher learning and the demands of adulthood.

Even though Buffy's home base begins to shift more consistently to her house over the course of season six, as she must assume full "adulting" after the death of her mother Joyce, the Magic Box remains a key location for Scoobie meetings, book research, and the performance of spells. By the end of the season, however, the shop is destroyed, much as the library before it, and the Scoobies have ultimately failed in their efforts to find an effective pedagogical space. In a way, the season represents the failure of the Scoobies to function on their own without a clear teacher/guardian/Watcher or a focused site of instruction and mentorship. This failure seems to hinge on the absence of Giles for the majority of the season—although Buffy's return from the dead and her almost debilitating identity crisis certainly contribute. Buffy repeated fails over the course of the season—as a Slayer, as a caregiver, as a student, as a provider, as an employee, as a friend, as a girlfriend, etc. But also Xander fails at his relationship with Anya, Willow fails in her attempts to control her magic addiction, Anya fails in her attempt to be a human, Dawn fails to do more than shoplift and whine the entire season—and even Spike fails at being a vampire. Their collective failures are largely a result of

Giles' failure—as Buffy is still, technically, the Slayer, and he is still, necessarily, her Watcher. So whereas the library was destroyed at the end of season three as a symbol of the Scoobies' graduating and moving on to more self-sufficient, adult lives, The Magic Box is destroyed as a symbol of everyone's failure to succeed in those self-sufficient, adult roles.

Everything changes with season seven, in which the teacher/student, teaching/learning paradigms come full circle and are restored. Not accidentally, the first episode of the season is titled "Lessons," and the first scene shows Buffy (finally) teaching her younger sister Dawn how to survive in the supernaturally dangerous world in which she unavoidably lives. Additionally, Sunnydale High School has been rebuilt and re-opens (seemingly out of nowhere), setting up a number of refrains in character and plot that will occur throughout the season. The episode even presents the forthcoming series overtly in terms of a return "to the beginning" when the First Evil manifests itself to Spike in the guise of all the series' "Big Bad" villains in chronological succession. The impended successes of the Scoobies this final season will thus stand in contrast to their failures in season six, successes that will stem largely from proper instruction and effective instructional spaces—instruction offered by Buffy within the space of her home. Indeed, Buffy's efforts in season seven literalize Churchill's admonitions about buildings, as, during the first half of the season, she engages in the construction of the space of learning for the Potential Slayers, and, during the second half, that space works on the entire gang—including Buffy—to further their education, their training, and their construction of community.

Although Jowett claims "domestic space [in *BtVS*] is not 'liminal,'" with the episode "Bring on the Night," Buffy successfully transforms her literal domicile into a kind of boarding school for potential Slayers, and she finally discovers a hybridized institutional-domestic living-and-learning space that not only effectively replaces the high school library but perhaps also surpasses it. In addition, the space not only transforms her into a more effective Slayer, one able to defeat the First Evil, but also allows her to transcend her student status to become the teacher. As successful homeschoolers will readily attest, the home can function as a very effective school, particularly under the influence of a capable educator. Mulcahy explains, "In the more mundane and multiple spaces of pedagogical practice, this space is frequently re-appropriated and remade. As spatial boundaries are crossed, the shape of pedagogy shifts" (66–67). Teaching in the home is not the same as teaching in a formal school setting, of course, but that space can be restructured to achieve the needs of the students. Buffy, albeit gradually (and we must remember that any such construction is a process) transforms her home, turning the living room into a classroom *and* dormitory, the kitchen into a cafeteria *and* teachers' lounge, and the basement and backyard into gymnasia. Luz argues how "the construction of place enhances the construction of knowledge and meaning" and that "the process of learning is built by and into the learning space." This undertaking by Buffy literalizes Luz's words, showing not only how the house can function as an effective pedagogical space, but also how the very process itself contributes to the positive learning experiences of the Potentials and the original Scoobies.

Early seasons of *BtVS* provide Buffy with the hybridization of the institutional-domestic space because she strives so hard to keep her "work" out of her home—and away from her often-unaccepting mother. After Joyce's death, however, and with the creation of Buffy's "Command Central" Slayer boarding school (Jowett), the Summers home fulfills the hybrid institutional-domestic role she experienced so developmentally during her formative years as the Slayer. As Kirkpatrick points out, season seven challenges the traditional Hero's Journey by making the mythical quest one accomplished by a community rather than an individual, and that transformation takes place within a domestic sphere. The heroic community of *BtVS* is, to use Kirkpatrick's word, a "gynarchical" one; thus the development of that community within the traditionally matriarchal space of a domestic home makes sense.[16] Whereas Giles worked most efficiently in the "masculine space" of the library for the first three seasons of the series, Buffy takes full advantage of the "feminine space" of her home. However, like Giles before her, Buffy is wise enough to recognize the value of community in the learning process; she takes full advantage of Willow and Xander, who increasingly function as faculty members of this Californian "Hogwarts," a faculty that will eventually include Spike, erstwhile high-school principal Robin Wood, and reformed Slayer Faith.[17]

Of course, the Potentials must learn elsewhere as well, particularly as a group, as the functional qualities of Buffy's home limit the kinds of learning that can take place there. As traditional schools must rely upon strategic field-trips to augment the spaces of student learning, so too must Buffy take the Potentials into the "field" to learn from specialized, local places. Mulcahy rightly points out how "peer learning is engaged in various places: in students' homes, campus cafes and school canteens" (64), and while season seven *does* show the Potentials learning in these kinds of domestic spheres, other, more relevant places include a construction site, the local cemeteries, the basement of the now-abandoned Sunnydale High School, and a nearby winery. Buffy expands the learning spaces of her "Slayer School" beyond just her house as any good educator does the space of the classroom, taking advantage of local locations as part of a place-based pedagogy.[18] By taking advantage of these local "field trips," Buffy practices what John Loughran calls "constructivist learning principles," a pedagogical approach that emphasizes "learning by doing" (121). A crucially impactful initiatory lesson—and practical demonstration—for the Potential Slayers takes place at one of Xander's build sites in "Showtime," when Buffy kills the first übervamp, thus inspiring her students like a dynamic chemistry teacher in a lab. In the next episode, "Potential," Buffy takes the Potentials into the cemetery to train with her and Spike—as Giles once did with her—with Spike acting in the capacity of a special "guest lecturer." In other words, Buffy as a teacher uses the various spaces and places at her disposal to provide her students with the best possible learning environments, liminal environments that serve different purposes at different times but which share their function to enhance the learning process.

By the end of season seven, Buffy's efforts to teach and train the Potentials come to hasty fruition, with most of her charges successfully "graduating" in the final episode, "Chosen," proof that her pedagogical efforts have succeed in teaching the women to become Slayers in their own rights. Their confrontation of the The First and its army of übervamps represent their final exams—or perhaps the ACT or SAT—and their success in destroying Sunnydale and sealing the Hellmouth is analogous to students' transitions from high-school students to educated adults. When stripped of its supernatural trappings, then, *BtVS* can be seen as an extended narrative metaphor for the process of learning (and living) that all students traverse on their real-life quests to become educated. This educational process is most conducive to student learning, on a crucially individual basis, when enacted within the confines of effective pedagogical spaces, spaces that fuse the formal, public, and institutional spaces with the nurturing, supportive, and domestic spaces of students' lives. The public school system is designed to help students create living/learning communities, but, as we see in with the destruction of the library, after graduation students are forced to navigate the world alone and create such communities independently. And while we, as educators, must do what we can within our *own* hybrid institutional-domestic spaces to facilitate our students' learning and sense of community, ultimately, like Giles—and later, Buffy—we must prepare them to find, create, and inhabit these kinds of spaces on their own.

Notes

1. Julia Williams Robinson, in her *Institution and Home: Architecture as a Culture Medium*, explores the "hypothesized dialectic of institution and home" (5). While she focuses primarily on the polarity between institutional and domestic spaces (65–75), we argue how the fusion or hybridization of those otherwise opposed spaces represent the best learning environments, particularly based on how they are imagined in *BtVS*.

2. Indeed, the series unerringly presents Buffy's house as the realm of the feminine, overseen initially by Buffy's mother Joyce and later by Buffy herself, as we will discuss later.

3. Admittedly, McLean is referring to libraries in terms of an older tradition, when they were run by monks, but this association makes sense as Giles deals with ancient and arcane texts.

4. For a different approach to the roles of space and place in *BtVS*, see Karen Sayer's "This Was Our World and They Made It Theirs."

5. In the season three episode "Revelations," Giles mentions Sunnydale has 12 official city cemeteries.

6. In an interview with Mim Udovitch for *Rolling Stone* magazine, Whedon reflects on his initial ideas for the *Buffy* television series: "Well, a TV show needs something that will sustain it, and a California girl fighting vampires, that is not enough. So I thought about high school and the horror movie, and high school as hell and about the things the girl fights as reflections of what you go through in high school." For more on the significance of this metaphor, see Tracy Little's "High School Is Hell."

7. See, for example, Jess Battis, who considers Giles' relationship with Buffy in terms of a positive—if colonial—father figure (93–95). See also Kirsten Stevens' "Meet the Cullens" and Christina Casano's "Love and Loyalty."

8. Many scholars have explored the overt connections between *Buffy the Vampire Slayer* and Joseph Campbell's ubiquitous work on mythology, the Monomyth, and the Hero's Journey. See, for example, Frances Early's "Staking Her Claim," Laurel Bowman's "*Buffy the Vampire Slayer*: The Greek Hero Revisited," Rhonda Wilcox's *Why Buffy Matters*, David Fritts' "Buffy's Seven-Season Initiation," and, particularly, Valerie Estelle Frankel's *Buffy and the Heroine's Journey*.

9. For an extensive discussion of the domestic space of Buffy's home, see Jowett's "The Summers House as Domestic Space in *Buffy the Vampire Slayer*."

10. Giles initially tries to teach Buffy in the traditional Watcher ways—giving her the *Vampyr* book to read in the pilot episode (which we never see her actually read), formally sparing with her in "The Pack," and trying to begin her weapons training with the quarterstaff instead of a crossbow in "Angel"—but, as we learn in "What's My Line? Part 2," Giles has refrained from expecting the same kind of isolated education typical of most Slayers because, with Buffy, "some flexibility is required." Indeed, he has not even given her a copy of the "Slayer Handbook" because, as he delicately informs her, "after meeting you, Buffy, I realized the Handbook would be of no use in your case."

11. The library becomes a regular "all night" haunt with "Beauty and the Beasts" when Giles converts a lockable storage space into a cage for the werewolf Oz. For the three nights of the full moon each month, the library becomes a literal domicile for Oz, Willow, and, more often than not, Xander.

12. See particularly the episode "Revelations."

13. Anderson's book explores the influence Winthrop's ideological emphasis on the domestic has had on the depiction of community in both the culture of the United States and its related art and literature. His findings and conclusions obviously extend to *Buffy the Vampire Slayer* as well, as our focus on the domestic and the creation of community demonstrate.

14. See note 10 above.

15. The one notable exception comes in "Hush," which marks the first time in season four when Giles is back on his "Watcher" game, even though he is not working in an official capacity. His research efforts *finally* pay off, *and* he effectively conveys that knowledge to the rest of the Scoobies—not coincidentally in a classroom.

16. See McLean 94.

17. Giles' role in the instruction of the Potentials is problematic, as his presence undermines Buffy's efforts as much as support them. In a sense, he is as much a student of the season as a teacher, as he takes a subordinate role in the instructional processes.

18. See Ball and Lai 262–270 for a thorough overview of the history and theory of this pedagogical approach.

WORKS CITED

Anderson, Douglas. *A House Undivided: Domesticity and Community in American Literature.* Cambridge: Cambridge University Press, 2009. Print.
"Angel." *Buffy the Vampire Slayer: The Complete First Season.* Episode 7. Writ. David Greenwalt. Dir. Scott Brazil. The WB. 14 April 1997. Twentieth Century Fox, 2002. DVD.
Bain, Ken. *What the Best College Teachers Do.* Cambridge: Harvard University Press, 2004. Print.
Ball, Eric L., and Alice Lai. "Place-Based Pedagogy for the Arts and Humanities." *Pedagogy:*

Critical Approaches to Teaching Literature, Language, Composition, and Culture 6.2 (2006): 261–287. Print.

Battis, Jess. *Blood Relations: Chosen Families in* Buffy the Vampire Slayer *and* Angel. Jefferson, NC: McFarland, 2005. Print.

"Beauty and the Beasts." *Buffy the Vampire Slayer: The Complete Third Season*. Episode 4. Writ. Marti Noxon. Dir. James Whitmore, Jr. The WB. 20 Oct. 1998. Twentieth Century Fox, 2003. DVD.

Bowman, Laurel. "*Buffy the Vampire Slayer*: The Greek Hero Revisited." University of Victoria, 2002: n. pag. Web. 15 Aug. 2016.

"Bring on the Night." *Buffy the Vampire Slayer: The Complete Seventh Season*. Episode 10. Writ. Marti Noxon and Douglas Petrie. Dir. David Grossman. UPN. 17 Dec. 2002. Twentieth Century Fox, 2004. DVD.

Buchanan, Ian. "Extraordinary Spaces in Ordinary Places: De Certeau and the Space of Postcolonialism." *Journal of the South Pacific Association for Commonwealth Literature and Language Studies* 36 (1992): n. pag. Culture and Communication Reading Room, 15 April 2015. Web. 7 May 2016.

Casano, Christina. "Love and Loyalty: Giles as Watcher, Father, and Partner." *Girls in Capes* 28 June 2013: n. pag. Web. 14 Aug. 2016.

"Chosen." *Buffy the Vampire Slayer: The Complete Seventh Season*. Episode 22. Writ. and Dir. Joss Whedon. UPN. 20 May 2003. Twentieth Century Fox, 2004. DVD.

Churchill, Winston. "House of Commons Rebuilding." 28 Oct. 1943. *Hansard 1803–2005*. UK Parliament, n. d. Web. 7 May 2016.

Early, Frances. "Staking Her Claim: Buffy the Vampire Slayer as Transgressive Woman Warrior." *The Journal of Popular Culture* 35.3 (2001): 11–27. Print.

Frankel, Valerie Estelle. *Buffy and the Heroine's Journey: Vampire Slayer as Feminine Chosen One*. Jefferson, NC: McFarland, 2012. Print.

"Fear Itself." *Buffy the Vampire Slayer: The Complete Fourth Season*. Episode 4. Writ. David Fury. Dir. Tucker Gates. The WB. 26 Oct. 1999. Twentieth Century Fox, 2003. DVD.

"The Freshman." *Buffy the Vampire Slayer: The Complete Fourth Season*. Episode 1. Writ. and Dir. Joss Whedon. The WB. 5 Oct. 1999. Twentieth Century Fox, 2003. DVD.

Fritts, David. "Buffy's Seven-Season Initiation." *Buffy Meets the Academy: Essays on the Episodes and Scripts as Text*. Ed. Kevin K. Durand. Jefferson, NC: McFarland, 2009. 32–44. Print.

Gee, Lori. "Human-Centered Design Guidelines." *Learning Spaces*. Ed. Diana G. Oblinger. Educause, 2006. N. pag. Web. 30 Oct. 2015.

"Graduation Day: Part 2." *Buffy the Vampire Slayer: The Complete Third Season*. Episode 22. Writ. and Dir. Joss Whedon. The WB. 13 July 1999. Twentieth Century Fox, 2003. DVD.

Graetz, Ken A. "The Psychology of Learning Environments." *Learning Spaces*. Ed. Diana G. Oblinger. Educause, 2006. N. pag. Web. 30 Oct. 2015.

"The Harvest." *Buffy the Vampire Slayer: The Complete First Season*. Episode 2. Writ. Joss Whedon. Dir. John T. Kretchmer. The WB. 10 March 1997. Twentieth Century Fox, 2002. DVD.

"Helpless." *Buffy the Vampire Slayer: The Complete Third Season*. Episode 12. Writ. David Fury. Dir. James A. Contner. The WB. 19 Jan. 1999. Twentieth Century Fox, 2003. DVD.

"Hush." *Buffy the Vampire Slayer: The Complete Fourth Season*. Episode 10. Writ. and Dir. Joss Whedon. The WB. 14 Dec. 1999. Twentieth Century Fox, 2003. DVD.

Jowett, Lorna. "The Summers House as Domestic Space in *Buffy the Vampire Slayer*." *Slayage: The Online Journal of Whedon Studies* 5.2 (2005): n. pag. Web. 5 Aug. 2016.

Kirkpatrick, Kim. "Scoobies and Potentials: The Slayer Community as Hero in *Buffy the Vampire Slayer*." *MP Journal* 1.4 (2006): n. pag. Web. 17 Oct. 2015.

"Lessons." *Buffy the Vampire Slayer: The Complete Seventh Season*. Episode 1. Writ. Joss Whedon. Dir. David Solomon. UPN. 24 Sept. 2002. Twentieth Century Fox, 2004. DVD.

Little, Tracy. "High School Is Hell: Metaphor Made Literal in *Buffy the Vampire Slayer*." *Buffy the Vampire Slayer and Philosophy*. Ed. James B. South and William Erwin. Chicago: Open Court, 2003. 282–293. Print.

Loughran, John. "Pedagogy: Making Sense of the Complex Relationship Between Teaching and Learning." *Curriculum Inquiry* 43.1 (2013): 118–141. Print.

Luz, Ana. "The [Design of] Educational Space: A Process-Centered *Built* Pedagogy." *International Conference on Engineering and Product Design Education*. Universitat Politecnica de Catalunya, Barcelona. 4-5 Sept. 2008. The Design Society, n. d. Web. 3 Feb. 2016.
McGregor, Jane. "Making Spaces: Teacher Workplace Topologies." *Pedagogy, Culture & Society* 11.3 (2003): 353-375. Print.
McLean, Barbara. "Women Writing, Women Teaching: Speculating on Domestic Space." *Canadian Woman Studies* 17.4 (1998): 94-97. ProQuest. Web. 17 Oct. 2015.
Mulcahy, Dianne. "The Salience of Space for Pedagogy and Identity in Teacher Education: Problem-Based Learning as a Case in Point." *Pedagogy, Culture & Society* 14.1 (March 2006): 55-69. Print.
"No Place Like Home." *Buffy the Vampire Slayer: The Complete Fifth Season*. Episode 5. Writ. Douglas Petrie. Dir. David Solomon. The WB. 24 Oct. 2000. Twentieth Century Fox, 2003. DVD.
"The Pack." *Buffy the Vampire Slayer: The Complete First Season*. Episode 6. Writ. Matt Kiene and Joe Reinkemeyer. Dir. Bruce Seth Green. The WB. 7 April 1997. Twentieth Century Fox, 2002. DVD.
"Pangs." *Buffy the Vampire Slayer: The Complete Fourth Season*. Episode 8. Writ. Jane Espenson. Dir. Michael Lange. The WB. 23 Nov. 1999. Twentieth Century Fox, 2003. DVD.
"Passion." *Buffy the Vampire Slayer: The Complete Second Season*. Episode 17. Writ. Ty King. Dir. Michael E. Gershman. Twentieth Century Fox, 2002. DVD.
"Potential." *Buffy the Vampire Slayer: The Complete Seventh Season*. Episode 12. UPN. 21 Jan. 2003. Writ. Rebecca Sinclair. Dir. James A. Contner. The WB. 24 Feb. 1998. Twentieth Century Fox, 2004. DVD.
"Real Me." *Buffy the Vampire Slayer: The Complete Fifth Season*. Episode 2. Writ. David Fury. Dir. David Grossman. The WB. 3 Oct. 2000. Twentieth Century Fox, 2003. DVD.
"Revelations." *Buffy the Vampire Slayer: The Complete Third Season*. Episode 7. Writ. Douglas Petrie. Dir. James A. Contner. The WB. 17 Nov. 1998. Twentieth Century Fox, 2003. DVD.
Robinson, Julia Williams. *Institution and Home: Architecture as a Cultural Medium*. Transformations 7. Amsterdam: Techne Press, 2006. Print.
Sayer, Karen. "This Was Our World and They Made It Theirs: Reading Space and Place in *Buffy the Vampire Slayer* and *Angel*." *Reading the Vampire Slayer: The Complete, Unofficial Guide to* Buffy *and* Angel. 2nd ed. Ed. Roz Kaveney. London: I.B. Tauris, 2004. 132-55. Print.
"Showtime." *Buffy the Vampire Slayer: The Complete Seventh Season*. Episode 11. Writ. David Fury. Dir. Michael Grossman. UPN. 7 Jan. 2003. Twentieth Century Fox, 2004. DVD.
Stevens, Kirsten. "Meet the Cullens: Family, Romance and Female Agency in *Buffy the Vampire Slayer* and *Twilight*." *Slayage: The Online Journal of Whedon Studies* 8.1 (2010): n. pag. Web. 15 Aug. 2016.
Udovitch, Mim. "What Makes Buffy Slay?" *Rolling Stone*, 11 May 2000. Web. 12 Feb. 2016.
Waller, Gregory A. *The Living and the Undead: Slaying Vampires, Exterminating Zombies*. Urbana: University of Illinois Press, 2010. Print.
"Welcome to the Hellmouth." *Buffy the Vampire Slayer: The Complete First Season*. Episode 1. Writ. Joss Whedon. Dir. Charles Martin Smith. The WB. 10 March 1997. Twentieth Century Fox, 2002. DVD.
"What's My Line? Part 2." *Buffy the Vampire Slayer: The Complete Second Season*. Episode 10. Writ. Marti Noxon. Dir. David Semel. The WB. 24 Nov. 1997. Twentieth Century Fox, 2002. DVD.
"When She Was Bad." *Buffy the Vampire Slayer: The Complete Second Season*. Episode 1. Writ. and Dir. Joss Whedon. The WB. 15 Sept. 1997. Twentieth Century Fox, 2002. DVD.
Wilcox, Rhonda. *Why Buffy Matters: The Art of* Buffy the Vampire Slayer. New York: I.B. Taurus, 2005. Print.
"Witch." *Buffy the Vampire Slayer: The Complete First Season*. Episode 3. Writ. Dana Reston. Dir. Stephen Cragg. The WB. 17 March 1997. Twentieth Century Fox, 2002. DVD.

A Home at the End of the World
The Future of Domesticity in the Whedonverse

LISA K. PERDIGAO

In Joss Whedon's *Avengers: Age of Ultron* (2015), the advent of AI causes a crisis on the homefront for the characters. This is not a surprising development, however, as *The Avengers* (2012) and *Agents of S.H.I.E.L.D.* (2013–) had previously depicted the impossibility of reclaiming home, at least in the traditional sense. In *Age of Ultron*, Clint Barton/Hawkeye is the only character for whom domesticity is rendered a possibility. The farmhouse, coded as the "safe house," is revealed to the other Avengers as a dream. Steve Rogers/Captain America cannot afford to live in his old neighborhood in Brooklyn while Natasha Romanoff/Black Widow and Bruce Banner/the Hulk say that they are unable to have "normal" family lives. Thor abruptly leaves the farmhouse, saying that he cannot find answers there. Ironically, although Barton had been under Loki's mind control in *The Avengers*, in *Age of Ultron*, he is the only Avenger able to resist Wanda Maximoff/Scarlet Witch's spell. That the revelation of Barton's idealized domestic life coincides with his resistance to programming is significant. Where Whedon resignifies what home represents to the characters in his earlier works, *Age of Ultron* represents the evolution of a concept: a systematic reprogramming of ideas about domesticity within the Whedonverse.

The endings of *Buffy the Vampire Slayer* (1997–2003), *Firefly* (2002–2003), *Serenity* (2005), and *Dollhouse* (2009–2010) hinge on the destruction and deconstruction of the characters' homes. In the *BtVS* series finale "Chosen," the characters face the abyss that was once home and watch the "Welcome to Sunnydale" sign fall into it. As this "Hellmouth is officially closed for business," they are forced to leave home; however, Giles reminds them that there is "another one in Cleveland" ("Chosen"). This suggests that the characters will relocate, finding a new home and sense of purpose. Where *Firefly*'s final episode, "Objects in Space," ends with meditations on the physical structure—and resiliency—of the characters' home, the spaceship *Serenity*, at the conclusion of the film *Serenity*, Captain Malcolm Reynolds encapsulates the series and film's representation of the ship when he tells River Tam, "Love keeps her in the air when she oughta fall down, tells you she's hurting 'fore she keens. Makes her a home." From its beginning, *Dollhouse* most explicitly challenges the idea of home as the Dollhouse manufactures and is manufactured from fantasies.[1] The series finale, "Epitaph Two: Return," depicts the dolls leaving the crumbling subterranean Dollhouse and looking toward the future and the possibility of finding a home in the real world. From the urban fantasy of *Buffy the Vampire Slayer* to the science fiction worlds of *Firefly*, *Serenity*, and *Dollhouse*, Whedon offers distinct visual representations of the resignification of home.

With *The Avengers*, Whedon's project of "assembling" the superteam is framed by a revisitation of the concept of home. The film begins with the characters' individual narratives and locations: Barton/Hawkeye is alone, "[u]p in his nest, as usual," at the NASA Joint Dark Energy Mission Facility; Romanoff/Black Widow is in the midst of an interrogation in an abandoned building; Rogers/Captain America is training at an empty Brooklyn gym; Banner/the Hulk is in a shack in Calcutta helping the poor; and Tony Stark/Iron Man returns from activating his self-sustaining clean energy reactor to the technologically-advanced Stark Tower. With the exception of Stark, who meets Pepper Potts at their shared home, the characters are depicted as isolated and their environments are (mostly) empty or outright abandoned. The opening scenes highlight what is at work in the film—bringing the individual characters and narratives out of isolation to forge the foundation of the expansive Marvel Cinematic Universe (MCU) to conclude Phase One.[2] After the first act of *The Avengers*, Whedon relocates the characters to a S.H.I.E.L.D. helicarrier that the characters individually and collectively refer to as home.[3] For example, after Loki wages an attack on the helicarrier, Stark says, "He hit us all right where we live. Why?" and Loki tells Agent Phil Coulson that his "floating fortress falls from the sky" (*The Avengers*). At its center, *The Avengers* represents threats to the security and stability of the home as well as the homefront.

The Avengers can be considered as exhibiting features of what Kristin J. Jacobson describes as "neodomestic fiction," works that "renovate the ideal home's usual depiction by positioning instability—as opposed to stability—as a key structure of quotidian American home life" (2).[4] Jacobson identifies neodomestic fiction as a product of a cultural shift in the early twenty-first century resulting from discrepancies in housing access and equity as well as rising foreclosure rates (1–2). This is not to say that the concept of home was ever a stable one. Betsy Klimasmith traces the history of the word's "changing definitions" in the *Oxford English Dictionary*—from "a village or town, a collection of dwellings" to "fixed residence of a family or household" to "the affective meaning of home"—before concluding that home is a contradictory space: "the nexus of the concrete and the fleeting; of place and 'conditions, circumstances and feelings'; of circumscribed and indefinite spaces" (4). Twenty-first century texts further problematize these definitions with their specific conditions, including the financial and social crises in the early twenty-first century for which Jacobson accounts.[5] Extending Jacobson's theories about the neodomestic realist contemporary novel to the Whedonverse science fiction films and television series yields possibilities for reconsidering how home figures in—and into—the future.

Jacobson's description of the three features of neodomestic fiction—relational domestic space, domestic mobility, and domestic renovation and redesign (4)—are well-suited for the Whedonverse more expansively and Whedon's work within the MCU specifically. As the world faces an extraterrestrial attack, home is an ideological concept that must be protected at all costs. As Ramzi Fawaz writes, "[P]ostwar superheroes produced complex and internally heterogeneous communities of fellow travelers—often brought together under the rubric of the superhero 'team' or chosen 'family'—who sought to use their powers for shaping a more egalitarian and democratic world" (11). The superheroes, tasked with defending the home, lack stable home environments of their own. Lisa Gotto argues that as superheroes "explore environments, navigate them, and thereby generate knowledge through space and spatial positioning" (47), the superhero genre "points to the emergence of new spatial sensibilities and viewing capacities" (41). The "domestic mobility" that Jacobson ascribes to both home as ideology and as physical space is especially evocative for the superhero genre. When S.H.I.E.L.D. Director Nick Fury tells Barton that he gave him security detail so that he could "keep a close eye on things," Barton replies, "Well, I see better from a distance" (*The Avengers*). As Scott Bukatman writes, "Superheroes exist to inhabit the city, to patrol, map, dissect, and traverse it" (195). In *The Avengers*, the assembled group offers distinct visions of what home comes to represent for the greater population—as viewed from above, away from, and within the city proper.

With the assembly of the Avengers comes conflicting ideologies, particularly those of Rogers/Captain America and Stark/Iron Man, who, respectively, represent tradition and innovation. When Coulson talks to Rogers for the first time, he tells him that he helped redesign the Captain America suit. Rogers asks, "Aren't the stars and stripes a little old-fashioned?" (*The Avengers*). Coulson replies, "With everything that's happening and the things that are about to come to light, people might just need a little old-fashioned" (*The Avengers*). Rogers is a "man out of time" and a "touchstone to the past" (*The Avengers*; "0-8-4"). Rogers' American idealism is central to the mission; however, it is strained in relation to the new conditions that the team faces with Loki's threat. Loki, "want[ing] a monument built in the skies with his name plastered," is drawn to Stark Tower, which is poised "to become a beacon of self-sustaining clean energy," for the site of the breach and Chitauri invasion (*The Avengers*). Stark Industries unites the two superheroes, as Tony Stark's father, Howard, was instrumental in Rogers' transformation into Captain America. However, the tower—what it represents—divides them. There is an ideological gap between the superheroes' conceptions of their relations to New York City: one wants to preserve the city of the past while the other wants to usher forth the city of the future. Klimasmith writes that "the formative power ascribed to environment, and specifically to architecture, would only become more complex with the rise of cities whose landscapes concretized a continual process of drastic and radical transformation" (5). That the Avengers engage in the Battle of New York is significant: they are fighting to protect the home and fighting about its very meaning.

At the end of *The Avengers*, a voice-over narration of the aftermath of the Battle of New York is accompanied by a sweeping shot of the city: Central Park is at the center, flanked by skyscrapers. The concept of home is rendered in expansive terms, as is the Avengers' mission. The news anchor states that "despite the devastation of what has been confirmed as an extraterrestrial attack, the extraordinary heroics of the group known as the Avengers has been to many a cause not only for comfort, but for celebration" (*The Avengers*). The city scene transitions to more intimate images of citizens' responses, which include praise, gratitude, questions, and critique. At the film's end, Thor takes Loki and the Tesseract home to Asgard and the rest of the Avengers go "their separate ways," "some, pretty extremely far" (*The Avengers*). However, Fury's promise of the Avengers' protection of the homefront is visually rendered onscreen as Stark and Pepper work on the renovation of the nearly-destroyed Stark Tower. As the camera zooms out from the pair and the construction materials that surround them, the trademark A of the Avengers is a sign of what is to come.

At the end of Phase One, the homefront is secured and restabilized, but, with *Agents of S.H.I.E.L.D.*, Whedon returns to the small screen to reexamine its relative security by bringing S.H.I.E.L.D. (Strategic Homeland Intervention, Enforcement and Logistics Division) into the foreground. Early in the pilot episode, S.H.I.E.L.D.'s purpose is clearly defined when Agent Maria Hill asks Agent Grant Ward what the organization means to him. He replies that "it means we're the line between the world and the much weirder world. We protect people from news they aren't ready to hear. And when we can't do that, we keep them safe" ("Pilot"). According to Coulson, S.H.I.E.L.D. is humanity's "last line of defense" ("Providence"). The series is framed as an extension of *The Avengers*' narrative; however, it introduces radical new ideas about what home signifies.

As Agent Hill says, "The Battle of New York was the end of the world. This—now—is the new world" ("Pilot"). The world in and of *Agents of S.H.I.E.L.D.* is made both familiar and strange. The pilot episode of *Agents of S.H.I.E.L.D.* begins with a long shot of the city, its skyline populated by skyscrapers. In a voice-over monologue, Rising Tide member and soon to be S.H.I.E.L.D. recruit Skye states, "The secret is out. For decades, your organization stayed in the shadows, hiding the truth. But now we know—they're among us. Heroes ... and monsters. The world is full of wonders..." as images from *The Avengers* appear onscreen: Thor's hammer, Captain America's shield, a Chitauri warrior, and a roaring Hulk ("Pilot"). The last image is clearly from the film, what Matthias Stork identifies as the film's "spectacular display of digital convergence, translating the comic book slogan 'Avengers Assemble' to the big screen through visualized iconography, by virtue of an uninterrupted 360-degree CGI-inflected tracking shot" (78). The triptych that unfolds in the opening sequence reveals the city restored, the city under attack, and the city protected, an encapsulation of the work in and of *The Avengers*. S.H.I.E.L.D.'s intervention in and enforcement of the homefront is proven successful. However, in the television series, S.H.I.E.L.D. becomes an embattled organization and concept, as the very idea of what is being protected—and from whom—is called into question.

The dismantling of the S.H.I.E.L.D. organization post–*Captain America: The Winter Soldier* (2014) sets the stage for the loss of the homefront in *Age of Ultron*, which realizes the illusory nature of home that *Agents of S.H.I.E.L.D.* suggests from its beginning. At the end of the television series' pilot episode, Coulson and Skye leave a white farmhouse, a safe house to which they relocated Mike Peterson's son, Ace. Peterson, a single father, joined Project C.E.N.T.I.P.E.D.E. with the hope of finding prospects to support his son other than working at a factory. However, the project goes wrong—or right—and transforms him into a weapon. At the end of the pilot, Coulson and Skye say that Peterson will return home soon; however, for three seasons, Peterson remains estranged from his son and home. There are no "safe houses" for the characters in *S.H.I.E.L.D.*: Skye, an orphan, is homeless, living in a van working with Rising Tide when she is discovered by S.H.I.E.L.D.; Melinda May loses her husband and home after crises within S.H.I.E.L.D.; Grant Ward burns his family's home to the ground after killing his family; and the Inhumans lose their safe haven, Lai Shi ("Afterlife"), at the end of season two. The white farmhouse depicted in the pilot episode is an illusory ideal that the characters—human and Inhuman—cannot attain.

Four days after the release of Anthony and Joe Russo's *Captain America: The Winter Soldier* (April 4, 2014), the *Agents of S.H.I.E.L.D.* episode "Turn, Turn, Turn" (April 8, 2014) featured the phrase #ITSALLCONNECTED in the bottom corner of the screen to emphasize the MCU's model of convergence. The safe house can be read as part of that project, as it becomes a recurring idea, symbol, and physical site in *Agents of S.H.I.E.L.D.* and the *Avengers* films. In the season two episode of *Agents of S.H.I.E.L.D.* "Love in the Time of Hydra," Coulson relocates Skye to a cabin called "The Retreat." It is described as "the house that Banner built" and a "safe house for people with powers" ("One Door Closes"; "Love in the Time of Hydra"). In the season two midseason finale, "What They Become," Skye's exposure to the Terrigen Mist causes her to undergo Terrigenesis, transforming her into "Quake" from the Marvel comics. S.H.I.E.L.D. Agent and scientist Leopold "Leo" Fitz tells Skye that if she was able to learn to control her body, she could have "Avengers-level powers, something like Captain America, even" ("Love in the Time of Hydra"). Fitz's partner, Jemma Simmons, replies, "I think it's best we keep in mind the unstable nature of Skye's power. If there is an Avenger equivalent, right now I'm afraid it's the Hulk" ("Love in the Time of Hydra"). The need to contain Skye becomes the focus of the episode and recalls the subplot within *The Avengers* of constructing a "cage" for the Hulk, lest he become uncontrollable. Skye trades one cage, as she calls the room where she is being kept on the S.H.I.E.L.D. "Bus" ("Airborne Mobile Command Station"), for another. The meaning of "safe house" changes from the pilot episode's depiction. Here it is viewed, at least from Skye's perspective, as a prison.

The scene of relocating Skye to Banner's cabin recalls the pilot episode in its framing. Again, Coulson and Skye travel alone. However, where the pilot episode ends with Skye joining S.H.I.E.L.D., in "Love in the Time of Hydra," she is removed from active duty and relocated to "one of Fury's old retreats." The traditional cabin is juxtaposed with advanced technology: the metal of the Quinjet appears alongside a rustic wood cabin on a lake in the first shot.[6] Skye's question "But who's it supposed to keep safe—the people with powers or everyone else?" signifies the shift in the meaning and purpose of the safe house ("Love in the Time of Hydra"). Coulson agrees to the more expansive definition, replying, "Both" before reassuring her, "Look, this is a safe place. You can relax here ... get a handle on your abilities" ("Love in the Time of Hydra"). The message on the touchscreen monitor punctuates this point: "RETREAT SECURED" ("One Door Closes"). In the episode "One Door Closes," Skye realizes that the safe house is a construct. The wood panels are just a façade; the safe house is actually made of a vibranium alloy (like the honeycomb-patterned walls in the Bus' "cage"), appearing to be the more literal prison that she imagined. On the metal surface is an undeniable imprint: the outline of the Hulk's fist.

"The Retreat" offers a shared space that physically and ideologically connects the narratives and characters of *Agents of S.H.I.E.L.D.* and *The Avengers*. As Coulson notes, "Rogers even spent a few weeks here after he defrosted" ("Love in the Time of Hydra"). Where Rogers awakens to the twenty-first century in an artificially-constructed World War II-styled hospital room in Joe Johnston's *Captain America: The First Avenger* (2011), the relocation of Rogers to the cabin suggests what the cabin is made to recall: a traditional American setting. However, upon closer inspection, its artificiality is exposed. The safe house is compromised, or perhaps it never really was: those claiming to be part of the "real" S.H.I.E.L.D. discover Skye's location and attempt to capture her. One safe house is then exchanged for another, signaling the "domestic mobility" that Jacobson describes. Gordon, an Inhuman, takes Skye to Lai Shi, where he says that she can be safe among others like her ("One Door Closes"). When Skye awakens in "Afterlife," Gordon repeats his promise: "Everything's gonna be okay. You're safe now." As Lincoln, Skye's "transitioner," tells her, with the exception of Gordon, no one knows where they are or the way "in or out"; as a result, they are kept "secret and safe from the outside world" ("Afterlife"). However, Skye, apparently suspicious of any safe house, adds, "Or it keeps us prisoners" ("Afterlife"). Lai Shi, Lincoln says, is not a "permanent place," more a "way station," suggesting Klimasmith's representation of home as the "nexus of the concrete and the fleeting; of place and 'conditions, circumstances and feelings'; of circumscribed and indefinite spaces" (4). And, despite its natural setting, Lai Shi is also revealed to be a construct: it is the utopian "no place," unable to be sustained, protected, and preserved.

Where Lai Shi is conceived as a safe haven for Inhumans who have evolved, *Avengers: Age of Ultron* depicts revolutionary advancements in AI meant to protect the world. In the "Age of Ultron," the home and its protectors are threatened by new technologies. The home (domestic and global, city and country) is physically and ideologically under attack. Where *Agents of S.H.I.E.L.D.* emphasized #ITSALLCONNECTED, *Age of Ultron* allows Whedon to come full circle, returning to a familiar concept of home.[7] The reappearance of the white farmhouse in *Age of Ultron* emphasizes a central and pervasive idea about how Whedon is reconceiving domesticity within the MCU. Where the pilot episode of *Agents of S.H.I.E.L.D.* depicts Coulson and Skye leaving behind the farmhouse and what it represents, in *Age of Ultron*, under Barton's direction, the Avengers are taken to a safe house to reassemble the team. Continuing—and evolving from—the narrative thread of *Agents of S.H.I.E.L.D.*, *Age of Ultron* actively rewrites the concept of home for the future.

Where *The Avengers* is staged around the Battle of New York, *Age of Ultron* relocates the Avengers to Sokovia, a fictional European country, to examine the impact of war on an international scale. The film begins in the perspective of the embattled Sokovians; the Maximoff twins, Pietro/Quicksilver and Wanda/Scarlet Witch, hold hands as Baron von Strucker announces on a loudspeaker, "This is not a drill. We are under attack!" (*Age of Ultron*). In the film, the twins symbolize the devastation brought by war, by the Avengers. Initially conceived as a "global peacekeeping initiative," Ultron comes to identify the Avengers as the real threat to peace and plans for the team's extinction (*Age of Ultron*). The twins support Ultron's claim that Tony Stark is the cause of destruction. When Ultron asks Pietro to think of the "big picture," Pietro references a "little picture" that he looks at every day (*Age of Ultron*). When Ultron tells him, "You lost your parents. I've seen the records," Pietro replies that "the records are not the picture" (*Age of Ultron*). Pietro does not reveal the picture, but he suggests its meaning and significance as he tells the story of how the twins lost their parents when their home was bombed.

As Rhonda V. Wilcox notes, Whedon ponders "the overwhelming fact of our ability to imbue [objects] with meaning" in the *Firefly* episode "Objects in Space" (158). *Age of Ultron* evidences Whedon's larger project of imbuing the concept and physical structure of home with meaning. The "little picture" that Pietro holds and reconstructs in his narrative details the eradication of the familial home during a most quotidian ritual: the family was eating dinner in their apartment when the first shell hit. The twins' parents fell through a hole in the floor as "the whole building start[ed] coming apart" (*Age of Ultron*). The children hid under the bed, three feet away from a shell produced by Stark Industries. Ultron understands the reason for the twins' survival of von Strucker's experiments, revenge against Tony Stark, and they become key components of his plan. He tells Pietro that Wanda will "tear [the Avengers] apart from the inside" (*Age of Ultron*).

As Ultron finishes his line, the scene transitions to a long shot of a rebuilt Avengers Tower (previously Stark Tower) marked with the Avengers A, a stark contrast to the devastated Sokovia. Both sites had experienced war on home soil, but where Avengers Tower is newly fortified, at least externally, Sokovia remains a crumbling fortress. Ultron uses Pietro and Wanda's personal histories as the catalyst and medium for revenge against the Avengers. There is a certain symmetry to his plan: by "tear[ing] them apart from the inside" (*Age of Ultron*), the team will be destroyed, like Pietro and Wanda's home. Reciprocity is central to the plot: Wanda accesses and manipulates their collective fears about the loss of home. It is her first and most potent line of attack that has a ripple-effect throughout the narrative.

The Avengers collectively experience Wanda's spell in the same way: they envision the loss of their families and homes. Stark's initial vision, which inspires him to create Ultron, is a distortion of the marble sculpture that appears at the end of the film celebrating the characters' heroic feats. In Stark's vision, the Avengers are dead, save for himself and Rogers, who tells Stark that he could have saved them. Romanoff's vision is of a tragic past rather than the future extinction of the Avengers. She remembers the "graduation ceremony" where she is sterilized. When Madame B tells her that the ceremony is necessary for Romanoff to take her place in the world, Romanoff replies, "I have no place in the world" (*Age of Ultron*). Rogers, the "man out of time," similarly has no place in a post-war world. While soldiers and civilians celebrate at a club, Rogers sees destruction everywhere: soldiers fight, and spilled wine on a shirt resembles a bullet wound. There is war even in peacetime. Agent Peggy Carter tells Rogers, "The war is over, Steve. We can go home. Imagine it" (*Age of Ultron*). But she—and everyone else—disappears, leaving him alone. He is haunted by the past that never was, the future that he realizes he has lost when he wakes up in the twenty-first century in *Captain America: The First Avenger*. Thor's vision bookends the others.[7] He is transported back home to Asgard where he learns from Heimdall that his power leads to his people's deaths. The Hulk is the last of Wanda's victims, but his vision is not depicted in the film, only the devastation that he causes in Johannesburg, South Africa. He realizes the other Avengers' worst fears.

Where the Avengers' ideas and fears about home—local and global—are manipulated, Barton's sense of home remains intact and guides the course of the narrative. Having "no place in the world," the Avengers leave for an uncertain future after being told by Agent Hill to remain in "stealth mode," "away from here" (*Age of Ultron*). Barton flies the team to a safe house, to *his* safe house that resembles the farmhouse in *Agents of S.H.I.E.L.D.* As they land, the Quinjet disappears into a thicket of trees and all that is left onscreen is the white farmhouse, an old barn, a meandering fence, and rolling green fields. Nancy Armstrong writes, "The opposition between city and country ... only enhanced the advantages of the domestic ideal" (69). After witnessing and participating in the destruction of Sokovian and South African cities, the characters struggle to make sense of this "domestic ideal." The characters reluctantly make their way into Barton's family home as Barton calls out, "Honey? I'm home," like a character in a 1950s sitcom.[8] The scene confuses the team members. Stark immediately tries to come up with an alternative narrative for the seemingly conventional family narrative: seeing Barton's pregnant wife Laura, he says, "This is an agent of some kind," and, when he sees Barton's two children, says, "These are smaller agents" (*Age of Ultron*). Barton tells them that this life predates his work with the Avengers: Fury helped him set up the safe house when he joined and kept it "off S.H.I.E.L.D.'s files" (*Age of Ultron*).

However, the farmhouse proves to be anything but safe for the Avengers. It inadvertently continues Ultron's plan—executed by Wanda—to "tear [the Avengers] apart from the inside" (*Age of Ultron*). It is a tangible reminder of what each of them will never have. Thor is the most uncomfortable at Barton's home; he steps on the children's Legos and awkwardly looms over Barton's daughter. As he looks at the girl, visions of the destruction in Asgard flash in his mind. Occupying Barton's home seems to evoke the images; however, the everyday objects and rituals of the family—Legos and the sound of the toaster—distract him from the mission. He tells Rogers, "I saw something in that dream. I need answers. I won't find them here" and abruptly leaves (*Age of Ultron*). It is fitting that Rogers remains alone on the farmhouse porch once Thor departs. An American flag hangs on the left side of the porch while the barn and a pickup truck are positioned on the right. The scene recalls Rogers boxing in a Brooklyn gym at the beginning of *The Avengers*; he is reanimated in the twenty-first century yet remains rooted in the past.

The safe house appears as a representation of Americana, a contrast to Avengers Tower and Ultron. The safe house, like Captain America, is a "touchstone to the past" ("0-8-4"). However, rather than reenter the house, Rogers pauses in the doorway. He hears the echo of Peggy's voice saying, "We can go home" (*Age of Ultron*). Rogers sighs before walking away. Here Rogers acknowledges that the traditional home is lost to him. *Captain America* comics writer Steve Englehart said, "I was very aware when doing Cap that I wanted to rehabilitate him as a character, and that meant facing up to his particular ambiance, which was Classic Americanism…. The fact that I was writing him in an era (1972) … when Americanism was in disrepute, just sharpened his focus, as far as I was concerned" (qtd. in Dittmer 85). Earlier in the film, when Rogers tells Sam Wilson/Falcon that he cannot afford a place in Brooklyn, Wilson says, "Well, home is home, you know?" asserting the connection between Captain America and the city (*Age of Ultron*). However, as Bukatman writes, "through the vehicle of the superhero, as through cinema and sociology, one recovers the city as new and shifting ground" (195). The "Age of Ultron" introduces radical questions about the hero's relationship to his home. The farmhouse, a more comfortable and perhaps attainable ideal for Rogers, is not a viable option.

While Rogers remains outside of the farmhouse, looking in, Romanoff sits inside, looking out, as she remembers, through flashbacks, the sterilization procedure that she underwent as part of her "training." Banner also experiences the aftermath of Wanda's spell from inside the home. While shaving, he remembers his violent attack on the city. Glimpsed from the inside, the farmhouse becomes a symbol of what the two characters will never have. Banner tells Romanoff that now that the world has seen the "real Hulk" for the first time, he has to leave. When Romanoff proposes that she run away with him, he asks, "Where can I go?," recalling the line from her vision; he, too, has "no place in the world" (*Age of Ultron*). The domestic narrative revealed at Barton's farmhouse is not their reality. Banner tells Romanoff,

"There's no future with me. I can't ever.... I can't have this. Kids. Do the math. I physically can't" (*Age of Ultron*). Romanoff responds, "Neither can I" and tells him the details of the "graduation ceremony." As Jacobson writes, "Neodomestic fiction reflects, provokes, and theorizes distinctive responses to conservative visions of the contemporary home and family" (38). Banner and Romanoff cannot take part in that conventional narrative. Family, the "one thing that might matter more than a mission," is taken out of the equation for the characters, and arguably for most of the members of the Avengers team. From their vantage point within—or just outside—of the farmhouse, home is an equally fantastic concept.

In *Age of Ultron*, Stark redefines—or at least clarifies—the Avengers' Initiative when he tells Rogers that their mission is to "end the team," "end the fight," and "go home" (*Age of Ultron*). Returning home is the goal for the superheroes. The "Avengers Initiative" and idea of building a team was conceived by Fury and broached to Stark in an *Iron Man* post-credits scene. In *Age of Ultron*, Fury is no longer the Director of S.H.I.E.L.D.; in fact, S.H.I.E.L.D., the organization protecting the homeland, no longer exists, at least officially. However, Fury's reappearance and call for the Avengers to reassemble highlight the importance of home. He gestures to Barton's farmhouse, saying that Ultron wants to see "all this, laid in a grave" (*Age of Ultron*). The Avengers' redefined mission is to protect the home symbolized by the farmhouse, something that will not—and cannot—be realized for them personally.

Home is a construct for all but Barton. Yet even Barton's home is destabilized: it is in the midst of renovations. Jacobson notes that "Home renovation both maintains and redesigns model domesticity; the home's shifting ideal architectures reveal entrenched and changing ideas about the social construction of the American family" (78).[9] In *Age of Ultron*, Barton's remodeling project involves "both literal renovation projects within the storyline as well as generic and symbolic restructuring" (Jacobson 78). Laura tells Barton, "Things are changing for us. In a few months' time, you and me are gonna be outnumbered" (*Age of Ultron*). Barton's roles as husband and father are in conflict with his role as Hawkeye; he is needed on this homefront as well. As the Avengers leave the farmhouse, the significance of retaining and restoring domestic life is highlighted, albeit in a playful way, when Barton, after replacing his plaid flannel shirt with body armor, promises his wife that he will finish reflooring the sunroom when he returns home. Her reply, "Yeah, then you'll find another part of the house to tear apart," gestures beyond their domestic narrative to identify the threat that Ultron represents. Barton promises a restored house and home with the simple line, "No. It's the last project. I promise" (*Age of Ultron*).[10]

The farmhouse is ideologically conceived and rendered visually as a contrast to the superhero's city. As Gotto writes, "Being capable of transcending the laws of physics, superheroes move through space in a special way" (47). Where the Avengers fly, bound, run, and race through the city, Vision—conceived as the evolved form of Ultron—appears to be an extension of the city, of space itself. Thor throws Vision through a glass wall, but before Vision reaches the skyscraper window, he gracefully stops and stares out at the city. Bukatman writes, "The superhero city is experienced in a rush but opened to contemplation: it is distinguished by this dialectic of exuberant motion and legible stasis" (177). Whedon uses rack focus to superimpose Vision upon the city. Michel de Certeau writes that the view from the summit of the World Trade Center—a now impossible vantage point—"is to be lifted out of the city's grasp. One's body is no longer clasped by the streets that turn and return it according to anonymous law.... His elevation transforms him into a voyeur. It puts him at a distance" (127). Vision is able to occupy a seemingly impossible vantage point within and above the city and its population. As James N. Gilmore notes, "the ultimate power of the digital man is in his ability to move across borders and spaces.... The digital man, it would seem, has the utopian capability to be anywhere and do anything" (23). When Vision is brought to life, he is the conduit between New York and Sokovia. He directs the Avengers to Sokovia, and with it, to a reconceptualization of home. Where *The Avengers* stages its war on the American homefront in the Battle of New York, moving the battle to Sokovia in *Age of Ultron* highlights contrasting ideologies similar to those of the skyscraper vs. the farmhouse. New York survives but Sokovia is destroyed.

In the last act, *Age of Ultron* reveals the resuscitation of home. As Sokovia is about to fall, a helicarrier appears to deliver the Sokovians to safety. Pietro asks, "This is S.H.I.E.L.D.?" and Rogers replies, "This is what S.H.I.E.L.D is supposed to be" (*Age of Ultron*). The organization protecting the homeland performs a deus ex machina; the helicarrier is a machine of the gods (plural if we count Vision), superheroes, and agents that saves mankind. Fury says, "She's dusty, but she'll do" (*Age of Ultron*), sounding a bit like *Firefly* and *Serenity*'s Mal.[11] Here is the most obvious representation of "domestic mobility" as the Sokovians leave their homeland for a new location. Where Loki had threatened a "falling fortress" in *The Avengers*, *Age of Ultron* restores S.H.I.E.L.D.'s function of protecting—and serving as—the home. It appears to civilians and superheroes alike as a marvel, recalling Rogers and Banner's initial reactions in *The Avengers*.

The film then offers a conceptual shift from the global to the individual home. As Barton and Romanoff arrive at the scene to transport themselves and the Sokovians to safety, Barton returns to his thoughts of and plans for his own home. He says, "I know what I need to do. The dining room. If I knock out that east wall, it'd make a nice workspace for Laura, huh? Put up some baffling. She can't hear the kids running around. What do you think?" (*Age of Ultron*). Romanoff plays along with the narrative, saying, "You guys always eat in the kitchen anyway," and Barton replies, "No one eats in a dining room" (*Age of Ultron*). Where Pietro is constantly reminded of the loss of the family scene at the dinner table, Barton actively rewrites it for his own family, even relocating the traditional spaces to more utilitarian and contemporary purposes. It is fitting, then, that Pietro offers the sacrifice play: when Barton falls under Ultron's fire after leaving the "lifeboat" to save a young boy, Pietro rushes in to shield Barton and the boy. Pietro becomes a physical embodiment of S.H.I.E.L.D., protecting the homefront. After the destruction of Sokovia and Ultron, the film returns to the farmhouse one last time. Barton appears in the kitchen, no longer dressed as Hawkeye. The Battle—and loss—of Sokovia was the "last project" for him. He is finally able to leave the team and finish restoring his own home.

Away from the farmhouse, Stark arrives at the new Avengers Facility where the remaining members of the team—including James Rhodes/War Machine, Vision, Wilson/Falcon, and Wanda/Scarlet Witch—reassemble. The location of the facility is outside of city and country—or perhaps in the liminal space between them. It is upstate New York, after all. The facility is built of metal and glass (with Stark's money, most likely something stronger) and surrounded by green. Saying, "[I]t's time for me to tap out," Stark tells Rogers, "Maybe I should take a page out of Barton's book. Build Pepper a farm, hope nobody blows it up" (*Age of Ultron*). When Rogers replies, "The simple life," Stark adds, "You'll get there one day" (*Age of Ultron*). Incidentally, Stark is the only Avenger who does not appear out of place at the farmhouse; he comfortably settles in, even finding time to work on a John Deere tractor.[12] Unlike the other Avengers, his vision is not of the loss of his family, his home with Pepper.

However, for the remaining Avengers, the concept of home is ultimately adapted and altered. Rogers replies, "I don't know. Family, stability.... The guy who wanted all that went in the ice 75 years ago. I think someone else came out" (*Age of Ultron*). When Stark asks, "You all right?" Rogers replies, "I'm home" (*Age of Ultron*). Echoing Mal's gesture at the end of *Serenity*, Rogers reclaims a sense of home in this new world. As Klimasmith notes, "'Home' operates best as an ideological space when defined in opposition to its surroundings" (3). As Phase Two of the MCU comes to a conclusion following *Age of Ultron*, the Avengers admit the impossibility of traditional domesticity for themselves but succeed in saving many Sokovians as their homeland is destroyed. Although the Avengers' actions in New York, Washington, D.C., South Africa, and Sokovia become points of contention and the cause for intervention in Anthony and Joe Russo's *Captain America: Civil War* (2016), Whedon's *Avengers* films highlight the possibility of recovering and restoring home. Bukatman writes that "the experience of the city (and the comic book) is less one of static order than dynamic negotiation" (174). The experience of home can be similarly mapped. Traditional ideas of domesticity are not a reality for the Avengers; however, by the end of the film, Rogers and Romanoff, two characters with "nowhere to go," find meaning and purpose, a resignified home fitting for the future.

NOTES

1. In the *Dollhouse* episode "Man on the Street," Echo says, "The Dollhouse deals in fantasy. That is their business, but that is not their purpose."
2. Phase One is the first of Marvel's three planned stages for big and small screen adaptations of the comics. It began in 2008 with the release of Jon Favreau's *Iron Man* and ended with *The Avengers*. Phase Two ran from 2012 to 2015, concluding with Peyton Reed's *Ant-Man*, which followed *Avengers: Age of Ultron*. The final phase, Phase Three, began with Anthony and Joe Russo's *Captain America: Civil War* (2016) and is slated to end in 2019.
3. Admittedly, the representation of the helicarrier as home is distinct from the representation of the spaceship *Serenity*. Barbara Maio notes that the *Serenity* is a "metaphoric home; so the rooms, public or private, are designed to have a sense of intimacy" (209–210). We do not have access to the private rooms within the helicarrier; instead, the focus is on shared environments—for example, the control room, lab, and cargo bay that establish the helicarrier as the hub of S.H.I.E.L.D. And yet S.H.I.E.L.D. offers the superheroes a sense of home, a representation of what they are fighting for.
4. Jacobson writes that the genre "does not represent a full break from its literary predecessors" but rather an "intensification and rearrangement of tensions and characteristics present at the time of domestic fiction's inception in the nineteenth century and its continued development in the twentieth century" (6–7).
5. Jacobson references neoconservatism, neoliberalism, the new urbanism movement, the aftermaths of 9/11 and Hurricane Katrina, the "rise and aftereffects of second-wave feminism," the affordable housing crisis, and suburban development (including the popularity of gated communities) as contexts that shape neodomestic fiction (36, 37).
6. The representation of "The Retreat" recalls Drew Goddard's film *The Cabin in the Woods* (2012) (for which Whedon co-wrote the screenplay and produced), suggesting that the seemingly natural setting is contrived, artificial, and not really "safe."
7. According to Stacey Abbott, *Serenity* marks "the point where Whedon's television and cinema career came full circle" (227). She adds, "Whedon's circle thus continues to turn" (Abbott 238). Whedon's *Agents of S.H.I.E.L.D.* and *Avengers* films highlight this convergence of universes: Whedonverse and Marvel Cinematic Universe.
8. In Gary Ross' *Pleasantville* (1998), twins David and Jennifer are transported into a 1950s television series by the same name. Their TV father, George Parker, constantly repeats the lines when entering the family home.
9. Jacobson traces developments in neodomestic fiction to material culture, arguing that "the booming remodeling period that characterized the early years of the twenty-first century figured in other areas of the era's domestic culture" (77).
10. In an earlier scene, Barton replies, "I answer to you. Yes, ma'am" (*Age of Ultron*) when on his cell phone. He originally tells Rogers that it is his girlfriend, but the revelation of his other life alters the picture. From the onset, Barton—and the film—upsets traditional and conventional representations of power dynamics within the home. Here he again follows his wife's lead, choosing to return to and remain within the domestic space after this last mission.
11. Fury's line also recalls Wilcox and Tanya R. Cochran's assessment of the *Serenity* spaceship: "Her pieces fall off and break, but somehow she keeps flying. And she is home" (7).
12. This scene recalls Stark repairing his Iron Man suit in Harley Keener's garage in

Shane Black's *Iron Man 3*. In both films—and spaces—Stark appears comfortable and "at home" in settings where he can work with his hands, similar to Barton.

Works Cited

Abbott, Stacey. "'Can't Stop the Signal': The Resurrection/Regeneration of *Serenity*." *Investigating* Firefly *and* Serenity: *Science Fiction on the Frontier*. Ed. Rhonda V. Wilcox and Tanya R. Cochran. London: I.B. Tauris, 2008. 227–238. Print.
"Afterlife." *Agents of S.H.I.E.L.D.* Season 2. Episode 16. Writ. Craig Titley. Dir. Kevin Hooks. ABC. 7 April 2015. Disney-ABC Domestic Television, 2015. Netflix. 15 May 2016.
Armstrong, Nancy. *Desire and Domestic Fiction: A Political History of the Novel*. New York: Oxford University Press, 1987. Print.
The Avengers. Writ and Dir. Joss Whedon. Marvel Studios, 2012. DVD.
Avengers: Age of Ultron. Writ. and Dir. Joss Whedon. Marvel Studios, 2015. DVD.
Bukatman, Scott. "A Song of the Urban Superhero." *The Superhero Reader*. Ed. Charles Hatfield, Jeet Heer, and Kent Worcester. Jackson: University Press of Mississippi, 2013. 170–198. Print.
The Cabin in the Woods. Writ. Joss Whedon and Drew Goddard. Dir. Drew Goddard. Lionsgate, 2012. DVD.
Captain America: The First Avenger. Writ. Christopher Markus and Stephen McFeely. Dir. Joe Johnson. Marvel Studios, 2011. DVD.
"Chosen." *Buffy the Vampire Slayer: The Complete Seventh Season*. Episode 22. Writ. Joss Whedon. Dir. Joss Whedon. UPN. 20 May 2003. Twentieth Century Fox, 2004. DVD.
De Certeau, Michel. "Walking in the City." *The Cultural Studies Reader*. 2nd ed. Ed. Simon During. London: Routledge, 2003. 126–133. Print.
Dittmer, Jason. *Captain America and the Nationalist Superhero: Metaphors, Narratives, and Geopolitics*. Philadelphia: Temple University Press, 2013. Print.
Fawaz, Ramzi. *The New Mutants: Superheroes and the Radical Imagination of American Comics*. New York: New York University Press, 2016. Print.
Gilmore, James N. "Will You Like Me When I'm Angry? Discourses of the Digital in *Hulk* and *The Incredible Hulk*." *Superhero Synergies: Comic Book Characters Go Digital*. Ed. James N. Gilmore and Matthias Stork. Lanham, MD: Rowman & Littlefield, 2014. 11–26. Print.
Gotto, Lisa. "Fantastic Views: Superheroes, Visual Perception, and Digital Perspective." *Superhero Synergies: Comic Book Characters Go Digital*. Lanham, MD: Rowman & Littlefield, 2014. 41–56. Print.
Jacobson, Kristin J. *Nedomestic American Fiction*. Columbus: Ohio State University Press, 2010. Print.
Klimasmith, Betsy. *At Home in the City: Urban Domesticity in American Literature and Culture, 1850–1930*. Durham: University of New Hampshire Press, 2005. Print.
"Love in the Time of Hydra." *Agents of S.H.I.E.L.D.* Season 2. Episode 14. Writ. Brent Fletcher. Dir. Jesse Bochco. ABC. 24 March 2015. Disney-ABC Domestic Television. Netflix, 2015. 15 May 2016.
Maio, Barbara. "Between Past and Future: Hybrid Design Style in *Firefly* and *Serenity*." *Investigating* Firefly *and* Serenity: *Science Fiction on the Frontier*. Ed. Rhonda V. Wilcox and Tanya R. Cochran. London: I.B. Tauris, 2008. 201–211. Print.
"Man on the Street." *Joss Whedon's Dollhouse: Season One*. Episode 6. Writ. Joss Whedon. Dir. David Straiton. Fox. 20 Mar 2009. Twentieth Century Fox, 2009. DVD.
"Objects in Space." *Firefly: The Complete Series*. Episode 14. Writ. and Dir. Joss Whedon. Fox. 13 Dec. 2002. Twentieth Century Fox, 2003. DVD.
"One Door Closes." *Agents of S.H.I.E.L.D.* Season 2. Episode 15. Writ. Lauren LeFranc and Rafe Judkins. Dir. David Solomon. ABC. 31 Mar 2015. Disney-ABC Domestic Television, 2015. Netflix. 15 May 2016.
"Pilot." *Agents of S.H.I.E.L.D.* Season 1. Episode 1. Writ. Joss Whedon, Jed Whedon, and Maurissa Tancharoen. Dir. Joss Whedon. ABC. 24 Sept. 2013. Disney-ABC Domestic Television, 2014. Netflix. 15 May 2016.

"Providence." *Agents of S.H.I.E.L.D.* Season 1. Episode 18. Writ. Brent Fletcher. Dir. Milan Cheylov. ABC. 15 April 2014. Disney-ABC Domestic Television, 2014. Netflix. 15 May 2016.
Serenity. Writ. And Dir. Joss Whedon. Mutant Enemy/Universal, 2005. DVD.
Stork, Matthias. "Assembling the Avengers: Reframing the Superhero Movie through Marvel's Cinematic Universe." *Superhero Synergies: Comic Book Characters Go Digital.* Ed. James N. Gilmore and Matthias Stork. Lanham, MD: Rowman & Littlefield, 2014. 77–96. Print.
"What They Become." *Agents of S.H.I.E.L.D.* Season 2. Episode 10. Writ. Jeffrey Bell. Dir. Michael Zinberg. ABC. 9 Dec. 2014. Disney-ABC Domestic Television, 2015. Netflix. 15 May 2016.
Wilcox, Rhonda V. "'I Do Not Hold to That': Joss Whedon and Original Sin." *Investigating* Firefly *and* Serenity: *Science Fiction on the Frontier.* Ed. Rhonda V. Wilcox and Tanya R. Cochran. London: I.B. Tauris, 2008. 155–166. Print.
Wilcox, Rhonda V., and Tanya R. Cochran, eds. "'Good Myth': Joss Whedon's Further Worlds." *Investigating* Firefly *and* Serenity: *Science Fiction on the Frontier.* London: I.B. Tauris, 2008. 1–11. Print.
"0-8-4." *Agents of S.H.I.E.L.D.* Season 1. Episode 2. Writ. Maurissa Tancharoen, Jed Whedon, and Jeffrey Bell. Dir. David Straiton. ABC. 1 Oct. 2013. Disney-ABC Domestic Television, 2014. Netflix. 15 May 2016.

About the Contributors

Kyle William **Bishop** is a professor of film and screen studies at Southern Utah University, where he directs the Honors Program. He has written articles on *Metropolis, Night of the Living Dead, Fight Club, Dawn of the Dead, The Birds, Zombieland, The Walking Dead,* and *World War Z,* and two monographs, *American Zombie Gothic* (2010) and *How Zombies Conquered Popular Culture* (2015), both from McFarland.

Dustin **Dunaway** is the assistant chair of English and Communication at Pueblo Community College, researching political economy in fandoms and co-cultures. He has presented on public pedagogy, sexism in "geek culture," the Beautiful-Is-Good Effect, gender roles and the problematic use of rape as female empowerment in fiction.

Valerie Estelle **Frankel** is the author of 50 books, including *Doctor Who—The What, Where, and How*; *Sherlock: Every Canon Reference You May Have Missed in BBC's Series 1–3*, and *How Game of Thrones Will End*. Many focus on women's roles in fiction: *From Girl to Goddess, Buffy and the Heroine's Journey* and *Women in Game of Thrones* (McFarland 2010, 2012 and 2014) and *The Many Faces of Katniss Everdeen*.

Julie L. **Hawk** teaches English at the University of West Georgia. She has published on 20th-century American literature and popular culture in several journals, including *Critique: Studies in Contemporary Fiction, The Journal of Popular Culture,* and *Slayage: The Online Journal of Whedon Studies*.

Kirk **Hendershott-Kraetzer** is a professor of humanities and co-director of the Global Citizen Honors Program at Olivet College, where he teaches film, creative writing, literature, Shakespeare, and composition and rhetoric. His research interest includes Shakespeare in film and television and the construction of knowledge and identity.

Juliette C. **Kitchens** is an assistant professor of writing and communication at Nova Southeastern University. Her research interests include popular culture, technology, community, and identity construction. She has published in *Studies in Popular Culture* and has presented at local and national conferences.

Melanie A. **Jensen** is a language arts teacher at Springville Junior High, inspiring students to read literature and write papers and creative works. She also works as a set dresser and prop designer for Hale Centre Theatre in northern Utah. Her writings about *Buffy* combine her love for pedagogy with her fascination with narrative spaces.

Melanie A. **Marotta** is a lecturer in the Department of English and Language Arts at Morgan State University. Her research focuses on SF, the American West, contemporary American literature, and ecocriticism, with a focus on the impact of space and place on identity formation.

Lisa K. **Perdigao** is humanities program chair and professor of English at Florida Institute of Technology. Her research interests are in the areas of American literature, film, television, comics, and YA literature. She is the author of *From Modernist Entombment to Postmodernist Exhumation: Dead Bodies in Twentieth-Century American Fiction* and articles on *Buffy the Vampire Slayer*, *Dollhouse*, *Firefly*, *Serenity*, *Community*, *Fringe*, and *Glee*.

Catherine **Pugh** is a writer and independent scholar. Working with horror and science fiction in all their forms, she is particularly interested in ideas of monstrosity and madness. Her research interests lie in the area of the transformative properties of cinematic insanity and real-life mental illness in regard to the body and external landscapes.

Karen **Walsh** is a part-time writing instructor at the University of Hartford. When not teaching, she waxes academic on all things popular culture from the anti-federalist nature of *Captain America: Civil War* to teaching new literacies through the illustrated Harry Potter.

Victoria **Willis** specializes in literary theory and rhetoric. Her research interests include music, science fiction and fantasy, popular culture and gender studies. She co-edited the collection *Geek Rock: An Exploration of Music and Subculture*, and her work also appears in *Reading Joss Whedon* and *The Journal of American Culture*. She has written for the blogs *Threadless* and *Professor Awesome's University*.

Index

Afterlife 68, 73
agency 4–8, 23, 26, 50, 104–106, 111–113, 119–120, 125–126, 130–131, 137, 139, 146, 150, 156
Agents of S.H.I.E.L.D. 3, 9n2, 68, 74, 83, 182, 185–188, 190, 195n7
Alien: Resurrection 12, 14–16, 76, 83
Angel 1–2, 6, 12, 21–22, 32–35, 37–38, 40, 43n14, 43n15, 48, 68, 70, 75, 77–78, 80, 83, 120n1
Angel: After the Fall 40, 68, 78
Angel and Faith 2, 83, 110, 111, 112, 120n1
Astonishing X-Men 69, 78–79
USS Auriga 14–15, 77
The Avengers 3, 12, 23–24, 32, 33, 36, 39, 40, 41, 76, 182–187, 193
Avengers: Age of Ultron 3, 6, 12, 23–24, 32, 35–36, 38, 40, 43n13, 43n17, 43n18, 68–69, 78, 83, 182, 186, 188–194, 195n10

Betty 14–15, 77, 83
boundary 28, 35, 37, 38, 50, 54–58, 63, 65n6, 102, 132, 136, 176
Buffy the Vampire Slayer 1–2, 7, 8, 9n2, 12, 13, 16–22, 23, 32, 33, 34, 37, 48, 59, 68, 70, 71, 75, 79, 104, 120n1, 122–123, 127–139, 142, 146, 165–178, 182, 183
Buffy the Vampire Slayer Season Eight 40, 68, 74, 79, 83, 109–111, 113, 144
Buffy the Vampire Slayer Season Nine 9, 105, 109–111, 114, 116, 119, 120n1, 143, 145, 148–151
Buffy the Vampire Slayer Season Ten 106, 111–112, 114–115, 119–120, 149–153, 155- 157, 159

Cabin in the Woods 3–4, 58, 68, 71–74, 76, 195n6
claustrophobia 30–32, 39, 42, 51
closed frame 6, 27–29, 31, 38–39, 42
community 7, 49, 62, 64, 68, 75, 76, 80, 87–88, 89, 90–92, 94–95, 97–102, 136, 157, 169, 170, 172–178, 179n13, 184

delivery 123–130, 131, 135–139
Dollhouse 1–3, 6, 12, 23, 32–34, 35, 36, 38, 39, 48–64, 65n6, 65n9, 65n12, 68, 69, 71, 73, 75–76, 182–183, 195n1

entanglement 4–5, 8–9, 11, 24

feminism 6, 7, 12, 13, 93, 107–108, 113, 117, 122–123, 132, 136–139, 147, 151, 153, 157; post 7–8, 142–164; second wave 105, 116; third wave 16, 152
Firefly 2–3, 7, 9n2, 9n4, 14, 24, 32–33, 35, 36, 38, 40–41, 48, 68, 69, 71, 72, 77, 80, 87–103, 182, 183, 189
Fray 1, 104–105, 108–109, 113–114

Gothic 33, 42n11, 51, 69–71, 72, 75, 79, 83, 84n1, 168

horror 12, 14, 17, 32, 50–51, 55, 58, 62–63, 72, 75, 179n6

identity 1–2, 6, 7, 9n1, 11–12, 14–24, 36, 48, 50, 55–56, 63–64, 65n6, 87–88, 93–98, 101, 131, 145–146, 148–149, 161, 163, 171, 176
In Your Eyes 68, 82

Leapfrog 68, 82

magic 7, 71, 74, 79, 105, 106, 108–119, 138, 144, 145, 149–152, 154–156, 169, 175; The Seed of Wonder 109–111, 114, 119, 149
materialism 4–5, 106, 165–167, 195n9; enchanted 110; vital 7, 105–106
Much Ado About Nothing 1, 3–4, 6, 27, 29–31, 35–36, 38–39, 41, 42n6, 76

neodomesticity 8, 146, 183–184, 192, 195n5, 195n9
non-place 6, 63–64

202 Index

object oriented ontology 4–5, 7, 105–106, 112
open frame 27–29

Panopticon 53, 55
parlor rhetoric 7, 123, 130, 131, 133–138
pedagogy 8, 176–177; built 165–166, 174
proxemics 5–6, 12–20

The Runaways 68, 81–82, 83

scythe 7, 104–120, 122, 137–138
The Searchers 28–29, 43n17
Serenity (film) 1, 6, 32, 35, 36, 38, 40, 59, 80, 93, 94, 102n4, 182, 194, 195n7
Serenity (ship) 2, 7, 9n2, 15, 32, 33–34, 35, 38, 40–41, 42n9, 43n17, 48, 76, 77, 80–82, 84, 87–95, 97–100, 101–102, 102n4, 183, 195n3, 195n11
Slayer 7, 17–18, 20–21, 34, 40, 70, 74, 107, 109, 112–113, 114, 117, 138–139, 142–145, 148–151, 154–158; first 108, 130–133, 136, 139, 173, 175–176; potentials 8, 37, 74, 79, 107–109, 113, 115, 116, 119, 129, 134–135, 138, 166, 176–178

subjectivity 4, 5, 136–137, 151–152
surveillance 35, 50, 52–53, 55, 56, 64; voyeurism 31, 33, 42, 42n8, 50, 53, 54, 193

technology 6, 11, 13, 16, 34, 35, 37, 39, 49, 51, 59, 65n6, 76, 89, 95–96, 100, 110, 151, 153, 168, 184, 187–188
total institution 6, 49–50, 53, 55, 56–57
transhuman 11, 12, 15–16, 18, 20–24
transparency 51–54

unhomely 7, 87–88

Vampyr 111, 149, 150–155, 168, 179n10

Willow: Wonderland 111, 114, 118, 119, 120n1
Wolfram & Hart 2, 22, 33, 34, 38, 78
work 32, 34–37, 38, 43n16, 49–50, 51–52, 61, 91, 100, 124–125, 130, 138, 142–143, 144, 145, 149, 151, 153, 154, 157–158, 160, 162–163, 169, 172, 174–175, 177, 179n15, 186, 195n12

www.ingramcontent.com/pod-product-compliance
Lightning Source LLC
Chambersburg PA
CBHW032058300426
44116CB00007B/804